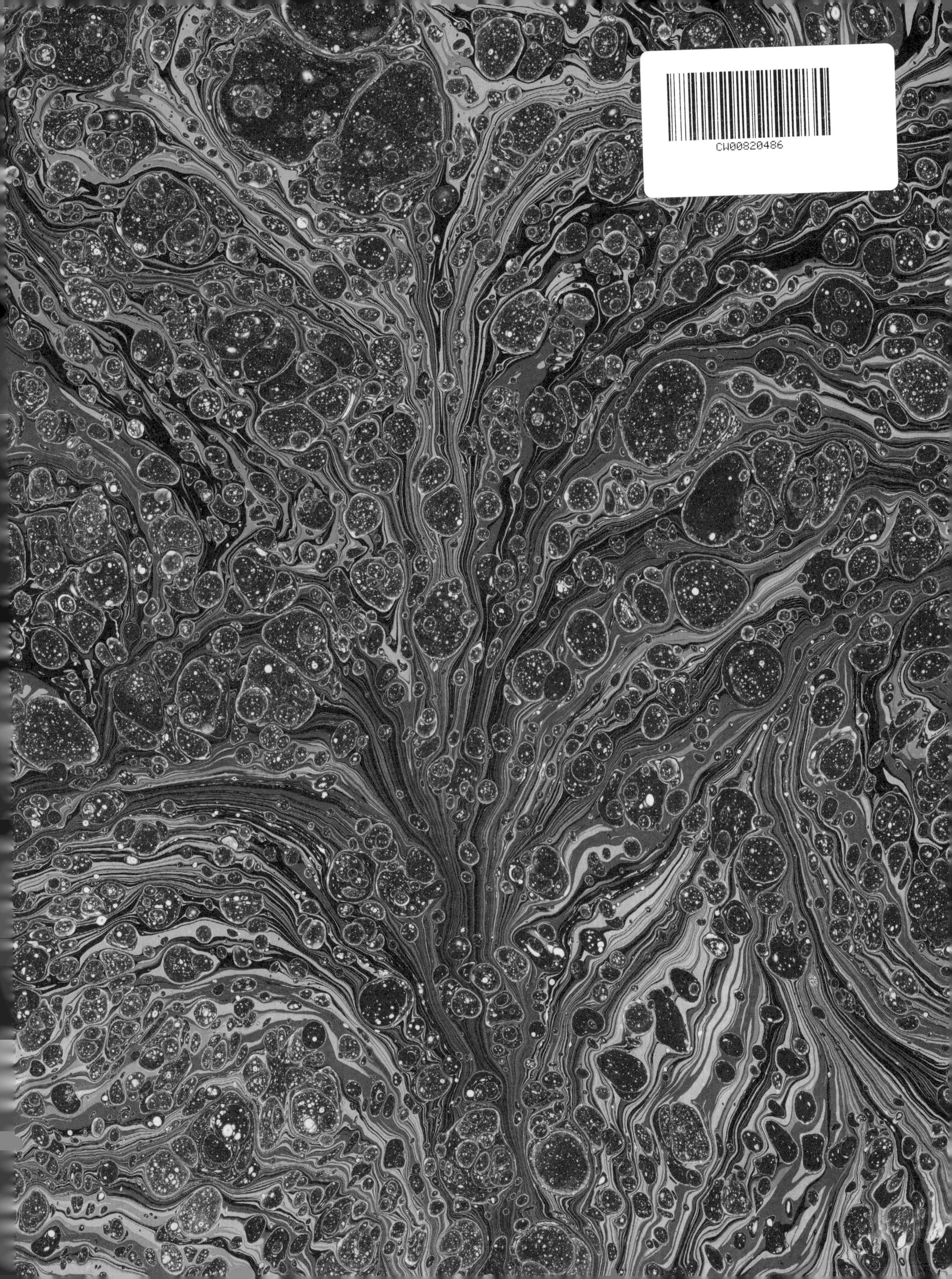
CW00820486

Moto Guzzi

Motorcycles since 1921

Jan Leek
and
Wolfgang Zeyen

Moto Guzzi

Motorcycles since 1921

Jan Leek
and
Wolfgang Zeyen

4880 Lower Valley Road • Atglen, PA 19310

Translation from the German by David Johnston.

This book was published under the title,
Moto Guzzi: Motorräder seit 1921,
by Motorbuch Verlag, Stuttgart, Germany.

Library of Congress Control Number: 2013939433

Design Adaptation by Mark David Bowyer.

Printed in China.
ISBN: 978-0-7643-4344-5

We are interested in hearing from authors with book ideas on related topics.

Published by Schiffer Publishing Ltd.
4880 Lower Valley Road
Atglen, PA 19310
Phone: (610) 593-1777
FAX: (610) 593-2002
E-mail: Info@schifferbooks.com.
Visit our web site at: **www.schifferbooks.com**
Please write for a free catalog.
This book may be purchased from the publisher.
Try your bookstore first.

In Europe, Schiffer books are distributed by:
Bushwood Books
6 Marksbury Avenue
Kew Gardens
Surrey TW9 4JF, England
Phone: 44 (0) 20 8392-8585
FAX: 44 (0) 20 8392-9876
E-mail: Info@bushwoodbooks.co.uk.
Visit our website at: www.bushwoodbooks.co.uk

Contents

Foreword

A book about Moto Guzzi is also a book about almost 100 years of motorcycle history. History also means stories, and no one could tell stories about Moto Guzzi better than Umberto Todero, who joined Moto Guzzi at the end of the 1930s and died in Mandello del Lario in February 2005 after a life in and for Moto Guzzi.

The hours we spent with Todero are for both of us some of our fondest memories associated with motorcycles. His enthusiasm for the brand, for motorcycles in general was infectious, simply thrilling.

Writing this book stirred all our memories of Todero, and not just for this reason we have dedicated a small chapter in this book to him.

We hope that we have created a factual history of Moto Guzzi. It is possible that we have told the story the way Todero told it to us. Perhaps because of this it is not entirely faithful to the truth, but we find his version entirely worth retelling.

We are not alone in hoping that Moto Guzzi is not history, that the brand will live on, something that has not always seemed certain in recent years. Under the direction of the Piaggio concern, however, the future seems assured.

Jan Leek
Wolfgang Zeyen

The two authors with "their" Guzzis: Wolfgang Zeyen (left) with the Dr. John's replica on the Dahlemer Binz, and Jan Leek (above) reunited with "his" old V7 Special while visiting its current owner in Sweden.

Motorcycles with Soul

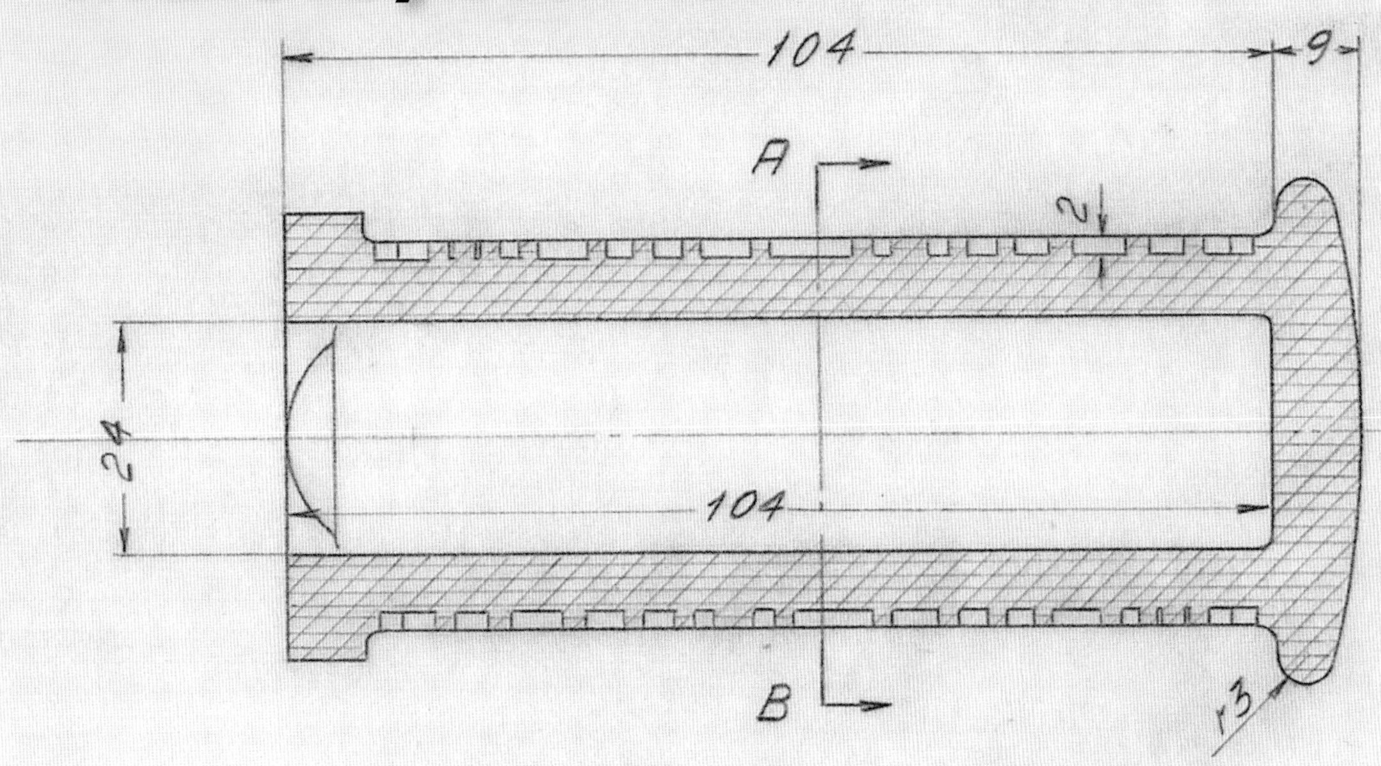

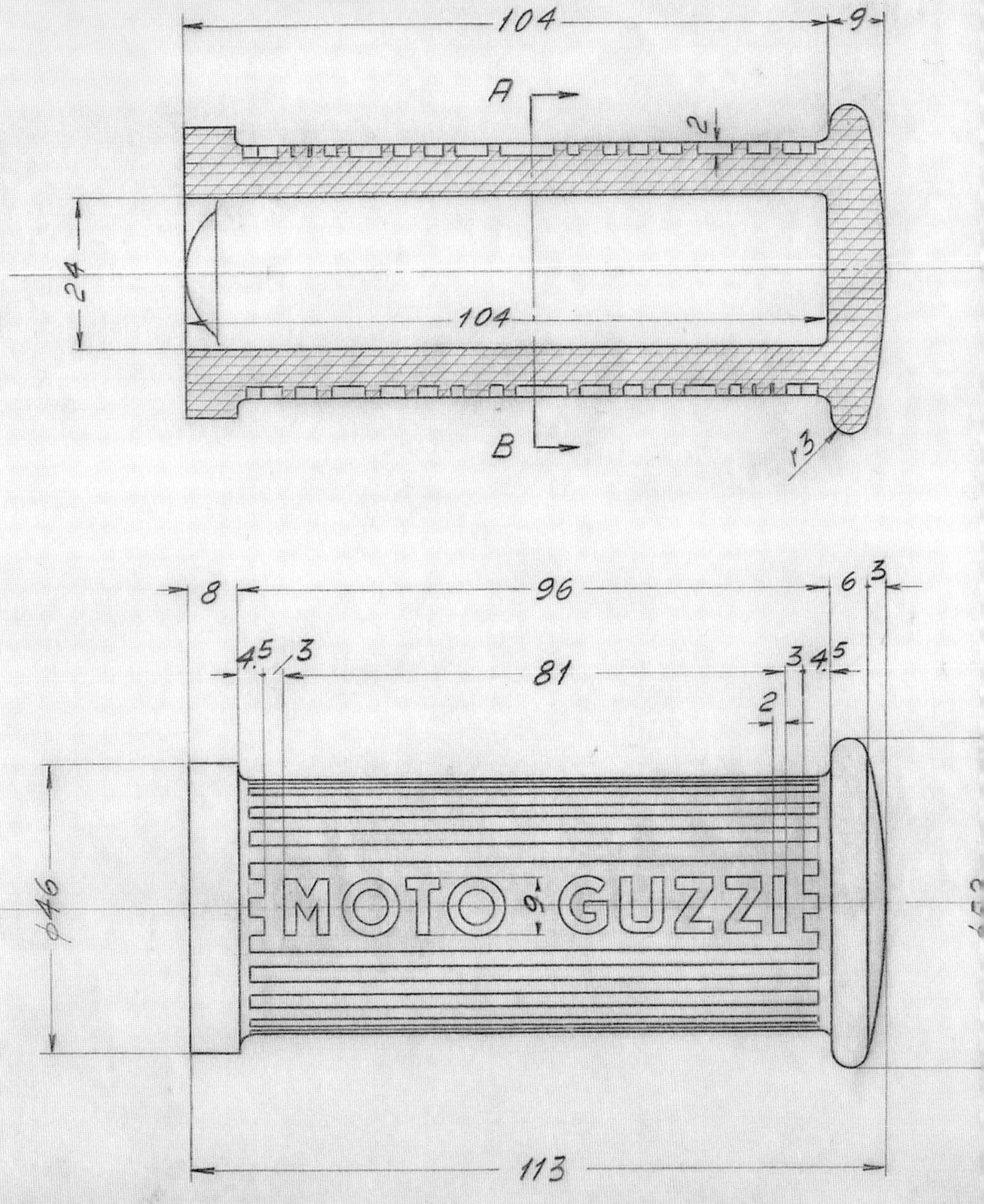

Motorcycles with Soul

In 1851 a small cannon was set up beside the peaceful harbor in Mandello del Lario. It is still there, pointing towards the peaceful spurs of Lake Como, at the edge of a green park where once a week market day is held beneath the thick trees. Behind us towers the Grigna massif with its pointed peaks, although they cannot be seen from here below. It is a distinctive feature for all travelers approaching the small city from the south. Just before Como the saw blade forms an ominous backdrop then disappears from sight, as the road takes up little space between the mountain range and the lake. Small romantic houses, exotic plants and narrow winding streets now shape the image. It is difficult to understand why the cannon was placed by the harbor. Just a hundred meters from the cannon there is a small piazza, also situated right beside the water. Beneath shade-giving arcades is the *Gelateria Constantin – dal 1925*. Now it is a peaceful and quiet place, but this idyllic ice-cream parlor has seen turbulent times. And the times were turbulent in the years after the war when the ice-cream parlor opened its doors for the first time and spread the checkered tablecloths.

Historical events did, in fact, play a part in the creation of the Moto Guzzi brand, as did geography. Ultimately, however, the history of Moto Guzzi differs more than a little from the other brands, and the history of the Italian motor industry is itself quite lively.

A map of Italy reveals a belt running along the River Po from Milan to Rimini, in which the Italian automobile and motorcycle industries are concentrated. This strip also marks the path of the old

The cannon has been on the shore of Lake Como for more than 200 years. With its baroque shape, the classically-styled California Vintage shows Guzzi's way to the future.

Alessandro Manzoni published his first novel. Titled *Promessi Sposi* (The Engaged Couple), it was the first work in modern Italian, and the author lived in Lecco, twenty kilometers south of Mandello.

The reason why Moto Guzzi settled in the mountains by Lake Como had an entirely different historical background. Carlo Guzzi was born in Milan in 1888. His family owned several houses in Mandello, and Carlo and his three sisters grew up in the small city. Carlo spent almost all of his spare time in the garage of a certain Giorgio Riparmonti, who worked on anything that had a crankshaft – engines for fishing boats, automobiles, and motorcycles. The young Guzzi was mainly interested in motorcycles, but their unreliability and design shortcomings soon led him to develop his own concept of what a good motorcycle should look like.

For decades the Guzzi factory has been wedged between the rail line and the slopes of the Gringa. Carlo Guzzi (above) was born in Milan but selected Mandello del Lario as his home as his family had property there.

Via Emilia trade route, and it is also one of Italy's few plains, with the river providing natural irrigation: in earlier times the Po regularly overflowed its banks. Unlike the mountainous regions, farmers were able to begin using machines early on, and for this reason the Po Plain became the showplace of Italy's industrial revolution. This background formed the basis for a technical revolution, which in turn gave birth to a prosperous automobile industry. Engines of all kinds thus have a long tradition in northern Italy, and author Giovannio Guareschi even has a Moto Guzzi flitting past in his stories about Don Camillo.

The cannon of 1851? Italy the state is not as old as the cannon. A Kingdom of Italy was not called into being until 1861. Naples (and Sicily) joined the union in 1866 and Rome in 1870. Political embroilments with France were just settling down when Austria stepped onto the stage and became the new bogeyman. In 1851, therefore, the cannon made good sense. By the way, this was the same time when

Before Carlo could turn his ideas into reality, the First World War broke out. The young Guzzi was called up and joined Italy's recently created air force – the *Aeronautica Militare* – as a mechanic. There he met two pilots, Giovanni Ravelli and Giorgio Parodi. Ravelli had become well known as a motorcycle racer before the war, and Parodi was also interested in racing. The two pilots quickly became interested in Carlo Guzzi's ideas. Together, they decided to build a motorcycle after the war.

Giorgio Parodi was the son of a well-known Genoan shipping magnate, Emmanuele Vittorio Parodi, and he was supposed to see to the financing. After the war he asked his father for financial support. The letter with his elderly father's reply, dated 3 January 1919, now hangs in the company museum beside the oldest Moto Guzzi. "Dear Giorgio, ... you can inform your two partners that I will provide 1,500 or 2,000 Lira for your first attempt, but only under the condition that, under no circumstances, will you exceed this sum. As well, I reserve the right to inspect your progress before I give my final approval to the project. If I am satisfied, I can foresee investing more, with no limit."

Old Parodi was obviously unaware that Giovanni Ravelli had been killed in a crash in September 1918, just a few days before the end of the war. The two remaining men, Carlo Guzzi and Giorgio Parodi, began work and built a first prototype.

The motorcycle was named the G.P., for Guzzi-Parodi. It was painted green and had to get by without the eagle wings on the fuel tank. The machine had a horizontally mounted single-cylinder engine with a bore of eighty-eight millimeters and a stroke of eighty-two millimeters. An overhead camshaft in the cylinder head was driven by a vertical shaft on the right. Four overhead valves controlled the gas cycle. The mixture was ignited by two spark plugs simultaneously – a Bosch magneto providing the necessary voltage. The crank mechanism and gearbox shared a common housing which could be kept small because of the external flywheel. The half-liter engine produced 12 hp.

The GP came with a four-valve engine, a very advanced design that proved too expensive for quantity production. For the first production Guzzi, therefore, the designer turned to a much simpler variant with two opposed valves.

Around this low-set power plant, Guzzi designed a double loop frame with an unsprung rear wheel. Part of the rear fender was incorporated into the supporting frame structure. A parallelogram front fork held the front wheel and the spring element was at the top, directly in front of the headstock. There was no front wheel brake, and Guzzi used a band brake on the rear wheel. The G.P. was capable of 100 kph, a terrifying speed when one imagines the gravel roads shortly after the war.

The motorcycle was undeniably a very advanced design, not revolutionary but very advanced: combustion chamber with four valves, a short bore-stroke ratio, primary drive using gear wheels, and all of this combined in one unit. None of these features was new, but they had never been combined in a single design; that was new.

The two young entrepreneurs were soon forced to realize, however, that their design was too costly for a production motorcycle. What the market needed after the Great War was not a racing machine but a robust vehicle for everyday use, with low fuel consumption and high reliability. Carlo returned to his drawing board and the result was the Tipo Normale of 1921.

The Normale was the first motorcycle with the name Moto Guzzi and the eagle on the tank. The latter was the emblem of the *Aeronautica Militare*, in memory of their late friend Ravelli. There were few differences between the two motorcycles, the prototype and the Normale. Guzzi's basic ideas were also good for this simplified version: horizontally mounted engine, low frame, external flywheel. The savings could be found elsewhere, for example the rear fender, which lost its supporting element. It was replaced by a simple steel section.

The exhaust valve was placed in the overhead position in the center of the combustion chamber and was activated by a pushrod from the rocker shaft. This placed the part most in need of cooling – the exhaust valve – directly in line with the airflow. The inlet valve was positioned on the side of the cylinder and was opened directly by the cam. Mixture preparation was entrusted to a British AMAC carburetor with separate float chamber. The single-cylinder engine produced all of eight horsepower, sufficient for a top speed of 80 kph.

The engine of the Tipo Normale had just two valves, one vertical and one overhead in the cylinder head.

As I said: despite several familiar ingredients, the Moto Guzzi was something new and it incorporated several innovations never before seen on a production motorcycle. One detail deserves special attention, namely the one-piece Bowden cables. These had just appeared on the market in 1921 and were still far from being an industry standard, but Carlo Guzzi did not hesitate for a moment to use them. Just a small thing? Certainly, but the sum of such details led to a perfect end result and also demonstrated the young designer's obsession for detail.

Carlo Guzzi's first machines proved that he was a master of his métier – and of technology. There was also no doubt that his business partner Giorgio Parodi – with his influential father in the background – had the requisite business know-how to establish a company. But all this still does not make a successful motorcycle manufacturer.

It is not enough to build good motorcycles. They also have to be sold.

Carlo Guzzi – fourth from the left – surrounded by motorcycle racers: far left is Carlo Agostini, one of the first Moto Guzzi employees and later chief mechanic in the racing division.

Marketing and Company Philosophy

In the Café Piccola, at the service station on the other side of the railroad tracks, the company's employees still drink their espresso beneath the poster of a Guzzi V7 Sport. They have since stopped drinking Grappa Bassano.

The Italian lifestyle, according to the cliché, is narcissistic, built on sensuous pleasure in every way and it is precisely this life-affirming attitude that makes motorcycles (and cars) objects of love south of the Alps, objects for feelings. The same philosophy – if in fact it is one – also allows technical weaknesses to be hidden under the cloak of "character." A ban on drinking grappa during the workday therefore sounds somehow reasonable.

It is exactly the same with advertising – do racing successes contribute something to marketing success? The basic question of whether advertising makes any sense, or how much, can never be answered satisfactorily, as the effects are not measureable. That's how it is today, that's how it was in the 1920s.

There must be something to it, however, both for racing sport and advertising. In any case these two factors contribute to the success of a new brand: racing is intended to arouse interest and advertising tells about it. And there is much to tell.

In those days the racing scene consisted mainly of long-distance races on public roads. That is how it began, and racing events as we know them today did not then exist. In any event, when Moto Guzzi took the stage, there was one permanent racetrack in operation and a second was to follow. The first permanent motor arena – motordrome – was opened in Brooklands, London in 1907, but it was an oval course for test purposes. The races held there were at the industry's discretion and served its purposes. The first "true" racetrack was probably Monza, in the royal gardens of Milan. The original track layout consisted of two banked turns with crossovers and alternate tracks between them. Track length was easily ten kilometers. It was opened in 1922, a year after the Moto Guzzi brand was established.

Ten kilometers might sound like a considerable distance now, but then it was nothing to speak of. Previous experience had been gained in races with entirely different dimensions: Mille Miglia, Targo Florio, Milan-Naples. In the early years of motor sports, races were held between the major cities of Europe. It was no different in Italy. The Alps were in the way, however, and Italy was therefore always a little uncoupled from the North-European events. Consequently such long-distance races continued in Italy until the terrible accident during the Mille Miglia in 1957, in which two drivers and twelve spectators were killed.

The first race in which a Moto Guzzi took part – unsuccessfully – was the Milan to Naples long-distance event in 1921. The new company entered two machines – the only two it had built so far.

At that time, the Guzzi operation encompassed a few hundred square meters – right in front of the small railway station, a hundred meters from the waters of the Lario, and several hundred meters from the towering rock face of the Grigna. The lack of space wasn't a serious problem and it wasn't until the 1950s, during its expansion phase, that the company suffered from a steadily growing shortage of space.

After this first unsuccessful attempt, the young company's sporting statistics improved suddenly and permanently. The furious opening act was a victory at the Targo Florio, which was held soon afterwards, and in the years that followed one triumph came on the heels of another, so that by the end of the 1920s, Moto Guzzi was an established racing stable. It was not surprising that the northern Italians gained significant market acceptance as a result.

This was reflected in its model program. In 1923 the Tipo Normale was replaced by the C2V racing machine. The abbreviation stood for *Corse 2 Ventila*. This racing machine, with its overhead valves, was to become the young company's most important motorcycle by far, and it established Moto Guzzi's reputation as a maker of sporty motorcycles.

For a time at least, the original Normale continued to be built alongside the new motorcycle, although it underwent a number of changes. Customer feedback flowed in during subsequent development. As a result, a circulation lubrication system was introduced, the second spark plug was eliminated, and there was a modest increase in power to 8.5 hp.

The Tipo Sport now entered production. It combined the Normale engine and the lighter and longer frame of the C2V. The engine received a significant boost in output, however, producing 13 hp at 3,800 rpm. Beginning in 1929, further development stages of the Sport series (Sport 14, Sport 15) resulted in the introduction of a drum brake on the front wheel and a Bosch electrical system. On the first Sports the two accessories could only be purchased as a package for an additional charge.

Then, as in the future, there was a joyous confusion of production models for the street and pure racing models, but that is also typical of the Italian motorcycle maker. As Carlo Guzzi's racing machines were based on production models, the line between road and racing machines became blurred.

An obvious exception was the four-valve motorcycle of 1924. With its valves arranged in parallel, this C4V replaced the overhead valve C2V. From this basic design were derived the 4V TT and the 4V SS, which in 1928 achieved a peak performance of 30 hp and a maximum speed of 170 kph. The first version allowed the company to claim European honors, winning the first title ever awarded, in Monza in 1924. The world championship was not created until 1949. And that wasn't all: at Monza the brand took first, second and fifth places. This success gained attention outside Italy and further international successes were to follow.

Technically, these racing engines differed from production machines, having needle bearings for the piston pins, differently coated cylinder liners, and much more – essentially minor items, but ones which contributed to a successful complete package. What created a link to the production models, however, was the engine installation: mounted longitudinally with horizontal cylinders.

All official histories of the company tend to portray random chance as foresighted entrepreneurship and inspired farsightedness, especially in chapters about the manufacturer's pioneering years, but in Moto Guzzi's case this is justified. Concentration on one engine philosophy was not only an important component in the success of the first two decades, but also an expression of a fully developed concept. Contemporary witnesses describe Carlo Guzzi as a down-to-earth man, which also explains his fixation on this simple design. But that is not the entire truth.

Photo taken during the muffed TT in 1926: Pietro Ghersi took second place, however he lost it after the race because his 250-cc racer had the wrong kind of sparkplug.

Of course, in 1932 he designed a 250 with the same layout, but at the same time several examples of a three-cylinder for the road appeared, following failed experiments with a four-cylinder racing machine in 1930. Was this the work of an excessively cautious designer of a company that had been in existence for just ten years?

More importantly, quite the contrary: was the concentration on a single cylinder not a much riskier game? For what would happen if the competition found a better solution and if the customers suddenly became interested only in twin-cylinders?

There was also another aspect: racing is actually a waste of money, as the huge commitment's impact on sales of the series product cannot be measured. And yet, it was precisely in this category that this supposedly conservative maker produced its most interesting motorcycles: a 250-cc with supercharger, a four-cylinder, and finally a 500-cc V-twin.

Racing undeniably helped make the brand known around the world. The year was 1926; the stage the Isle of Man. The island gained worldwide fame in 1907 when the first TT races were held there. As racing of any kind was forbidden in the British Isles, enthusiasts exploited a legal loophole on this small island between England and Ireland.

Italian riders had already tried their luck there. Carlo Guzzi designed a 250 for racing, with a square layout and an overhead cam and master shaft. Pietro Ghersi was sent to the island with the small machine, which weighed just 105 kg. The results were encouraging – the fastest lap time and a second place finish – but because of a form error Ghersi was denied second place. At that time all products used on every racing motorcycle taking part in the TT had to be listed – oil, chain, sparkplugs, tires and so on. During the race Ghersi changed the sparkplugs, replacing them with a brand other than the one he had declared – a trifling matter, but against the rules. The performance did gain attention, however, and in Italy Moto Guzzi's string of successes continued.

To Carlo Guzzi, however, this was not the most important thing. In his designs he valued suitability for daily use, and in 1928 he and his brother, Giuseppe, developed a torsion-resistant, rear wheel suspension, something then considered an impossible thing to do. While there were rear wheel suspensions on the market, apparently no one had taken the trouble to thoroughly analyze and work out the entire problem. But that was precisely the boss's trademark: going into detail. A characteristic of the new chassis was a low-mounted box with four coil springs, which were under pressure and gave the motorcycle 110 millimeters of suspension travel at the rear end.

Brother Giuseppe drove the GT to the Arctic Circle and back, resulting in the motorcycle being named the Norge (Norway). The machine was powered by the engine from the Sport 14. The GT was later fitted with a developed engine that improved sales numbers. Less than eighty examples of the Norge were sold. What survived, however, was the rear wheel suspension, and Guzzi retained this basic design on his single-cylinder machines into the 1960s.

The last years of the decade were a period of upheaval for Moto Guzzi, and there was quite an intermingling of model variants. For example, the Sport 14 was offered in various versions with no change in the company catalogue. No mention was made of the introduction of an electrical system, and equally suddenly drum brakes were to be found on the machines, front and rear, without it being documented in any way.

When the 1920s came to an end, the factory was employing 500 people. At the beginning of the decade, in 1921, there had been less than a dozen people who manufactured just seventeen motorcycles. This decade was full of contrast – technical advances on the one hand, ancient propulsion technology (belt drive) on the other. Charles Lindbergh flew solo across the Atlantic; the Hindenburg flew around the world; architecture found new lines; classic authors made their debut – Hemingway, Joyce, Hesse, Kästner. It was a fast decade, the Jazz Age – and in 1922 Benito Mussolini became head of state. In 1925 he became dictator.

The 1930s

The beginning of the 1930s cannot exactly be painted in glowing colors. History itself is, of course, ignorant of any numerical graduation. It was mere chance, therefore, that the world economic crisis occurred in 1929 and put an end to the Roaring Twenties. Jazz fell silent and hopes for a peaceful decade diminished.

Against this background, Carlo Guzzi began spending more time on economical designs suitable for everyday use. Proof of this can be found in the continued development of the inlet-over-exhaust,500-cc line, but also in the introduction of the small P.E. 175, which was to fill a market niche in a tax-favorable category.

And then there was also the matter of the four-cylinder racing machine and the three-cylinder tourer.

It was clear to Carlo Guzzi that racing success lent itself extremely well to advertising, and as a technician he also understood that multiplying the number of cylinders made possible higher revolutions, in other words, higher performance. Unfortunately, the designs of many of his competitors only translated this fact into better performance to some extent. But why didn't it work? Quite simply: increased weight reduced maneuverability, especially in turns, which negated any performance gains in straight-aways. Chassis and suspension design had not yet reached the point where increased performance immediately translated into improved lap times.

Guzzi nevertheless designed a four-cylinder with sharply inclined cylinders and a supercharger. Supercharging works best with multi-cylinder engines, and it was well known that Moto Guzzi had only single-cylinder machines to offer. What the single-cylinder had in its favor, however, was its lightweight. The four-cylinder Guzzi could not keep up with the single-cylinders. After extensive testing in the winter of 1931-32 the project was cancelled. On the racetrack, single-cylinders were still superior in handling and weight, and no one could seriously argue that they weren't more economical, cheaper and all in all more practical for everyday use.

But the lessons learned from the four-cylinder led Carlo Guzzi to a new idea. Even if the concept's performance potential could not be realized, the multi-cylinder engine had other advantages. Guzzi, therefore, transferred his ideas to a three-cylinder GT machine. It was a strange, very advanced design, and like all futuristic visions was well ahead of its time. Several examples were built in 1932 and 1933, however they found no acceptance on the market.

Omobono Tenni – decades later a special model of the V11 Le Mans was named after him. He fascinated the spectator masses in the same way that Valentino Rossi does today. Tenni was killed in an accident at the 1948 Bern Grand Prix.

Tourist Trophy 1935: posing behind the 250 Monoalbero are, from the left: Giorgio Parodi, Stanley Woods, Omobono Tenni, a brother-in-law of Woods, and three mechanics.

Start of the 250-cc race at the 1935 TT: Stanley Woods pushes the 250 to the starting line. He recorded Guzzi's first victory on the island.

A pity actually, for from today's perspective the machines were nice-looking and possessed very modern lines for the time.

It is ironic, but Italy's war against Abyssinia, planned since 1932, begun in 1935, can perhaps also be described as very advanced. Unexpectedly, fierce resistance led Mussolini to the idea of using terror bombing and poison gas to bring the country to heel. The British freed the country from Italian domination in 1941.

The Italian military, thus, saw action before the outbreak of the Second World War and Moto Guzzi motorcycles gained their initial experience in Africa. By then, Mussolini was "Il Duce," the dictator, and as such he tried to expand the military. It might sound clichéd, but man is always most inventive when it comes to killing his fellow men.

Technology was making vast strides in those days and technical advancement was given a high priority in Italy, just as it was in Germany at the same time and for the same reasons.

And, as in Germany, great importance was given to the "motorization of the people." Automobiles remained prohibitively expensive, but small inexpensive motorcycles were within reach of many. The state did its part by eliminating taxes on motorcycles up to a certain engine displacement. In Italy, this limit was set at 175 cc. The tax concession ran out in 1933, one year after the company had introduced the P175. As a result, Guzzi authorized an increase in displacement for his

Close to the finish: Stanley Woods steers the Bicilindrica past Governor's Bridge. The Briton also won on the bigger machine, achieving Guzzi's biggest success to date.

small model, which mutated into a 250. This P 250 was also built as the P.E. 250, with rear wheel springs and a top speed of 100 kph. It formed the basis of a new generation of Moto Guzzi motorcycles. In 1937, after another increase in displacement to 247 cubic centimeters, the 250s also justified their designation.

They gave rise to numerous variants, with and without suspension, with and without chrome and other details. In 1939, all of the knowledge and improvements flowed into the design of the P.E. model, from which, in turn, was developed the Airone, one of the most important models built by the manufacturer in the postwar period.

But that was all in the future, and at the end of 1933 the company stood on the brink of a new era. With the Series V, it now had a modern, 500-cc engine with angular overhead valves. This model laid the foundation for the GTV, with the first two letters standing for a suspension frame. There was also a G.T.W., essentially the same motorcycle but equipped with a more powerful, 22-hp engine – a fine example of Moto Guzzi's policy at the time of building motorcycles for everyday and sporting use. And the idea paid off, for in 1934 Moto Guzzi was the leading Italian motorcycle maker. The company's staff grew to 700 workers.

At the beginning of the 1930s the national racing sport committee announced a new racing series for close-to-production motorcycles. The notion of using street machines for racing purposes was supposed to reduce costs and enable amateurs to also take part in races without having to face overpowering factory teams. Italy's number one reacted with the G.T.C., a derivative of the GTV and W. A further development, a lighter production racer, appeared in the program as the Condor in 1939.

By then, Benito Mussolini had consolidated his power and begun a reorganization of the state apparatus. The motorcycle industry was also affected, at least indirectly. As in Germany, where the NSKK, or National Socialist Motorist Corps, took part in motor sports, in Italy Mussolini saw to it that racing drivers were drafted by the traffic police – *Milizia del la Strada* – where they did what they were best at: riding. They also had their own championship, which was carried out on Condor motorcycles. Essentially, it was the first one-make cup, at least in Italy, if not worldwide.

Moto Guzzi was also dominant in international racing sport. Its 250s were unbeatable, at least until the German DKW with supercharging made its appearance and dominated the scene. In response, Guzzi fitted his 250s with superchargers, no easy undertaking, as a single-cylinder engine with supercharger is difficult to control. Not until 1939 did these consolidation measures bear their first fruit, but the greatest successes were the new world records, set over an hour and in the flying kilometer. This design led to further experiments with a fuel injection system, which was taken up again after the war.

The make's greatest success, however, came in the races on the Isle of Man in 1935. As previously mentioned, single-cylinder machines were still the rule in racing sport and also dominated everyday use. On the other hand, by that time V-twins were also commonplace on the streets. Such machines appeared regularly in England, although they were rarely seen on racetracks. The speed trials at the Brooklands track, at the gates of London, were an exception. Instead of a curvy racetrack it was a high-speed oval, and there the weight difference was of no great significance. At that time JAP was establishing itself as the engine supplier for all of Europe, especially V-twins of all sizes. The same thing was happening in the USA, where Harley-Davidson and Indian – plus several other makes – continued to pursue the twin-cylinder philosophy. This did not mean, however, that advanced, multi-cylinder designs had no chance on the racetrack. BMW, which introduced its Boxer in 1923, was best proof of this. And the GRB developed in the 1920s, which mutated into the OPRA Rondine and was later bought up by Gilera, was a four-cylinder in-line. In 1933 the OPRA project was revived by the newly founded CNA and later inspired the four-cylinders by Gilera and, after the war, by MV Augusta – not least because the designer Pietro Remor had a hand in the development of all three machines.

In Sweden, Husqvarna tinkered with a V-twin for racing purposes, but then in 1935 the company ended its involvement. The year before, in 1934, Husqvarna had engaged the already legendary Englishman, Stanley Woods, to race on the Isle of Man. It was almost enough to claim victory, but the Swedish-English combination lost when it ran out of fuel.

Moto Guzzi hired Woods for the 1935 senior class on the island. And the Italians certainly had a reputation to defend: since their convincing performance in the 250 class in 1926, the TT 250 was just as mature as it was reliable and dominated its class. The 500, on the other hand, was obsolescent despite its four-valve technology and had to be replaced. But with what? The love of experimentation displayed by other manufacturers gave Carlo Guzzi no rest and his four-cylinder of 1930 is proof of this. As he saw it, the logical consequence was to build a 500-cc V-twin from the successful 250. This logic bore fruit, as the machine dominated not just the racetrack, but also long-distance races on public roads. Moto Guzzi won the Milan to Tarent long-distance race five times, then the "Grand Prize of Nations" (the traditional name for the annual international races at Monza) three times. It also regularly won the Italian championship before the war and exactly as many times after the war.

During its very first trials at Monza, the twin-cylinder Moto Guzzi, still without a suspension, achieved lap speeds in excess of 175 kph.

The V-twin's first great success, however, was its convincing victory on the island in the Irish Sea. The engine, which initially produced 44 hp, was uprated to 50 hp for use abroad, and the motorcycle had a rear wheel suspension, a novelty in racing sport. And that was not all: a lever on the left side of the fuel tank enabled the driver to change the damping himself during a race.

In the third of seven laps, Woods was forty-seven seconds behind the leading Norton driver Jimmie Guthrie, but then began an attempt to overtake him. As the drivers started individually and only lap times counted, it was therefore impossible to immediately choose the winner. Jimmie Guthrie waited nervously as Woods shot across the finish line – with, as it turned out, a four second lead.

As he had done the year before with the Husqvarna, Woods set a new lap record, improving on his previous time by more than a minute. He beat the race record by a full seven minutes!

Incidentally, several days before, Woods had also won the Junior TT on a 250 despite adverse weather conditions. The Moto Guzzi team returned to Mandello with two victories in one of the most important meets on the calendar.

The victory also helped the rear-wheel suspension make a breakthrough, and the number of motorcycles with suspensions – even on the streets – grew steadily. Almost simultaneously with the introduction of rear wheel suspension a new name moved into the consciousness of racing enthusiasts: Omoboni Tenni, nicknamed "Capellone." The latter he owed to his wild and magnificent head of hair, which now and then resembled a cap. The thirty-year-old was at the Isle of Man when Woods achieved his double victory, but he was forced to withdraw. He returned to the island in 1937 – no longer as a young star who had enthralled spectators in the Twenties, but as a perpetual talent whose best days were already behind him. But that year he showed everyone. He – and Guzzi – achieved what no one had done before: Omoboni Tenni became the first non-Briton to win the TT class on a motorcycle not made in Britain.

At the time, that was simply a sensation, for the TT was not just any race. First run in 1907, the Tourist Trophy was the most important and prestigious race in the world, a legend; the race that separated the boys from the men. With an overall length of sixty kilometers, changing track surfaces, curves, hairpin turns and often changeable weather conditions, the bumpy course deserved just one title: "extraordinary."

Two years later, however, Italy found itself facing entirely different challenges, and memories of the racing successes faded. Six years later they were just that – memories.

The War Years

At one end of the present day company museum in Mandello, there is a structure, almost like a small tower. During the last days of the Second World War, Umberto Todero sent light signals from there to the partisans on the other side of the lake. The future development engineer had been with Moto Guzzi less than six months when the Second World War broke out. Strangely enough, Italy did not join the party at first. Despite its forays into North Africa and the Spanish Civil War in the 1930s (which is often characterized as a prelude to the Second World War), Italy stayed out in the beginning. Not until June 1940, with France on the verge of surrender, did Mussolini declare war on England and France. One month later, when France fell, Mussolini obtained some territorial gains, but that was it. After failed military adventures in Africa and Greece, militarily and politically Italy was in shambles. The disaster had reached such an extent that her German ally offered – or was forced to lend, depending on your point of view – its support. The fact is, however, that after 1941 Germany's influence grew steadily and by the end of 1943 it was largely in control of most key functions. Mussolini's Italy was no longer an equal partner in the alliance; it had become a supplier of raw materials to the German war industry. This was shown by the deliveries of food to the Germans, which left barely enough to feed the native population.

Mussolini – on the far left – inspects a sniper unit. The soldiers are riding GT 17s, the first Guzzi built solely for military use.

Italy lost Libya, its North African colony, in the spring of 1943, and when Allied forces overran Sicily the king placed Mussolini under house arrest. Marshall Badoglio was given the task of signing the surrender in September 1943. Germany reacted by sending more military units to Italy, and from then on the front extended right across the country. German paratroops freed Mussolini from his imprisonment, after which the Duce tried to create a pro-German republic. In April 1945, however, he was on the run. He and his mistress were caught by partisans near Mandello and hanged. The war in Europe ended one month later.

It is perhaps not surprising that the two nations that dominated motorcycle racing after the First World War – namely England and Italy – also developed and built motorcycles during the war. Of course, this was done at the behest of the respective ministries, but nevertheless, despite the war, motorcycles were always a topic. In retrospect, the military motorcycle seems to have been no more than an error in reasoning. Basically the only ones who could do anything with it were dispatch riders, and all other tasks were better accomplished by Kübelwagens and Jeeps.

Of course, no one realized this when, in 1928, Moto Guzzi revealed the G.T. 16, the first service motorcycle suitable for off-road use. Experience gained with it resulted in the G.T.17, which had a shorter tank (on account of a passenger seat), adjustable rear

In the 1950s the Moto Guzzi wind tunnel – wedged close to the slopes of the Gringa – performed valuable service in the development of fairings for the Grand Prix machines.

suspension, and twin shock absorbers. There were various equipment options for military use, including a fixed machine-gun.

Then, in 1939, the company revealed the newly developed Alce (Moose). The long-legged machine, with its fork fairings, replaced the G.T.20 shown the year before and had the S-Type engine complete with automatic oil valve pump and a modified running gear that provided better ground clearance. As well, the wheels were the same size and could be changed quickly, which was not always the case with the braking systems then in use. Like the G.T.20, it had an inlet-over-exhaust engine, the last time a Moto Guzzi motorcycle used this type of valve train. While just over 200 of the G.T. interim model were built, Moto Guzzi produced approximately 7,000 examples of the Alce. Ten percent of these were equipped with a sidecar.

Various developed versions appeared during the war, including the Trialce, a three-wheeler, of which more than 1,740 were built. With a top speed of 70 kph it was not particularly fast, but this is not surprising considering that it weighed more than 330 kg. There was even a take-apart version of the Trialce conceived for use by airborne troops.

A proper motorcycle-sidecar combination on the German example was also developed. It had fat tires and a selectable drive for the sidecar's sprung wheel. The machine also had a one-sided rear wheel mounting – all-in-all a promising development that never entered production.

For in those turbulent times, there were other concerns, and by the spring of 1945 motorcycle production had almost come to a halt. After the German occupation of northern Italy, the factory was converted into an armaments plant that manufactured gun barrels and other military equipment, under German supervision.

But even these dark days came to an end; the black nightmare ended with the death of Mussolini. Black? Yes, because Mussolini's men wore black trousers, not brown, because black was the fascist color. Incidentally, in those days "fascist" was not a derogatory term, rather a symbol of discipline and order. The word was derived from "*fascio*," the bundle of sticks with an axe carried by the old Roman lictors (a special class of Roman civil servant, with special tasks of attending and guarding magistrates of the Roman Republic and Empire).

When the dictatorship ended, the creative minds in Mandello soon returned to the building of motorcycles.

There were no new developments in the true sense. The program of the early postwar years used components from the prewar period. The Alce, Moto Guzzi's last inlet-over-exhaust motorcycle, was dropped from production, and its successor, the Superalce, was equipped with the V-twin engine. Production of a 500-cc version of the GTV resumed after the war, and from 1947 it was equipped with telescopic shock absorbers. It later gave birth to the Astore, with encapsulated valve system and aluminum cylinders and cylinder heads and even later to the Falcone. By then, the war was finally in the past.

The Economic Miracle

In the harbor basin of Mandello, there is a cannon from the time when the state of Italy was created. The young republic was just seventy years old when Moto Guzzi resumed its activities on the shore of Lake Como. The mid-1900s were turbulent times, and there, beside Lake Como, the first novel in modern Italian, *Promessi Sposi*, was written. Today the cannon is nothing more than a decoration in the nice green area beside the lake and fills this new role well.

The final year of the war was also a turbulent time, as the Germans were exploiting every factory in northern Italy to the fullest. With the aid of the young engineer Umberto Todero, a partisan group set up a radio transmitter in the tower at the end of the racing department in the factory's second floor. The same space today houses a museum.

On the other side of the lake, near Dongo, Benito Mussolini was captured and executed by partisans in April 1945. By the way, after the liberation of Italy a number of German soldiers stayed on as workers in the Moto Guzzi factory. By doing so, they missed out on the economic miracle in their own country but experienced firsthand the golden era of Italian motorcycle design, the 1950s.

No period, neither in the field of motorcycle racing nor motorcycle technology, is surrounded by such an aura as the years between 1945 and 1960. It was then that the motorcycle grew to become a mythical instrument for adventure, sport and excitement. This despite the fact that, in practice, it was a pragmatic tool for mastering the everyday: small, plain two-strokes without affectations. Despite this, motorcycle riders became heroes and their machines objects of desire.

As in Germany, there was a great need for transport during the postwar period. Most of the factories used by the prewar manufacturers had not been affected by the war and, as the German military had kept the workshops working, production was able to resume almost immediately. In the case of Moto Guzzi, it had the added advantage that production of motorcycles had not stopped entirely during the war. Postwar production began with the basic 500-cc design of 1933, but also the 250-cc Airone, which had been introduced in 1939. This small machine was initially used by the authorities, but a civilian version became a bestseller.

Between 1947 and 1955, there were actually just three model lines in Mandello: the single-cylinder 500s, first the GTV and W and from 1950 the various models of the Falcone; the 250-cc range, with two versions of the Airone beginning in 1949; and the Galetto scooter, with 160, later 170, and finally 192-cc engines. These were, in fact, sufficient to saturate the market. There were larger motorcycles for racing and use by the authorities, medium ones for use on the public roads, and the very special Galetto for use as a means of transportation.

An important new postwar entry was the Motoleggera 65, powered by a 64-cc, two-stroke engine with rotary valve induction. The company had no previous experience with two-stroke engines, but the model was a huge success and, typical for the brand, was equipped with all sorts of technical innovations, although in simplified form. Motorcycles for the low

BiS WANN
HAB' iCH ZEiT?

BiS OSTERN '99!

Die MOTO GUZZI-Start-Aktion '99.
Checkpoint: Ihr GUZZI-Partner!

MOTO GUZZI

Cross country ride after the war; the small single-cylinders were also a success off the pavement. This is a brochure from 1999. The caption at the top reads: "How much time do I have?"

cost market segment were of course designed with economy in mind, and the front suspension consisted of pressed steel girder forks. The main frame consisted of a diagonal central tube and the rear wheel suspension was two horizontal springs. These were small details, but typical for the Moto Guzzi brand.

As early as 1947, several models were equipped with hydraulically damped suspension elements. The first was the Airone, with then modern telescopic forks. And it was an upside down design for better stiffness! As well, one side was designed so that the lateral play of the forks could be adjusted.

These innovations and developments were not enough, however, to create a myth from this model range. Racing series also sprang up immediately after the war, and participants entered everything they could lay their hands on. This included many prewar Guzzis mixed with modified street models. There were no significant differences between the technologies of the two categories.

Since its early history, Moto Guzzi had used racing for developmental work. Racing and especially racing successes were also important PR instruments. There was no reason to break with this tradition. And so, not long after the end of the war, factory racing machines again appeared on the tracks.

The technical characteristics of these motorcycles clearly broke with the company's traditions and the brand's standard philosophy, however. There were as many variations of cylinder number and layout as one could desire. The single-cylinders of the prewar years survived in the form of the 500-cc Dondolino, which was replaced by the Gambalunga. The prewar Bicilindrica with its 120-degree V-twin 500-cc engine, was updated with modern suspension elements, the last time in 1951.

There was also a parallel 250-cc twin-cylinder, however it was soon replaced by a smaller variant of the quarter-liter Gambalunga – the Gambalungino. At the same time, the racing division was working on an inline, four-cylinder, mounted longitudinally, with shaft drive. This machine was very contrary, with a novel brake power distributor between the wheels, but after two years of development work (and two racing victories) the project was abandoned as the motorcycle was too difficult to ride. The second version had a frame that also served as a bearer for a full fairing, an example of the creative thinking of the Guzzi designers, who can actually be summarized in two names: Umberto Todero and Giulio Carcano. Carcano joined Guzzi in 1937, Todero in 1939, and after the war both presented properly worked-out designs for the racetrack, culminating in the 500-cc V8. And yet, it was a single-cylinder that brought five world championships in the 350-cc class home to Mandello, topped off by a title in the 250-cc class in the first world championship in 1949.

Love of detail stood for Giulio Carcano, a perfectionist of the old school. Almost a renaissance man, he was also responsible for the construction of a wind tunnel in 1950, close to the mountains in the factory's inner courtyard. For the first two years, two aircraft engines powered the tunnel, and even though there were as yet no noise abatement laws, the din produced by two such engines, without damping against a rock face, was a bit too much for the small village.

When the wind tunnel drive was switched to electricity, the grid was unable to handle the load and wind tunnel tests had to be carried out at night. But it was a great help; for example, a special scale measured the up- and down-thrust of a fairing, while a large board with lamps enabled the rider to work out the most favorable seating position.

The culmination of this meticulous work was a 350 racing machine, vintage '57. "That was the most beautiful one, at least if someone asks me," said one of the two designers, Umberto Todero. "It certainly represented the apex of single-cylinder development. For Guzzi, Giulio Carcano was a great stroke of luck. Carcano pretty much taught me everything I know today. He was my teacher, my professor. He was the greatest in his field, a genius." The late forties and early fifties were the heyday of the then thirty-year-old company. After the war, Carlo Guzzi's creative powers were no longer what they had once been, and

Carcano dominated technical development with his almost boundless engineer's spirit. From time to time, the older Guzzi reined in the young engineer, when he appeared to be throwing too much money out the window on Grand-Prix sport. The years 1956 and 1957 were the culmination and highlight of development. On the one hand, there was the legendary eight-cylinder racing engine; on the other, the unbelievably well engineered 350-cc single-cylinder which, in their last Grand-Prix year (1957), gave the Italians their fifth world championship in the 350-cc class.

Guzzi also entered its proven single-cylinder power plants in the 250- and 500-cc classes. But while the 250-cc Guzzis brought three world championships – 1949 and 1951 under Bruno Ruffo and 1952 under Enrico Lorenzetti – home to Mandello, the Guzzi riders on the 500-cc single-cylinders won numerous Grand-Prix races, but failed to win a world championship.

When the famous Bicilindrica was finally sent into well-deserved retirement in 1951, Giorgio Parodi sought a solution to the 500's problems outside the company – the Guzzi singles rarely made a trick against the fast, four-cylinder, Gileras and MV Augustas. He commissioned the Roman engineer Gianini to design a modern, competitive, 500-cc racing machine. The result was a motorcycle with a longitudinally mounted, four-cylinder, inline engine and shaft drive. The machine was not exactly a success, however. The designer had difficulty getting to grips with the load change reactions of the longitudinally mounted engine. Only once in 1953, in Hockenheim – where it was equipped with a mechanical integral brake system – under Lorenzetti, and in 1954, in Mettet (Belgium), under Fergus Anderson, did the four-cylinder cross the finish line in first place. For a racing machine with the flying eagle on the tank, that was, of course, not quite enough.

In Mandello during the winter of 1954-55, a decision was made in favor of an entirely new concept – the eight-cylinder's keel was laid. One of these V8 engines may be seen in a glass case in the Moto Guzzi museum, along with two complete motorcycles. The two engineers decided on a transversely mounted engine with a ninety degree angle between the cylinders – which ensured perfect mass balance – a total of four gear-driven overhead cams, two valves per cylinder, eight tiny 20-millimeter Dell'Orto carburetors, liquid cooling, and a six-speed transmission – on account of the anticipated narrow power band.

The design and construction times were extremely short. Concept work began in September or October and by the following spring the engine was already running on the test bench. The eight-cylinder produced over 60 hp in initial trials and – contrary to expectations – had an amazingly broad power band. It reached almost 12,000 rpm, but at higher revolutions – and these were essential for higher performance – there were vibration problems in the crank drive. Carcano and Todero returned to their drawing

boards and designed a two-part crankshaft whose halves were joined by Hirth gearing. Todero had the new crankshafts produced in Germany by the Albert Hirth GmbH, in Stuttgart-Zuffenhausen.

The eight-cylinder occasionally appeared on the racetracks in the summer of 1955, but the machine's first proper season was 1956. It was to be a season filled with failures and problems. The powerful engine undoubtedly had great genes, but its reliability left much to be desired. Nevertheless, at Hockenheim, Ken Kavanagh turned in the fastest lap – at an average speed of 199 kph! The bike was certainly fast. Not until the spring of 1957, however, did the Otto Cilindri record its first – and unfortunately only – victories. Giuseppe Colnago won the first heat of the Italian championship in Syracuse, on Sicily's east coast, and Dickie Dale the Coppa d'Oro in Imola.

The machine was denied any further victories. The complicated technology repeatedly brought the Guzzi technicians to the brink of desperation. A political decision to withdraw from racing sport along with Moto Mondial and Gilera took the racing division in Mandello completely by surprise. Bill Lomas had already withdrawn, but he brought a V8 to England and carried out tests there. John Surtees, several times world champion and later also an F1 world champion, was already scheduled to test the V8 when news of the decision by three Italian manufacturers seeped through. It was later discovered that, in the high rpm range, the V8 demonstrated a linear performance increase with no noticeable curtailment of reliability.

Much later, John Surtees got the opportunity to ride one of these newly built machines at a veterans' race in Masano, in 1986.

The 1950s were undoubtedly a great time for Moto Guzzi. Racing successes made the company known beyond the borders of Italy. But management failed to make capital from this outstanding image, and there were scarcely any new developments in production machines.

The 250-cc Airone entered production in 1938 and the machine, which produced 12 hp in its final versions, continued to be built almost unchanged until 1957. The small, two-stroke engines, which appeared in 1946 were an entirely new field. There were still two of these small two-stroke engines in the 1960s – the 50-cc Dingo and the 40-cc Trotter.

There was also a proper grown-up motorcycle in the program, the Astore. It was a development of the prewar GTV with a 500-cc single-cylinder engine that only just produced 20 hp. It remained in the program until 1953, when it was replaced by perhaps the most famous and best-known Moto Guzzi ever – the Falcone. For many, many years, it was Moto Guzzi's only single-cylinder 500-cc machine. Production of the Falcone continued up to and including the 1967 model year, in two versions – the Sport and the Turismo, which were technically identical. Both produced 23 hp at 4,500 rpm and achieved about 135 kph on the street.

The period of the late 1950s and early 1960s was certainly not a high point in Guzzi history, as the company suffered many misfortunes. Small street machines like the Stornello and the Lodola were added to the lineup. The latter was something special, however, as it was the last design from the pen of Carlo Guzzi. For the designer of so many famous and successful motorcycles, this job was, of course, not terribly exciting. As well, the motorcycle market was losing significance because of growing prosperity and the resulting trend toward automobiles. At the end of the 1950s Moto Guzzi had more than 21,000 employees and was one of the largest makers of motorcycles in the world. It also had subsidiaries in Spain and Turkey.

A real ray of hope was the Lodola, perhaps no great success in the marketplace, but nevertheless a motorcycle with sporting genes in its veins. The initial version broke with tradition, in that it had clearly modern traits, and not just in terms of technology. The 174-cc engine produced nine horsepower, a respectable figure at that time. The entire valve train was spring-mounted to avoid undesirable vibration. As well, the valves were opened by an overhead camshaft. The timing chain had an automatically tensioned slide rail. The duplex frame was joined to a sheet metal construction in the center, all in all a typical Italian 175, in red of course!

Following the cessation of all racing activities after the 1957 season, Moto Guzzi, in fact showed interest in a *regolarita*, what we would call *enduro* today. Several motorcycles based on the Lodola were built for this purpose. This displacement category had long had its own class in this segment of the sport, and 1958 was a development year for the small team. Five Guzzis took part in the 1959, six-day event. Four of these were in the Trophy Class, with displacements of 175 and 235 cc. They were otherwise technically identical, with overhead cams and four-speed gearboxes. Unfortunately, the team placed second. Guzzi decided not to enter the following year, but in Milan, in November, it displayed a production version of a 235-cc Lodola Regolarita.

Numerous good results followed in the years 1961-64, while, simultaneously, development of the street version continued. The 235-cc Gran Turismo, a street bike, followed in 1959, unfortunately with pushrods for the valve drive. In private hands, the overhead valve version often had to suffer in the matter of servicing, and the first 235-cc factory bikes also had pushrods. Later, the overhead cam reappeared on the factory bikes. The production Lodola produced eleven horsepower at 6,500 rpm, about the same as the 175-cc model in its second version.

For 1961 there was also a 247-cc overhead cam Lodola with a five-speed gearbox, but in 1964 these motorcycles were, in fact, only used in Italian races. There were also dirt bike versions of the small 125-cc Stornello, one of which was offered to the public via official channels in the 1964 model year.

But the workforce was simply too large for the sales figures that were achieved at the beginning of the 1960s. Many hand-finishing manufacturing processes were kept in-house for a long time. In the 1970s Guzzi was still making its own forks, as well as drum brakes and the chrome coating of the cylinder bores.

In addition to its purely economic problems, at that time the company was also shaken by a serious leadership crisis. Founding father Emanuele Vittorio Parodi and his nephew, Angelo, had died during the war. Giorgio Parodi himself suffered from lingering consequences of wounds suffered during the war and died in Genoa, in the mid-1950s. Carlo Guzzi was now more than seventy years old, ill, and weak. He died in November 1963. From the founding generation only Enrico Parodi, Giorgio's brother, who had been with the company since 1942, was left.

On 25 February 1966, a state-controlled receiver took over the company, and after that it was administered for about a year by a committee set up by irritated lending institutions. One of its first measures was to reduce personnel costs. The technical leaders of the company, including chief engineer Carcano, were shown the door. They were supposed to be rehired by the newly founded company, SEIMM (Società Esercizio Industrie Moto Meccaniche), which took over the firm soon afterwards, on 1 February 1967.

Once again, Carcano would not have it. He would gladly have worked for the new leadership, but being thrown out and then rehired, that did not sit at all well with the proud chief engineer; he considered it in poor style. He left the engineering business behind and turned to his second love, boat building. Several successful America's Cup yachts came from his drawing boards. The Italian sailors owed their Olympic victory in Melbourne, Australia, to him, by the way. Carcano designed a special rudder arrangement for them that reduced roll.

The once so proud brand had fallen into a deep depression. Whether it was because of sudden changes in the market or bad decisions on the part of management made no difference. By the end of 1957, Moto Guzzi had won 3,320 international races, forty-seven Italian championship titles, eleven victories on the Isle of Man, and fourteen world championship titles, if one includes the manufacturer's titles. The company's motorcycles also won four world championship titles in the 350 category and three in the 250 class.

Monza, September 1956

Monza 1956, the start of the 350 class race: working through the night, the Guzzi team had lightened the Bill Lomas' machine (12), marking the beginning of the company's light construction program of 1957. The reason – the new and faster four-cylinder Gileras ridden by Geoff Duke (2) and Libero Liberati (4).

Monza, in September 1956: Moto Guzzi's racing director and designer Giulio Cesare Carcano had called this meeting after training for the Italian Grand Prix. Also present were Umberto Todero – also a member of the racing Division – and drivers Dickie Dale, Ken Kavanagh and Bill Lomas. There was just one topic: the new and unexpectedly fast Gilera 350. The machine was actually supposed to have made its debut the following year, but now the four-cylinder Gilera with Libero Liberati in the saddle, was in the pole position. There was no need for the Guzzi men to worry, however.

After all, they already had the world championship title in the 350 class in their pocket. But to simply forego such a victory, in the witch's cauldron of the Monza autodrome? Where all of Italy was watching?

The Guzzi's advantages were its handling, low center of gravity, and especially its outstanding single-cylinder engine producing about 35 hp. The new Gilera had about seven more horsepower, and of course that mattered on the ultra-fast course at Monza. In training, the four-cylinder machine's lap times had been about three seconds better than the three Guzzis.

During training for the GP in Monza in 1956 it became clear that the days of the single-cylinder Guzzis might soon be past. Bill Lomas (standing in left of the photo) was already world champion before this last race.

During the race, Bill Lomas' machine ran just as fast as Liberati's Gilera. But a crash in the Lesmo curve robbed the Briton of any chance of victory. Instead, Dickie Dale took second place on the lightweight Guzzi behind the Gilera – ahead of a four-cylinder MV and three, three-cylinder DKWs.

The 1956 season was over. But by this race in the royal park in Monza at the latest, at least one thing had to be clear to the Guzzi men: if they wanted to continue their series of victories that had begun in 1954 – brand world champions from '53 to '56 – they would first have to achieve more performance and second go on a proper weight-reducing diet. That winter in Mandello, the lights seldom went out in the offices of the racing division.

Umberto Todero took care of the engine. All that was retained was the design principle – a single-cylinder four-stroke in a horizontal installation with two overhead cams and twin valves. The 350-cc engines used to date were designed with a rather short stroke (bore x stroke: 80 x 69.5 mm), in order to be able to install large valves in the combustion chamber – 41

Carcano made a proposal. He could add another horsepower during the night, but it would come at the cost of stability. Bill Lomas, who was already the certain world champion after victories with the 350 Guzzi in the Netherlands, in Germany, Ulster and in Imola and Floreffe, agreed. What did they have to lose? But could they not also save more weight?

They could! Between training runs and the actual race, all excess weight was removed from the three racing bikes with the numbers 12, 14 and 16. The bench seat was tossed into the corner, replaced by a simple aluminum plate with a small piece of foam on it. The extra protection against spark failure in the form of a second battery was removed. By the next morning the three Guzzis were several kilograms lighter.

Moto Guzzi more or less owned the 350 world championship in the 1950s, winning a total of five titles. The last was won by Keith Campbell (above left).

Bill Lomas (1) had a poor season in 1957 due to injuries. Here he is seen leading Bob McIntyre (20) and Libero Liberati on their Gileras at Imola. Liberati took the 500-cc world championship that year.

(inlet) and 36 (outlet) millimeters. It was a design that promised good peak performance. This version of the 350-cc power plant produced 35 hp at 7.800 rpm.

Todero's thinking during that winter of 1956-57 went in an entirely different direction. A high top speed was well and good, but in racing were not the best possible lap times the only thing that counted, pure and simple? And could not this goal be most easily achieved through the best possible rate of acceleration? And what he, Todero, could contribute to this was the broadest possible power band, one that would enable the rider to accelerate out of the corners a little better than his competitors.

No sooner said than done. Todero lengthened the stroke to seventy-nine millimeters and reduced the bore of the light metal cylinder to seventy-five millimeters. The valves were also made smaller. From the valves, which now measured thirty-nine (inlet) and thirty-three (outlet) millimeters, Todero expected a higher gas velocity and with it a better cylinder charge, even at relatively low revolutions.

Perhaps the most interesting racing motorcycle of all time, simply because its engine wasn't really powerful. This example is the 1956 version.

The new single's weight was also reduced by several pounds. The battery ignition was replaced by a magneto, the second sparkplug was eliminated, and the valves were closed by just one spring instead of two. Even the crankcase was modified. Its walls were made much thinner and stiffening ribs provided additional strength.

Meanwhile Carcano was not sitting on his hands. The chassis of the new 350 was his project. The frame was made of extremely light steel tube. A fat central tube of welded thin sheet metal accommodated the steering head and also served as a reservoir for the dry sump lubrication system. The diameter of the front wheel brake shrank from 220 to 200 millimeters, as in future it would have less weight to deal with. The spokes in the two wheels also had to lose weight. They were now only half as thick as those of the previous year's machine. Even the tires became narrower – and all of this just to save weight. Of course all of the nuts and bolts, which for strength reasons could not be made of aluminum, were drilled out or undercut.

The slim full fairings, which also encompassed the front wheel, were a work of art. They were lovingly hand made from magnesium sheet by the Spengler body makers. A protective finish was out of the question for Carcano – too much weight.

A coating of bichromate of potash – a potassium compound – protected the magnesium, which was susceptible to corrosion. This is why the Guzzi racing motorcycles of that era were not finished in the usual Italian red. Potash is green after all. The 1957 season was at the door, time was pressing. Umberto Todero worked with the engines on the performance test bench. His testing method was murderous for the delicate racing engines. Todero measured performance over the entire rpm range in 200 rpm increments. In each case, a single was run at full throttle at a certain rpm for at least a minute. At the end of this torture, the engines were producing a full 38 hp at 8,000 revs. And when the finished machines were finally sitting on their narrow wheels, there were only smiling faces to be seen in Mandello. The 350 weighed just ninety-seven kilos – a sensational figure. And that at a time when there were still no composite materials.

The first test rides in Imola were extremely satisfactory. As a rule, Bill Lomas achieved the same lap times he had with the previous year's machine in dry conditions. Even the narrow tires seemed to have no adverse effects; in fact the tires got up to temperature more quickly.

Just a few weeks later, however, disaster struck: during the first race of the season in Imola, the Coppa d'Oro, Lomas was involved in a bad crash which injured him and put him out of action for a long time. And Liberati and Bob McIntyre won the first two Grand Prix races – both on four-cylinder Gileras. But then the new Guzzi and Lomas' replacement, Keith Campbell, struck back. A second place finish on the Isle of Man and victories in Holland and Belgium secured him and Moto Guzzi the sought-after world championship in the 350 class. It was Australia's first title and Guzzi's last.

Guzzi was also active in the 250 and 500 classes – in both cases with proven single-cylinder power plants. But while the small 250-cc Guzzis at least brought three driver world championships – 1949 and 1951 under Bruno Ruffo and 1952 under Enrico Lorenzetti – to Mandello, the Guzzi riders on the 500-cc single-cylinders won numerous Grand Prix victories but no world championships.

When the famous Bicilindrica was finally sent into well-deserved retirement in 1951, Giorgio Parodi began seeking a solution to the 500's problems outside the company – it rarely made an impression against the fast four-cylinder Gileras and MV Augustas. He engaged the Roman engineer Gianini to design a modern competitive 500-cc racing machine. The result was a motorcycle with a longitudinally mounted engine and shaft drive. But the machine didn't turn out to be a piece of luck. The four-cylinder only crossed the finish line first on two occasions: in 1953 in Hockenheim – and then equipped with a mechanical

The side-view of the powerful V8 engine does not tell that the entire drive package weighed just 65 kilos, including the specially-designed Dell'Orto carburetors. Eight sat close together between the cylinders.

Mechanical breakers occasionally caused problems. It is said that not even the rider could tell if the engine was running on all eight cylinders. With typical dry humor, Bill Lomas said years later: "But if the engine was running on all eight, you sure noticed it."

integral brake system – and 1954 in Mettet (Belgium). That wasn't very often for a racing machine with the flying eagle on the tank.

In Mandello in the winter of 1954-1955, a decision was made in favor of an entirely new concept – the eight-cylinder's keel was laid. The two engineers decided on a transversely mounted engine with a ninety degree angle between the cylinders – which ensured perfect mass balance – a total of four gear-driven overhead cams, two valves per cylinder, eight tiny 20-millimeter Dell'Orto carburetors, liquid cooling, and a six-speed transmission – on account of the anticipated narrow power band.

The design and construction times were extremely short. Concept work began in September or October and by the following spring the engine was already running on the test bench. The eight-cylinder produced over 60 hp in initial trials and – contrary to expectations – had an amazingly broad power band. It reached almost 12,000 rpm, but at higher revolutions – and these were essential for higher performance – there were vibration problems in the crank drive. Carcano and Todero returned to their drawing boards and designed a two-part crankshaft, whose halves were joined by Hirth gearing. Todero had the new crankshafts produced by the Albert Hirth GmbH in Stuttgart-Zuffenhausen.

The eight-cylinder occasionally appeared on the racetracks in the summer of 1955, but the machine's first proper season was 1956. It was to be a season filled with failures and problems. The powerful engine undoubtedly had great genes, but its reliability left much to be desired. Nevertheless, at Hockenheim, Ken Kavanagh turned in the fastest lap – at an average speed of 199 kph! The bike was certainly fast. Not until the spring of 1957, however, did the Otto Cilindri record its first – and unfortunately only – victories. Giuseppe Colnago won the first heat of the Italian championship in Syracuse, on Sicily's east coast and Dickie Dale the Coppa d'Oro in Imola.

The machine was denied any further victories. The complicated technology repeatedly brought the Guzzi technicians to desperation. A political decision to withdraw from racing sport, along with Moto Mondial and Gilera, took the racing division in Mandello completely by surprise. Bill Lomas had already withdrawn, but he brought a V8 to England and carried out tests there. John Surtees, several times world champion and later also an F1 world champion, was already scheduled to test the V8 when news of the decision by the three Italian manufacturers seeped through. It was later discovered that, in the high rpm range, the V8 demonstrated a linear performance increase with no noticeable curtailment of reliability.

Much later John Surtees got the opportunity to ride one of these newly built machines, at a veterans' race in Masano in 1986.

Umberto Todero – Life in Guzzi

A life for Moto Guzzi – Umberto Todero began as an apprentice with Moto Guzzi and then steered the company's racing program in its golden years, always with great enthusiasm: in the box with Ken Kavanagh, with the stopwatch, and (right) often with a well-deserved victory on Sunday.

The beginning of the nineties: the two authors of this book are visiting Moto Guzzi. Umberto Todero – the company's chief engineer – is going to talk to us about the V 7 models and everything that came after them. We have to wait a while, until Dr. John Wittner – we have just had a look at his factory racing machine – can finally pull Todero away from his actual work. Then, finally, a not very tall, older gentleman is standing before us – gray, a full head of hair, a little bit round about the hips – but a bundle of energy, probably unlike anyone else in the company. Engineer Todero is already approaching seventy. He places his hand on Dr. John's arm: "Shall we go into the museum? It's such a lovely place to talk. But John, you will have to translate everything. My English is so bad." The rogue flashes in his eyes. He knew exactly what was coming next. "But your English is first class, far better than our collected Italian." Todero demurred, smiled, felt flattered.

The man at the door handed the engineer the keys to the factory museum. We climbed the narrow stairway that led upward into the elongated room in which long rows of Guzzis were set out on the left and right. In front were the new production machines – Le Mans III, Mille GT – ten meters farther the Sixties with the first V 7, the Nuovo Falcone, precisely in the center the first Guzzi, the two surviving eight-cylinder racing machines, and right behind them the Grand Prix racers and the prototypes. Todero closed the door behind us, rushed with small, quick steps through a good thirty years of motorcycle history, and headed straight towards the two eight-cylinders.

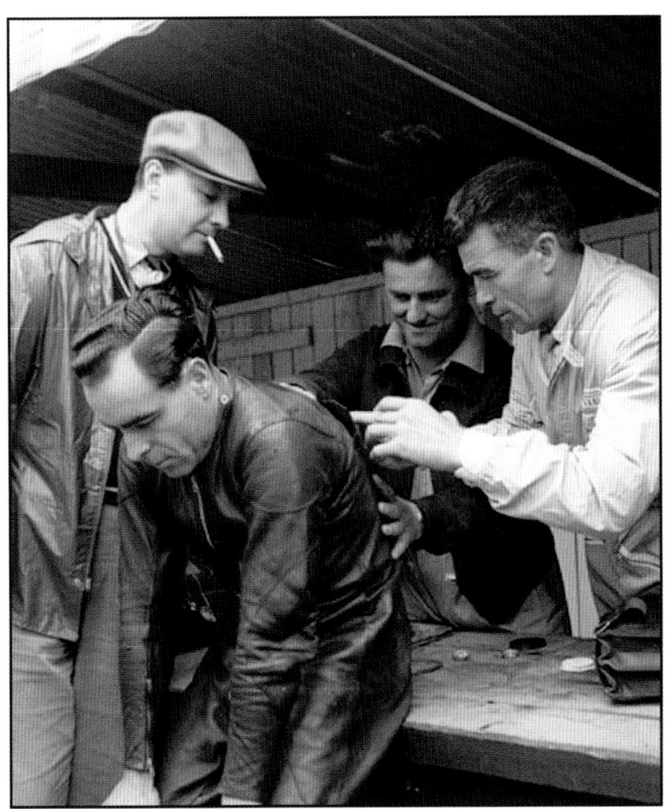

Todero stops in front of a 350 racing machine, a 1957. "That was the most beautiful one, at least if you ask me. It surely represents the apex of single-cylinder development. You know, Carcano joined us in 1937. It was a great stroke of luck for Guzzi. Carcano basically taught me everything I now know. He was my teacher, my professor. He was the greatest in his field, a genius."

A mechanic in green overalls enters the museum and asks Todero something in Italian. On his instructions he unscrews a few parts from a single-cylinder display piece and disappears again. "We are restoring one of the last 350 Grand Prix machines. The engine will be running again in a few days." When asked about missing parts, Todero reacted with a broad smile. 'Why would we need old parts?

The inner circle: Umberto Todero in a discussion with Enrico Cantoni and Giulio Carcano (from left to right). Rider Dickie Dale listens attentively. What exactly is up with Ken Kavanagh's back (above left) is unclear.

Todero is not someone one would call a great storyteller. He finds the hoopla about his person extraordinary, but he feels flattered nonetheless. The engineer seeks to start the conversation – "Do you know, has someone told you?" – searching for English words, speaking with his hands, his left hand repeatedly reaching for the arm of one of his listeners, seeking to hold his attention. And we hang on every word – three people, all of whom know at least the basics of the stories the gray-haired man is telling. But while Todero is talking, the old machines seem to come to life. Motorcycle history suddenly becomes alive, close enough to touch.

Umberto Todero began working at Moto Guzzi in March 1939, when he was sixteen years old. His monthly salary then was 350 Lire. The letter confirming his hiring is signed by Angelo Parodi the father of one of the two founders of the company – with fascist greetings, of course. Todero, of course, got to know both founders of the company – Carlo Guzzi and Giorgio Parodi.

The V8 now occupies a place of honor in the museum (above). Right: probably the first test ride with the Guzzini 65 before its record-setting rides in Switzerland in 1948 with Raffaele Alberti as rider.

After all, we still have all the original drawings. If something is missing we simply make a new part."

By then Todero had long since reached retirement age, but every morning he still entered through the red factory door and went to his office, where he brooded over his drawings and lived the Moto Guzzi legend.

Umberto Todero died in February 2005 and with him the motorcycle community lost one of its greatest ambassadors. Todero is buried in the cemetery in Mandello del Lario – within sight of the test track at the back of the Guzzi factory.

V7 – The Beginning of a New Era

A new era actually begins every day, but the first half of the 1960s was a strange time. The mood and the beliefs of the 1950s were still valid, including the Cold War and rock and roll. To society the motorcycle was as dead as other extinct animals from an era no one wants to see return. Only the enthusiasts committed themselves to this scene, brave souls desperately holding on. The motorcycle was dead. Motorcycle industries continued to exist in three European countries, but they were a community separated from the rest of the world. It was as if England and Italy were refusing to open the window to glance out at the rest of the world. For BMW in Munich, disastrous sales figures were indications of the company's future concentration on automobiles and soon other areas of technology. In 1969 just 4,863 new motorcycles of all brands were registered in Germany.

Among "real" motorcycle riders, the appearance of Japanese motorcycles was still regarded as a flash in the pan.

The mid-Sixties were when the first Moto Guzzi V7 models were conceived and designed. The Italian state needed a new police motorcycle and every contract of this kind was a life and death struggle, not a bad image as we shall see.

Umberto Todero worked on the basic concept of the motorcycle, together with Giulio Carcano and Cantoni, and built the first prototypes, which began testing in 1964. The engine was based on a Carcano design originally intended for the Fiat 500 automobile. Almost the entire development department disappeared in the big housecleaning. Then in 1967, Lino Tonti, a man who had now and then made a name for himself in Italian industry, took over the design department. Several years earlier he had designed the so-called Linto, a racer whose engine consisted of

Best regards from Perry Rodan: the engine and propeller in the wind tunnel look like something from an old movie. The wind tunnel ran for many, many hours, especially in the 1950s.

two Aermacchi single-cylinders. Many were sold, but few saw the finish line. Umberto Todero once said, "If someone is going to someday build a one-and-a-half-cylinder with three and a half valves, then it will have to be Tonti. Our inspection room over the racing department is full of such Tonti miscarriages." The prototypes often went into production too quickly.

Moto Guzzi had to vindicate itself with the new V 7, and would do so, but the turbulent times of the 1960s could have meant the final end.

They were difficult times for Moto Guzzi, in large part because of slumping sales figures, a problem faced not just by Moto Guzzi. Curiously, at the same time the Japanese motorcycle industry was overrunning the world. Under its old leadership, virtually the founding generation, over the years Moto Guzzi had created a super modern and complete production organization in step with the times. It was so complete that even engines were cast there and telescopic forks and brake systems manufactured. Everything needed for a complete motorcycle was made in-house. The company also had an extensive social program, with child day care, vacation facilities, housing, and a sports program. Bearing witness to this is the yacht club at the southern entrance to Mandello, which still exists.

During the 1960s, the only member of the founding generation and its descendants still with Moto Guzzi was Enrico Parodi, also a son of the founder. He is described as a charismatic person, but he made several unfortunate decisions that shook the financial base of the entire Parodi corporation. These included interests in the defense and electrical industries, but also major real estate holdings.

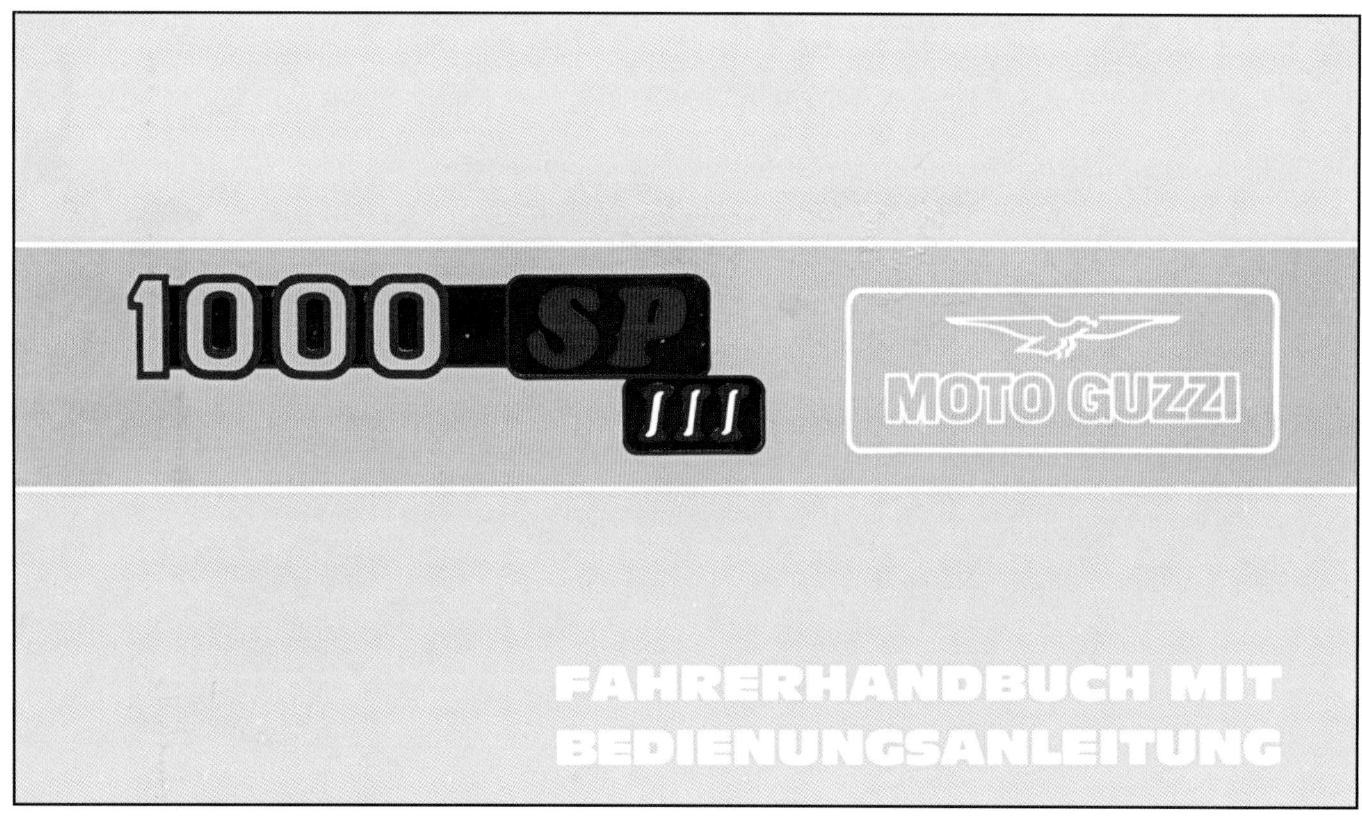

Owner's handbook and operating manual for a 1000 SP III: these books even contained instructions for setting the valves – almost unthinkable today.

Even before the first drawings of the coming V7 were completed, Moto Guzzi undertook an important step towards reorientation. Mofas, a Milan company, was brought into the program. 1963 saw the appearance of the first Dingo, a development of its own with a pressed steel frame and two-stroke engine. There were two versions, one with pedals and step-through frame, one with foot pegs and an elongated gas tank.

Nothing changed, however, and on 25 February 1966 the manufacturer was placed under a state-controlled receiver, a sort of trust committee with representatives of the bank and the IMI *(Instituto Mobiliare Italiano)*. One of the first steps was to reduce personnel in all areas, and one of those who had to go was chief designer, Giulio Carcano. Not until the 1990s did he accept an invitation to a company anniversary and, although he was reserved with personal comments, from then on he found himself part of the family again. In the interim, he had worked on designing regatta sailing vessels, a field where his forward-thinking solutions were welcomed.

The *Societá Esercizio Industrie Moto Mechaniche* (SEIMM) was created on 1 February 1967, and for three years it served as Moto Guzzi's leaseholder with an option to purchase, which in fact happened. The SEIMM was, in fact, the IMI reborn. Its first president was Luciano Francolini. After a year, he was replaced by Donato Cattaneo, who remained until the de Tomaso days. The general manager was Romolo de Stefani, formerly of Bianchi and Ducati. He brought Lino Tonti with him to Mandello.

One of the first steps was to trim the fat. Models that had sold poorly in recent years disappeared from the line: Lodola, Zigolo and Galetto were the most notable. The Stornello, in 125 and 160 cubic centimeter versions, received much attention, and at the same time there was activity on the new V7 project.

For Moto Guzzi the de Tomaso era began in 1973. The native of Argentina expanded the Guzzi palette with many smaller models.

Production of the police motorcycle began in 1966 and the demand in the civilian market was also so strong that plans were drawn up for a touring motorcycle. Mandello sensed dollars and first tested the market in November 1965, when it displayed a civilian version of the V7 at the Milan show.

The soundness of the concept is demonstrated by the fact that, forty years later, the same engine layout and transmission system still form the basis for all production at Mandello. The first civilian model in 1967 produced 42 hp from a V-twin with a displacement of 703 cc. The longitudinally mounted engine was ideally suited for shaft drive and a flange-mounted four-speed gearbox. In addition to the engine and gearbox, the motorcycle's electrical system was also ideally suited to touring, with a 32-Ah battery and a 300-Watt alternator, usually found only in automobiles. The sturdy frame also had no problem transporting bags and baggage across Europe.

This first model was made until July 1969, when it was replaced by the Special, with a 757-cc engine and a rounder design in white. The technology is described in detail elsewhere in the book, but the facts mentioned here are of significance to the brand's commercial development.

If the market in the 1960s was in transition, in the 1970s it was no less confusing, at least at the beginning. The early Seventies showed that the Fifties were over, true to the saying that the Sixties had never even existed. Outmoded thinking still ruled late in the 1960s, and in every area. The cutoff point, represented by the 1968 generation, was not so badly chosen, and

Long-distance racing in 1985: pit stop by the Martinek team during the eight-hour race at the Nürburgring – the only one ever held on the new GP track.

not just with respect to politics and ideology. The four-cylinder Honda CB 750 appeared on the market in 1969. In autumn of the same year, BMW unveiled its new /5 generation of motorcycles. The three-cylinders from BSA and Triumph had been on the market for a year and a half. In 1968 Kawasaki presented the 60-hp Mach III with 500 cubic centimeters and in 1970 the 750-cc three-cylinder two-stroke.

It sounds slightly arrogant now that Moto Guzzi wanted to answer such competitors with a heavy touring bike, but the brand, in fact, did it, although only under the conditions that prevailed at the time. BMW's top model, the R 69S, in fact had the same rated output – 42 hp – as the V7 from Mandello. If that was not enough of a yardstick!

Ivano Beggio incorporated Moto Guzzi into his Aprilia empire in May 1999. But he took on too much, and at the end of December 2004 Guzzi went to the Piaggio Group.

The new design has since become synonymous with the brand, even more; a Moto Guzzi is today a motorcycle with a transversely-mounted V-twin and shaft drive and nothing else.

The SEIMM era lasted until 1973 The V 7 series earned the company new respect and, above all, export success. In Germany the fat Guzzis were imported by Fritz Röth of Hammelbach and were all sold to private individuals. After the 850 GT, before the 850 T – or in 1974 – the Mobylette GmbH, in Brackwede took over the importing of Guzzis. The 850 T 3 came to Germany under the direction of the Deutsche Motobecane GmbH, in Bielefeld.

In 1973, Alejandro de Tomaso, who had been born in Buenos Aires in July 1928, took over the factory in Mandello. The native of Argentina had immigrated to Italy in 1955 and earned himself a good reputation as a racecar driver and later as a builder of sports cars. And since 1971, Tomaso had held seventy-five percent of the shares in Benelli. By combining two such large companies in the same trade, like Moto Guzzi and Benelli, de Tomaso hoped to be able to do something against the Japanese superiority. The opinion of insiders was: "de Tomaso is a very practical-thinking man, reserved, a little publicity-shy, but with ideas and initiative." Ever since he had been in Italy, de Tomaso had lived in a hotel in Modena. He simply had no desire to take on the responsibility for a house and home.

De Tomaso's plan was only possible if capacities in the motorcycle field were combined. And so he tried to coordinate the capacities and model lines of the two firms. He was determined to halt the Japanese advance with many new and modern motorcycles. Suddenly the program included machines with Asian-sounding names, such as the 350 GTS with a transversely mounted four-cylinder engine – 250- and even 125-cc versions of this engine already existed – and the 250 TS with a twin-cylinder two-stroke. Styling also became increasingly important. One example of this is the 254. Unveiled in 1975, the machine had a transversely mounted 250-cc, inline, four-cylinder engine that produced 27 hp at 10,500 rpm. The buyers obviously wanted four-stroke engines – after all the

Japanese were selling such bikes like hotcakes – and so they would have them. The motorcycle's styling was highly unusual and broke any number of rules that had proved good and proper over the decades. The instruments were placed on the tank, for example. As a result, a rider of normal stature could read almost nothing while riding.

The Guzzi community gave this sophisticated styling something less than a warm welcome. These negative spin-offs were also extremely contentious within the company. An example of such a misshapen motorcycle is the 850 T5. It was in no way a bad motorcycle; nevertheless, in the mid-1980s it became a shelf-warmer. The "crackle and pop" styling of the fairing and seat appeared to be entirely responsible, along with the trendy 16-inch tires.

The company did better with the "small" V-twins (V 35, V 50, V 65 and V 75) that made their appearance in 1977. The stylists returned to classic inspirations, and the use of V-twin engines caused the success of the big Guzzis to rub off on the small V-twins.

In 1988 Fratelli Benelli and SEIMM were both integrated into Guzzi Benelli Moto (G.M.B. S.p.A.). It sold the Benelli factory and integrated Innocenti (which also belonged to de Tomaso). Moto Guzzi now rediscovered its identity. Motorcycles like the Mille GT or the 1000 S combined modern technology – the new, angular cylinder, for example – with familiar classic styling elements. The days of depression were over. The eagle spread its wings again.

Gianfranco Guareschi won a total of three twin-cylinder races in Daytona on the MGS.

However, the eagle did not properly get wind beneath its wings again until the American dentist, Dr. John Wittner, won the American long-distance championship with one of his own designs. He made an agreement with de Tomaso by handshake, resulting in the new, four-valve, sports machines from Mandello. At the same time, however, the twin-valve California remained the central model in the program.

When de Tomaso retired for health reasons, in 1996, a holding company, the Trident Rowan Group Inc. (TRG) was created to put the company back on its feet. The mid-class models had already been dropped from the program, with the exception of the V 65 Custom/Florida and its derivative, the Nevada 750.

The program was quite clear, but commercial success was not guaranteed. The holding company went public in 1999, and with the new capital a number of new products were offered, including the V 11 Sport, which was to spearhead the attack. And the factory was put up for sale.

But what was there to sell? The new four-valve Daytona RS sport bike, the twin-valve V11 Sport and Sport 1100, two versions of the California, the 750 Nevada, the Quota touring-enduro, and the eccentric V 10 Centauro.

At the same time, Honda's CBR 600 F had just completed its eleventh year in production and thus solidified its cult status. The Honda Transalp was just thirteen years old; the VFR was given an 800-cc power plant with fuel injection. The Italian competitor Ducati, had just unveiled the 996, a development of the 916, and it was difficult even for dedicated Guzzi enthusiasts to grant any sort of cult status to the eagle from Mandello.

In May 1999, the brand was bought up by Ivano Beggio, who had begun the production of motorcycles at Aprilia (long active in the bicycle field). Despite initial concerns, the new master was able to calm the fan community to some degree: he insisted on maintaining the identity of the Guzzi brand and, despite his modernization measures, was determined to protect traditions.

Unfortunately, Beggio overreached himself. True, the model line was much modernized and quality improved almost visibly. The range of models was tightened, initially concentrating on cosmetic developments of the V11 Sport (Le Mans and Café Sport) and, of course, more variants of the California, which differed only in equipment – Jackal, Stone, Special, Titanium, etc. It quickly became obvious that that was what the fan base wanted – simple cruisers.

But the competition wasn't asleep at the switch, and the market became saturated with cruisers from just about every manufacturer.

Beggio and Aprilia were standing on shaky ground and the company threatened to go under. The small Brevia, a modern design with one foot in the future – or at least in the present – was unveiled in 2002. That same year, an exciting design was shown in Cologne: the Griso. It was a street fighter with exciting lines.

But what difference would it make, if the brand disappeared from the market? The demise of the scooter market was ultimately its salvation.

In the 1980s, the scooter giant Piaggio had acquired the Gilera brand, in order to protect itself against unpleasant surprises in the small motorcycle market. In the intervening years, it had unveiled a number of motorcycle-like scooters as well as studies with Japanese 600-cc engines.

This time, the story had a happy ending; Piaggio was allowed to buy Moto Guzzi and projects that had languished were suddenly realized. The Bravo 1100 and Griso 1100 were completed for 2005. A new Nevada – a completely new design and a very important one, especially for the home market – appeared, followed soon afterwards by a new 850 generation of the Bravo and Griso. The factory now had large two- and four-valve machines, with the same basic design for the models between 850 and 1100 cubic centimeters. The Nevada was the only product with a unique design. Of course, all this was primarily an economy measure, despite a visible expansion of the model line, which successfully combined the phenomena of riding pleasure and tradition. In its Vintage model, the California manifested the brand's long V-twin tradition and displayed it visually. As a sport model had been absent for two years, in autumn 2006 the factory unveiled a 1200 Sport. It was powered by the 1151-cc engine that also powered the new Griso and the fully faired touring model.

Entirely new was a larger 850 with a 946-cc power plant and a mixture of cruiser and street fighter under the name Bellagio 940.

With this model offensive, the traditions from Mandello continue to live – and hopefully will for a long time.

The various Griso models helped Moto Guzzi bring a fresh wind to its palette of models. The motorcycles also impress in their quality of workmanship.

Prewar Motorcycles

GP and Tipo Normale 1921–24

Construction of the first Guzzi prototypes extended into mid-1920. Work began in the cellar of the Guzzi family home and was later moved to the Ripamonti engine mechanic's garage. The prototype was called the GP (Guzzi – Parodi), was painted green and lacked eagle wings on the tank. The machine had a horizontally mounted four-stroke single-cylinder engine with a bore of 88 millimeters and a stroke of 82 millimeters – making it a short-stroke engine. In the cylinder head there was an overhead cam driven by a vertical shaft on the right side. Four overhead valves controlled the gas exchange. The mixture was ignited by two spark plugs simultaneously – a Bosch magneto providing the necessary voltage. The crank mechanism and gearbox shared a common housing which could be kept small because of the external flywheel. The half-liter engine produced all of twelve horsepower.

Around this low-set power plant, Guzzi designed a twin-tube frame with an unsprung rear wheel. Part of the rear fender was incorporated into the supporting frame structure. A parallelogram front fork held the front wheel and the spring element was at the top, directly in front of the headstock. There was no front wheel brake and Guzzi used a band brake on the rear wheel. The GP was capable of 100 kph, a terrifying speed when one imagines the gravel roads shortly after the war.

The GP was undeniably a very advanced design, not revolutionary but very advanced. Combustion chamber with four valves, a short bore-stroke ratio, primary drive using gear wheels, and all of this combined in one unit. None of these features was novel, but they had never been combined in a single design – that was new. But the two young entrepreneurs were soon forced to realize that their design was too costly for a production motorcycle. What the market needed, after the Great War, was not a racing machine but a robust

Moto Guzzi built just seventeen examples of the Tipo Normale. It was the first Guzzi to wear the eagle on the tank – in memory of co-founder Ravelli.

vehicle for everyday use, with low fuel consumption and high reliability. And so Carlo Guzzi had to go back to his drawing board. The result was the Tipo Normale of 1921.

The Normale was the first motorcycle to bear the name Moto Guzzi and the eagle wings – the emblem of the Aeronautica Militare, in memory of Ravelli. The horizontally mounted engine, the low frame, the external flywheel – the Normale had these too. Savings were found elsewhere, for example the rear fender, which lost its supporting element. It was replaced by a simple steel section.

The exhaust valve was placed in the overhead position in the center of the combustion chamber and was activated by a pushrod from the rocker shaft. This placed the part most in need of cooling – the exhaust valve – directly in line with the airflow. The inlet valve was positioned on the side of the cylinder and was opened directly by the cam. Mixture preparation was entrusted to a British AMAC carburetor with separate float chamber. The simple single-cylinder engine produced all of eight horsepower at 3,200 rpm, sufficient for a top speed of 80 kph. Sino Finzi won the first race for Moto Guzzi riding this machine, the notorious Targa Florio in Sicily. Moto Guzzi delivered all of seventeen examples of the Normale by 1921.

Tipo Normale

Production Period:	1921-1924
Number produced:	17
Engine:	1-cyl., inlet over exhaust valve arrangement
Displacement:	498 cc
Bore x Stroke:	88 x 82 mm
Compression:	4:1
Power output:	8 hp (5.9 kW) at 3,400 rpm
Mixture preparation:	AMAC, 1 inch; Bosch magneto
Clutch:	multi-plate wet clutch
Gearbox:	3 gears, primary gear wheel, chain
Frame:	steel tube frame and sheet metal sections
Wheelbase:	1380 mm
Front suspension:	parallelogram front fork
Rear suspension:	none
Front tire:	26 x 3.00
Rear tire:	26 x 3.00
Front brake:	none
Rear brake:	drum, hand and foot operated
Empty weight:	130 kg
Tank capacity:	10 liters
Maximum speed:	85 kph

The GP (above left) had a modern four-valve engine, however it proved too expensive for the conditions of the day. The simpler twin-valve engine (above) was used in the Normale.

Tipo Sport 1923–28

With minor modifications, the Tipo Normale remained in the production until 1923. The first production Guzzi was then replaced by the Tipo Sport, which had the lighter running gear of the C2V racing machine and the engine of the Normale – although a clearly more powerful version. The single produced 13 hp at 3,800 rpm. Maximum speed was 100 kph. More than 4,000 were built by 1928. A development of this model was the Sport 14 with much larger cooling ribs on the cylinder and cylinder head. More than 4,000 examples of this motorcycle were built in just two years. The last version of this machine, the Sport 15, began leaving the production line in 1931. Numerous modifications to the engine and running gear helped give the machine a modern look and somewhat improved performance. Nearly 6,000 examples of this type had been sold by the time war broke out in 1939.

Tipo Sport	
Production Period:	1923-1928
Number produced:	4,107
Engine:	1-cyl., inlet over exhaust valve arrangement
Displacement:	498 cc
Bore x Stroke:	88 x 82 mm
Compression:	4.5:1
Power output:	13 hp (9.6 kW) at 3,800 rpm
Mixture preparation:	AMAC, 1 inch; Bosch magneto
Clutch:	multi-plate wet clutch
Gearbox:	3 gears; main gear, chain
Frame:	steel tube
Wheelbase:	1430 mm
Front suspension:	parallelogram fork
Rear suspension:	none
Front tire:	26 x 3.00
Rear tire:	26 x 3.00
Front brake:	none
Rear brake:	drum, hand and foot operated
Empty weight:	130 kg
Tank capacity:	10 liters
Maximum speed:	100 kph

GT and GT 16 1928–34

Beginning in 1928 Moto Guzzi offered the GT, which later became the GT 16, alongside the Sport models. Both of these machines had what the competition had long characterized as "life-threatening nonsense" – a rear wheel suspension. Some years earlier Carlo Guzzi had recognized the weak point of all motorcycles – including his own: the rigid mounting of the rear wheel. For if the rear end bounced from one bump to the next on the frequently uneven roads of the day, half the time in the air, then it could hardly contribute to the machine's riding stability. Previous attempts to incorporate rear wheel suspensions had all failed because of unstable main frames – in part because today's materials were not available at the beginning of the century.

In the mid-Twenties, Carlo Guzzi and his brother Giuseppe set out to find the solution to this problem. He designed a solid triangular swing arm, whose upper end was hinged to the main frame. Long rods exerted pressure on a spring assembly (consisting of four

The GT was the first Guzzi with the "life-threatening" rear suspension.

GT and GT 16

Production Period:	GT: 1928-1931; GT 16: 1931-1934
Number produced:	832 (combined)
Engine:	1-cyl., inlet over exhaust valve arrangement
Displacement:	498 cc
Bore x Stroke:	88 x 82 mm
Compression:	4.5:1
Power output:	13.2 hp (9.7 kW) at 3,800 rpm
Carburetor:	Amal
Clutch:	multi-plate wet clutch
Gearbox:	3 gears; main gear, chain
Frame:	steel tube
Wheelbase:	1430 mm
Front suspension:	parallelogram fork, friction damping
Rear suspension:	coil springs, friction damping
Front tire:	26 x 3.00/3.50 x 19
Rear tire:	26 x 3.00/3.50 x 19
Front brake:	drum
Rear brake:	drum
Empty weight:	150 kg
Tank capacity:	11 liters
Maximum speed:	100 kph

springs) beneath the engine. Friction discs provided the necessary damping.

Acceptance by the buying public was minimal, and just eighty examples were built. Obviously no one believed that the suspension really was stable. Even a trip to the North Cape on the GT by Giuseppe Guzzi did little to help. It did, however, result in the machine being nicknamed Norge. Sales did not improve until Guzzi began using the rear wheel suspension in racing sport. More than 700 examples of the GT 16 follow-up version were sold by 1934.

The spring packet in the rear wheel suspension was hidden in a box beneath the engine. The swing arm is an upside-down cantilever version with its pivot point at the top.

With about 4,000 sold, the Tipo Sport 14 was the best-selling motorcycle of its day in Italy. The fork came from the racing machines of the same era.

Tipo Sport 14	
Production Period:	1929-1930
Number produced:	4,285
Engine:	1-cyl., inlet over exhaust valve arrangement
Displacement:	498 cc
Bore x Stroke:	88 x 82 mm
Compression:	4.5:1
Power output:	13.2 hp (9.7 kW) at 3,800 rpm
Mixture preparation:	AMAC
Clutch:	multi-plate wet clutch
Gearbox:	3 speeds; main gear, chain
Frame:	steel tube
Wheelbase:	1430 mm
Front suspension:	parallelogram forks, friction damping
Rear suspension:	none
Front tire:	26 x 3.00
Rear tire:	26 x 3.00
Front brake:	drum
Rear brake:	drum
Empty weight:	130 kg
Tank capacity:	11 liters
Maximum speed:	100 kph

Tipo Sport 14 1929 – 30

As Moto Guzzi became Italy's biggest manufacturer of motorcycles in 1929, it is not surprising that the Tipo Sport 14 outsold all other types in the years that followed, with more than 4,000 made during its two years in production. Refinements were added based on experience with the Sport, making the Sport 14 an entirely new generation of motorcycle. The frame was changed, the new forks from the GT and the racing machines were used, as were new brakes and a new electrical system – the magneto was replaced by a separate alternator driven by the clutch. The engine received its own oil circulation system to the valve mechanism, and it was instantly recognizable on account of its larger cooling vanes.

C 2V, 2VT, GT 2VT	
Production Period:	1923-1927/1928-1930/1931-1934
Number produced:	not known
Engine:	1-cyl., overhead valves
Displacement:	498 cc
Bore x Stroke:	88 x 82 mm
Compression:	5.25:1
Power output:	17 hp (12.5 kW) at 4,200 rpm
Mixture preparation:	AMAC; Bosch magneto
Clutch:	multi-plate wet clutch
Gearbox:	3 speeds, main gear, chain
Frame:	steel tube
Wheelbase:	1410 mm
Front suspension:	parallelogram forks, friction damping
Rear suspension:	none
Front tire:	26 x 3.00
Rear tire:	26 x 3.00
Front brake:	none at first; drum brake introduced in 1928
Rear brake:	drum
Empty weight:	130 kg
Tank capacity:	11 liters
Maximum speed:	120 kph

The GT 2VT was sold until 1934 and some examples came with lights.

C 2V, 2VT, GT 2VT 1923 – 34

These racing machines differed from the inlet-over-exhaust Normale mainly in having two overhead valves activated by pushrods. When the four-valve machines for the factory riders appeared in 1924, the C 2V was offered to private buyers. After a production pause it reappeared in 1928 as the 2VT with the new saddle tank and the chassis of the Sport 15. The final model, the GT 2VT with rear wheel suspension, was sold until 1934. As several examples were equipped with lights, it can be assumed that they were also ridden on the roads – the power output of 17 hp must be a convincing argument!

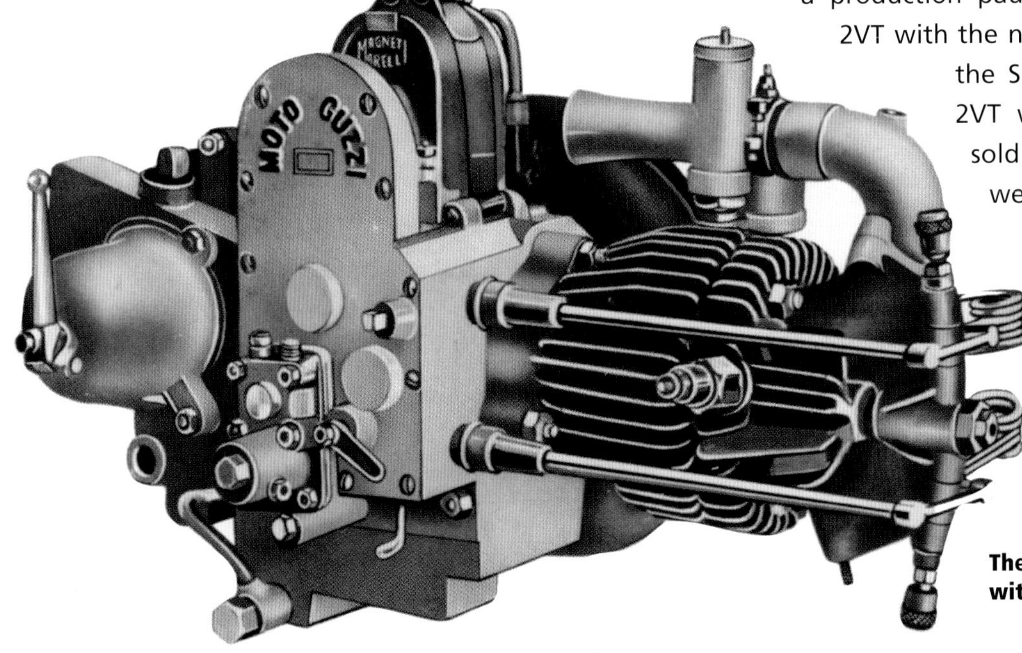

The engine had two overhead valves with external valve springs.

The C4V came with an overhead camshaft and four valves. This motorcycle won the European championship title.

C 4V, 4V TT, 4V SS	
Production Period:	1923-1927/1927-1928/1928-1933
Number produced:	486 in total
Engine:	1-cyl., overhead cam, four valves
Displacement:	498 cc
Bore x Stroke:	88 x 82 mm
Compression:	6:1 (C 4V)
Power output:	22 - 32 hp at 5,500 rpm (C 4V – 4V SS)
Mixture preparation:	AMAC 28.5 mm; Bosch magneto
Clutch:	multi-plate wet clutch
Gearbox:	3 speeds, main gear, chain
Frame:	steel tube
Wheelbase:	1380 mm
Front suspension:	parallelogram forks, friction damping
Rear suspension:	none
Front tire:	27 x 2.75
Rear tire:	27 x 2.75
Front brake:	wedge disc brake introduced in 1927; drum brake in 1928
Rear brake:	drum
Empty weight:	130 kg
Tank capacity:	10 liters
Maximum speed:	130 kph (C 4V)

C 4V, 4V TT, 4V SS 1924 – 33

C stands for Corsa (race) and 4V for four valves. This model was the first to wear the red clothing of master tailor Carlo Guzzi. He was finally able to use the overhead camshaft he had favored since the prototypes. The basic design was otherwise very close to production, sharing most components with the production versions. It was an immediate success, winning the first European Championship. It was also offered as a sport bike and was therefore entered in various races by private riders. With time it suffered from several age-related weaknesses (for example, the hand shifter), but it was an historically-important motorcycle nonetheless, as it was able to acquit itself well against the competition.

This 250 was offered mainly to private customers. It was more or less a smaller copy of the C4V.

250 Monoalbero 1926 – 40

This 250 was only offered to private buyers until 1933, after which it was employed as a factory racer. In every respect it was a smaller copy of the C 4V, but it was an independent design from the ground up. Two variants were produced simultaneously between 1930 and 1933, the factory racer with foot shifter and four-speed gearbox. Private riders had to be satisfied with the old systems on their TT or SS. New commercial models were later developed from the factory machines and these remained competitive even in the postwar years. The early models had a bronze cylinder head. Another obvious difference was the forks; the factory machines had English trapezoidal forks. In 1935 they were also fitted with rear wheel suspension.

250 Monoalbero	
Production Period:	1926-1933
Number produced:	377
Engine:	1-cyl., overhead cam, four valves
Displacement:	247 cc
Bore x Stroke:	68 x 68 mm
Compression:	8:1
Power output:	15 hp at 6,000 rpm
Mixture preparation:	Binks 25 mm; Bosch magneto
Clutch:	multi-plate wet clutch
Gearbox:	3 speeds, main gear, chain
Frame:	steel tube
Wheelbase:	1360 mm
Front suspension:	parallelogram forks, friction damping
Rear suspension:	none
Front tire:	27 x 2.75
Rear tire:	27 x 2.75
Front brake:	drum
Rear brake:	drum
Empty weight:	105 kg
Tank capacity:	12.5 liters
Maximum speed:	125 kph

Tipo Sport 15 1931–39

Modern times arrived with the introduction of the Sport 15. One innovation was the so-called "saddle tank," which practically sat on top of and around the upper tubular frame. As well, the tires and brakes were made larger. A luxury version, with plenty of chrome, could be had in the third production year. The tank was chromed with painted sides. The engine used a by then common T-shape connecting rod, which on Moto Guzzi bikes had only been seen on the four-valve factory racers. Most of the changes thus affected the power plant, even though, in principle, the horizontally mounted inlet-over-exhaust single remained basically unchanged.

Tipo Sport 15	
Production Period:	1931-1939
Number produced:	5,979
Engine:	1-cyl., inlet over exhaust valve arrangement
Displacement:	498 cc
Bore x Stroke:	88 x 82 mm
Compression:	4.5:1
Power output:	13 hp (9.7 kW) at 3,800 rpm
Mixture preparation:	Amal/from 1935 Dell'Orto; Bosch magneto
Clutch:	multi-plate wet clutch
Gearbox:	3 speeds, main gear, chain
Frame:	steel tube
Wheelbase:	1430 mm
Front suspension:	parallelogram forks with friction damping
Rear suspension:	none
Front tire:	3.50 x 19
Rear tire:	3.50 x 19
Front brake:	drum, 177 mm
Rear brake:	drum, 200 mm
Empty weight:	150 kg
Tank capacity:	11 liters
Maximum speed:	100 kph

The Sport 15 was the first Guzzi with a saddle tank that no longer sat atop the frame tube but actually partly encompassed it. Very modern lines.

Tre Cilindri 1932–33

Beginning in 1932, Carlo Guzzi tried the 500-cc class with something other than a single-cylinder. He designed a three-cylinder inline engine, also horizontally mounted, which produced 25 hp at 5,500 rpm. Only a few examples of the Tre Cilindri were made, however, each completely by hand. One machine has survived to the present day. The Tre Cilindri weighed all of 160 kilos, had just one side-mounted carburetor, and was capable of 130 kph. Until the V 7 it was the only production motorcycle that was not powered by a single-cylinder. A very similar three-cylinder engine was produced in 1940, but it was intended for a 500-cc racer and was equipped with a supercharger. The power plant produced over 65 hp.

Tre Cilindri	
Production Period:	1932-1933
Number produced:	not known
Engine:	3-cyl., overhead valves
Displacement:	495 cc
Bore x Stroke:	56 x 67 mm
Compression:	4.9:1
Power output:	25 hp (18.4 kW) at 5,500 rpm
Mixture preparation:	Amal; battery ignition/coil
Clutch:	multi-plate wet clutch
Gearbox:	3 speeds, main gear, chain
Frame:	steel tube with sheet metal sections
Wheelbase:	1440 mm
Front suspension:	parallelogram forks with friction damping
Rear suspension:	four coil springs, friction damping
Front tire:	3.25 x 19
Rear tire:	3.25 x 19
Front brake:	drum
Rear brake:	drum
Empty weight:	160 kg
Tank capacity:	11.5 liters
Maximum speed:	130 kph

In 1932 Carlo Guzzi attempted a 500-class motorcycle with more than one cylinder. Only a few examples of the machine, with its longitudinally-mounted three-cylinder engine, were built.

P 175/250 1932 – 40

Introduced in 1932, the P 175 was a cheap, tax-privileged machine with the same basic features as the by then well-known 250s and 500s. The engine was a completely new design with overhead valves. A 250 replaced the 175 when changes to the laws eliminated the tax benefits. The 250 was built in a succession of variants, the second with rear wheel suspension. There was also a sport version (PES) as well as a cheap version with sheet metal parts on the chassis (PL, later Ardetta).

P 175/250	
Production Period:	1932-1940
Number produced:	approx. 7,000; all variants
Engine:	1-cyl., overhead valves
Displacement:	174/238 cc
Bore x Stroke:	59 x 63/68 x 64
Compression:	5.5:1
Power output:	7 hp (5.21 kW) at 4,200 rpm/
	9 hp (6.6 kW) at 4,000 rpm
Mixture preparation:	Amal 18 mm; Bosch magneto
Clutch:	multi-plate wet clutch
Gearbox:	3 speeds, main gear, chain
Frame:	steel tube
Wheelbase:	1320 mm
Front suspension:	parallelogram forks with friction damping
Rear suspension:	sprung/unsprung alternately until 1937
Front tire:	3.00 x 19
Rear tire:	3.00 x 19
Front brake:	drum
Rear brake:	drum
Empty weight:	115 kg
Tank capacity:	10 liters
Maximum speed:	90/100 kph

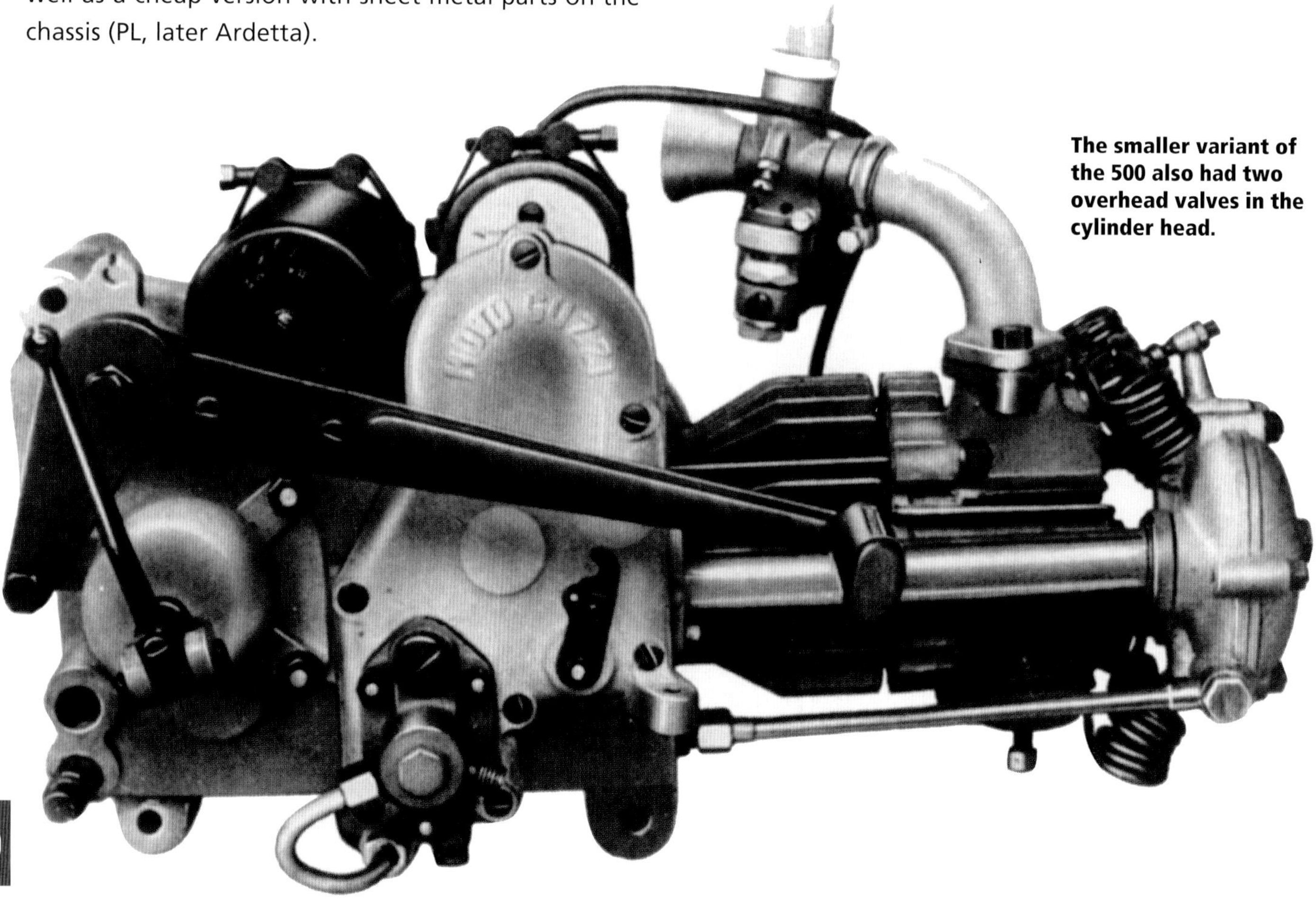

The smaller variant of the 500 also had two overhead valves in the cylinder head.

V, GTV, GTW 1934 – 48

The successful single-cylinder recipe was also used on the V of 1933, but with the difference that the engine had overhead valves. This provided good performance potential and from the V were developed the GTV and the more powerful GTW with 22 hp. Both had rear wheel suspension. The GTC Sport of 1937 to 1939 was another development of the V. With raised exhaust pipes, 3.00 x 20 front wheel and 17-liter tank, the Sport was capable of 150 kph. Production of the GTC totaled 161 machines.

The GTV continued to be built after the war, initially with rear wheel suspension from 1945 to 1947. The 1948 model introduced telescopic forks and hydraulic shock absorbers in the rear. The engine now had just one exhaust port and the exhaust a muffler. A 200-mm front wheel brake was introduced soon after production began, and, because of the fork, there was also a new fender. Beginning in 1949, the GTV was replaced by the Astore.

Powered by the 22 hp engine, the GTW flourished after the war and was built for two years: 1948 and 1949. Apart from sportier handlebars and aluminum rims, it was identical to the GTV.

V, GTV, GTW	
Production Period:	1933-1940/1940-1948
Number produced:	approx. 2,500 by 1940
Engine:	1-cyl., overhead valves
Displacement:	498 cc
Bore x Stroke:	88 x 82 mm
Compression:	5.5:1
Power output:	18.9 hp (13.9 kW) at 4,300 rpm
Mixture preparation:	Amal; Bosch magneto
Clutch:	multi-plate wet clutch
Gearbox:	4 speeds, main gear, chain
Frame:	steel tube with sheet metal sections
Wheelbase:	1400 mm
Front suspension:	parallelogram forks with friction damping; telescopic forks introduced in 1947
Rear suspension:	sprung/unsprung
Front tire:	3.25 x 19
Rear tire:	3.50 x 19
Front brake:	drum
Rear brake:	drum
Empty weight:	160 kg
Tank capacity:	12 liters
Maximum speed:	120 kph

The 500-cc engine of the V, GTV and GTW had excellent performance potential: 18 hp at 4,000 rpm was an excellent figure at that time.

S and GTS 1934–40

In addition to the sportier GTV and GTW, in 1934 the company introduced the S and GTS models for everyday use. The latter had the GTV's sprung frame, but otherwise it was identical to the S. Both were also the last with the inlet over exhaust valve arrangement, with less power, but had the new four-speed gearbox. For this reason, it also became the first Moto Guzzi police motorcycle, the beginning of a long tradition, and during the war it mutated into a military machine, the Alce. The S and GTS were very popular and almost 7,000 were sold by 1940.

S and GTS	
Production Period:	1934-1940
Number produced:	approx. 6,000
Engine:	1-cyl., inlet over exhaust valve arrangement
Displacement:	498 cc
Bore x Stroke:	88 x 82 mm
Compression:	4.6:1
Power output:	13 hp (9.7 kW) at 4,000 rpm
Mixture preparation:	Amal; magneto ignition
Clutch:	multi-plate wet clutch
Gearbox:	4 speeds, main gear, chain
Frame:	steel tube, sheet metal sections
Wheelbase:	1400 mm
Front suspension:	parallelogram forks with friction damping
Rear suspension:	sprung (GTS)/unsprung
Front tire:	3.25 x 19
Rear tire:	3.50 x 19
Front brake:	drum
Rear brake:	drum
Empty weight:	147 kg (S, unsprung)
Tank capacity:	12 liters
Maximum speed:	105 kph

The S and the GTS (above) were the first Moto Guzzi built for the authorities. The Airone, here the version with the encapsulated valve train, developed into a much-loved model.

Airone	
Production Period:	1939-1957
Number produced:	not known
Engine:	1-cyl., overhead valves
Displacement:	247 cc
Bore x Stroke:	70 x 64 mm
Compression:	6:1
Power output:	9.5 hp (7 kW) at 4,800 rpm
Mixture preparation:	Dell'Orto SBF 22; Marelli magneto ignition
Clutch:	multi-plate wet clutch
Gearbox:	4 speeds, main gear, chain
Frame:	steel tube, sheet metal sections
Wheelbase:	1370 mm
Front suspension:	parallelogram forks with friction damping
Rear suspension:	sprung; friction damping
Front tire:	3.00 x 19
Rear tire:	3.00 x 19
Front brake:	drum
Rear brake:	drum
Empty weight:	135 kg
Tank capacity:	10.5 liters
Maximum speed:	95 kph

Airone 1939–57

After the successful introduction of the PE models, ultimately with a 250-cc engine, an extremely modernized version appeared for the 1939 model year. In 1940 – christened the Airone – it was fitted with a pressed-steel frame and a four-speed gearbox and formed the basis for a police motorcycle that was also built after the war. In 1947 the hydraulically dampened telescopic fork and hydraulic damping on the rear wheel were added. The following year the valve drive was encapsulated, and at the same time the Airone Sport appeared with 13.5 hp and a top speed of 120 kph. The series subsequently divided itself into Turismo and Sport versions until production ended in 1957.

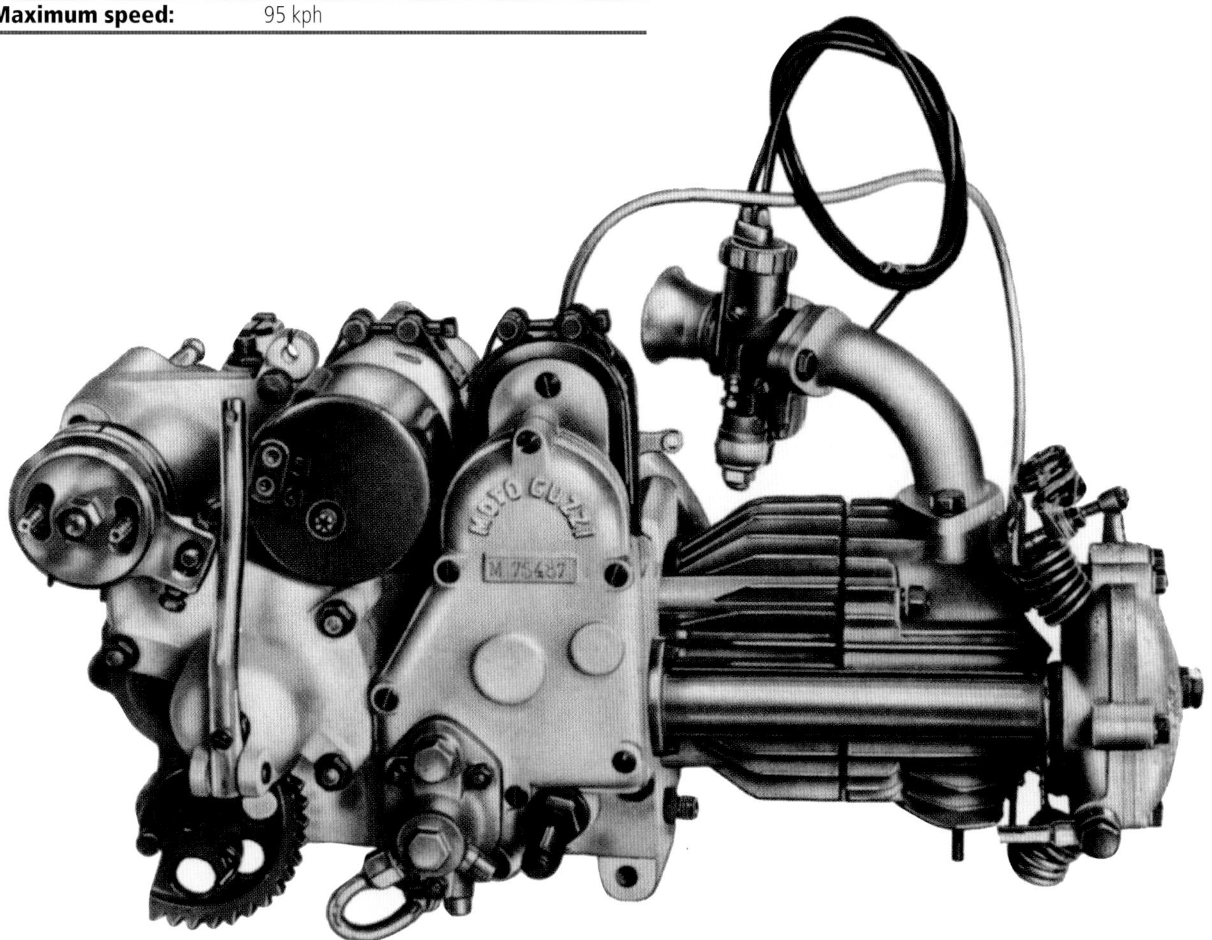

The 250-cc engine of the Airone barely produced ten hp at 4,800 rpm. This version still has the exposed valve train.

Quattro Cilindri 1930

The increased use of superchargers in racing machines was the real inspiration for this forward-looking design. Despite a lengthy testing period, especially on the racetrack in Monza, the machine never entered production, and the testing, which began in autumn 1930, ended in spring 1931. True to his basic concept, Carlo Guzzi designed an engine with four horizontal cylinders. The Cozette supercharger was located on the gearbox and the collector for the four combustion chambers resembled a tube over the exhaust openings. The steel tubes of the frame were joined by aluminum parts in the middle and beneath the engine. This obsolescent design resulted in running gear weaknesses, and the valves were not encapsulated.

Quattro Cilindri	
Production Period:	1930
Number produced:	not known
Engine:	4-cyl., overhead valves
Displacement:	492 cc
Bore x Stroke:	56 x 60 mm
Compression:	5:1
Power output:	45 hp (33 kW) at 7,800 rpm
Mixture preparation:	supercharger; Bosch magneto ignition
Clutch:	multi-plate wet clutch
Gearbox:	3 speeds, main gear, chain
Frame:	steel tube with aluminum sheet sections
Wheelbase:	—
Front suspension:	parallelogram fork with friction damping
Rear suspension:	none
Front tire:	—
Rear tire:	—
Front brake:	drum
Rear brake:	drum
Empty weight:	165 kg
Tank capacity:	12 liters
Maximum speed:	175 kph

Despite extensive testing in Monza, the Quattro Cilindri was never used in a production motorcycle. The engine had four horizontal cylinders.

Bicilindrica 500 — 1933–35/ 1946–47

When Carlo Guzzi had the bright idea to make a 500-cc twin-cylinder from the successful 250 racers, he could not imagine that the basic concept would still be holding its own on racetracks almost twenty years later. Or that the same layout would be adopted by Ducati forty years later. The initial version had the lines of its single-cylinder sister, but development continued and it formed the basis for Moto Guzzi's first really big success in the international arena, the victory on the Isle of Man in 1935. Development of the model continued after the war, and in 1948 it received a telescopic fork, a new body in 1949, and an anatomically fitting tank in 1950. The final refined version was built in 1951.

The Bicilindrica was essentially a combination of two 250 engines.

Bicilindrica 500	
Production Period:	1933-1935
Number produced:	not known
Engine:	V-twin, overhead camshaft
Displacement:	495 cc
Bore x Stroke:	68 x 68 mm
Compression:	8.5:1
Power output:	44 hp (32.4 kW) at 7,000 rpm
Mixture preparation:	two Dell'Orto 28 mm; magneto ignition
Clutch:	multi-plate wet clutch
Gearbox:	4 speeds, main gear, chain
Frame:	steel tube, sheet metal sections
Wheelbase:	1390 mm
Front suspension:	parallelogram fork with friction damping
Rear suspension:	none
Front tire:	3.00 x 21
Rear tire:	3.25 x 20
Front brake:	drum
Rear brake:	drum
Empty weight:	151 kg
Tank capacity:	20 liters
Maximum speed:	180 kph

Condor 500 1930–40

When a new racing class for approved road machines was introduced, Moto Guzzi responded with the Condor. It was first presented as an improved GTC, itself an improved performance GTV, and was then called the GTCL (for Lario). It was not a big seller, not even after it was finally offered as the Condor in 1939. It was mainly used by the Highway Police, a para-military organization, whose ranks included many well-known motorcycle racers of the day. Technically it was a dressed-up GTC, but with a different frame which was also used for a supercharged 250 and the Albatros and Gambalunghino racing 250s. The rear part of the frame was made partly of aluminum, and this material was also used in the engine. Even the friction plates for the rear wheel suspension were made of aluminum.

Condor 500	
Production Period:	1938-1940
Number produced:	69 (as Condor)
Engine:	1-cyl., overhead valves
Displacement:	498 cc
Bore x Stroke:	88 x 82 mm
Compression:	7:1
Power output:	28 hp (20.6 kW) at 5,000 rpm
Mixture preparation:	Dell'Orto SS 32M; magneto ignition
Clutch:	multi-plate wet clutch
Gearbox:	4 speeds, main gear, chain
Frame:	steel tube, sheet metal sections
Wheelbase:	1470 mm
Front suspension:	parallelogram fork with friction damping
Rear suspension:	sprung, friction damping
Front tire:	2.75 x 21
Rear tire:	3.00 x 21
Front brake:	drum
Rear brake:	drum
Empty weight:	140 kg (with street equipment)
Tank capacity:	18 liters
Maximum speed:	160 kph

The Condor was not a big sales success. The first machines went to the Italian highway police, which employed many racing riders at that time.

Albatros 250 1939–49

The first time that the name Giulio Carcano appears in the history of Moto Guzzi is in connection with the development of the Albatros in 1939. In company with Carlo Guzzi, it was on this project that the young engineer gained his first experience. Like the Condor, the Albatros was licensed for road use but was also capable of performing as a racer. It could thus be used in production racing as well in racing classes as a pure racer. It wasn't cheap, but it was still popular and was also used by the factory. The racing machines sold until 1933 and did not find a successor until the Albatros in 1939. In the intervening period, there were only factory machines for the 250 class. The model made a comeback after the war, but in 1949 it was replaced by the Gambalunghino.

Albatros 250	
Production Period:	1939-1949
Number produced:	not known
Engine:	1-cyl., overhead cam, vertical shaft
Displacement:	247 cc
Bore x Stroke:	68 x 68 mm
Compression:	8.5:1
Power output:	20 hp (14.7 kW) at 7,000 rpm
Mixture preparation:	Dell'Orto SS 30M; magneto ignition
Clutch:	multi-plate wet clutch
Gearbox:	4 speeds, main gear, chain
Frame:	steel tube, sheet metal sections
Wheelbase:	1430 mm
Front suspension:	parallelogram fork with friction damping
Rear suspension:	sprung, friction damping
Front tire:	2.75 x 21
Rear tire:	3.00 x 21
Front brake:	drum
Rear brake:	drum
Empty weight:	135 kg (with street equipment)
Tank capacity:	20 liters
Maximum speed:	140 kph

The Albatros was the first motorcycle designed for Moto Guzzi by Giulio Carcano; there was also a street-legal version of the racing machine for the production sport classes.

Like other multi-cylinder designs by Moto Guzzi, the Tre Cilindri was also luckless.

Tre Cilindri 500 1940

Gilera had just celebrated great international success with its supercharged four-cylinder. BMW had won the Tourist Trophy on the Isle of Man, also with a supercharged power plant. Moto Guzzi subsequently developed this three-cylinder, which in many respects broke from the company's design philosophy. The engine, with its sloped cylinders, had two overhead camshafts driven by a chain on the right. The frame was open below, and the power plant was suspended in a central bearer with screwed-on side structures. Unfortunately, the machine was only entered once, in Genoa in May 1940. The war prevented it from seeing further action. As superchargers were forbidden in international racing sport after the war, the machine became a museum piece.

Tre Cilindri 500	
Production Period:	1940
Number produced:	—
Engine:	4-cyl., double overhead cam
Displacement:	492 cc
Bore x Stroke:	59 x 60 mm
Compression:	8:1
Power output:	65 hp (48 kW) at 8,000 rpm
Mixture preparation:	Cozette supercharger; magneto ignition
Clutch:	dry clutch at the crankshaft
Gearbox:	5 speeds, main gear, chain
Frame:	steel tube/sheet metal
Wheelbase:	1470 mm
Front suspension:	parallelogram fork with friction damping
Rear suspension:	sprung, friction damping
Front tire:	2.75 x 21
Rear tire:	3.00 x 21
Front brake:	drum
Rear brake:	drum
Empty weight:	175 kg
Tank capacity:	22 liters
Maximum speed:	230 kph (factory specification)

Moto Guzzi at War

GT 17 1932 – 39

Moto Guzzi had been building motorcycles specially equipped for military use since 1928, but the GT 17 was the first pure military machine and it saw use with the Italian Army in Abyssinia in 1935-1936. It was powered by the inlet-over-exhaust engine – standing inlet, overhead outlet – with 13.2 hp and a three-speed gearbox. In principle, the technology was the same as that of other production Guzzis, but several equipment alternatives were available for military roles, including a submachine-gun on the front of the tank. There were also several baggage systems for the transport of ammunition boxes or heavy machine-guns. The front and rear spring stiffness was adjustable. Many of these machines remained in service even after the introduction of the GT 20.

GT 17	
Production Period:	1932-1939
Number produced:	4,810
Engine:	1-cyl., standing inlet valve, overhead exhaust valve
Displacement:	498 cc
Bore x Stroke:	88 x 82 mm
Compression:	4.7:1
Power output:	13 hp (9.7 kW) at 4,000 rpm
Mixture preparation:	Dell'Orto MC 26 F, Marelli magneto ignition
Clutch:	multi-plate wet clutch
Gearbox:	3 speeds, primary gear, chain
Frame:	steel tube with sheet metal sections
Wheelbase:	1500 mm
Front suspension:	parallelogram fork with friction damping
Rear suspension:	sprung with friction damping
Front tire:	3.50 x 19
Rear tire:	3.50 x 19
Front brake:	drum, 177 mm
Rear brake:	drum, 200 mm
Empty weight:	196 kg ready to ride
Tank capacity:	11.5 liters
Maximum speed:	100 kph

The GT 17 was the first purely military motorcycle made by Moto Guzzi. It proved itself in the Abyssinian campaign long before the Second World War.

GT 20 1938

Visually, the GT 20 differed little from the GT 17, but technically there was more to find than initially struck the eye. The engine was now the S version, with the four-speed gearbox, and the motorcycle clearly had more ground clearance for off-road use. The fork could be disassembled for quick repairs, however it was not adjustable as had been the case on the GT 17. The higher placement of the engine was made possible by relocating the oil tank – under the gas tank. One practical detail was the covering of the flywheel.

GT 20	
Production Period:	1938
Number produced:	248
Engine:	1-cyl., standing inlet valve, overhead exhaust valve
Displacement:	498 cc
Bore x Stroke:	88 x 82 mm
Compression:	4.7:1
Power output:	13 hp (9.7 kW) at 4,000 rpm
Mixture preparation:	Dell'Orto MC 26 F, Marelli magneto ignition
Clutch:	multi-plate wet clutch
Gearbox:	4 speeds, primary gear, chain
Frame:	steel tube with sheet metal sections
Wheelbase:	1440 mm
Front suspension:	parallelogram fork with friction damping
Rear suspension:	sprung with friction damping
Front tire:	3.50 x 19
Rear tire:	3.50 x 19
Front brake:	drum, 177 mm
Rear brake:	drum, 200 mm
Empty weight:	180 kg ready to ride
Tank capacity:	13.5 liters
Maximum speed:	90 kph

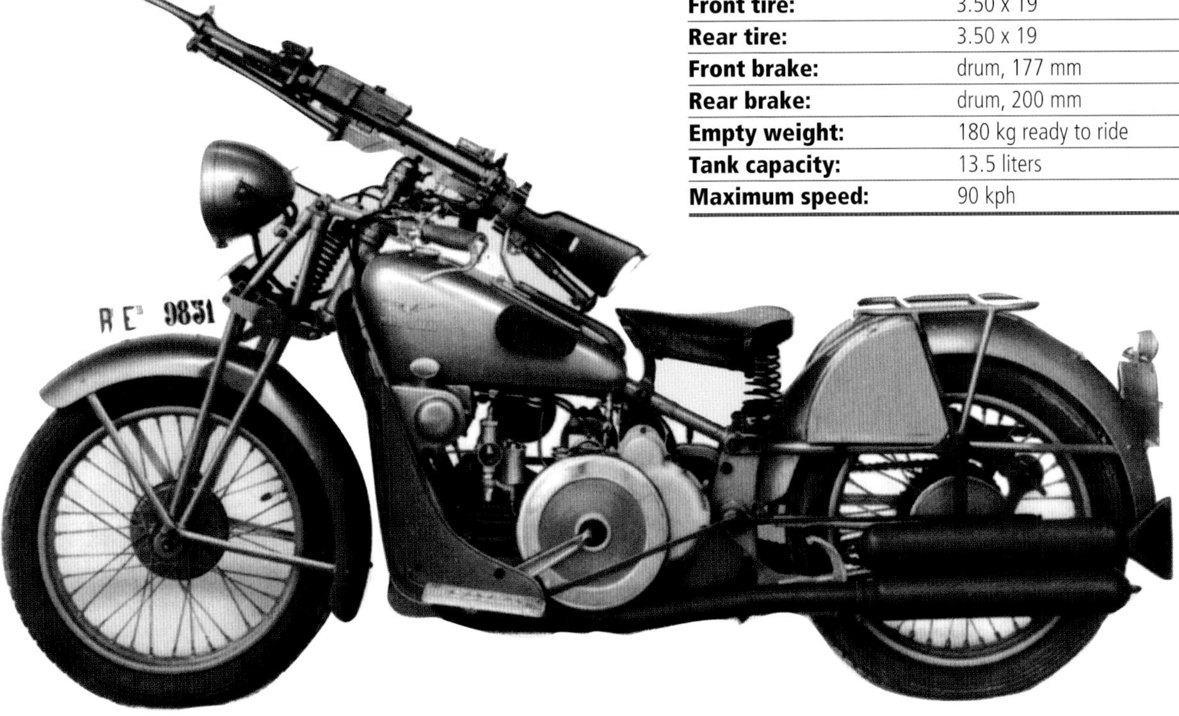

Alce 1939 – 45

The Alce was custom made for the army, but it was based on the GT 20 and superficially was very similar in appearance. The tilt stand was a sturdier design and the oil pump valves operated automatically. Like all military machines, it was delivered as a one- or two-seater, depending on its function, and there was a multitude of equipment details, mounts for the transport of ammunition or heavy machine-guns, for both versions. A reverse-roll locking mechanism made it possible to park the motorcycle in steep terrain. Ready to ride and fully loaded, the motorcycle-sidecar version of the Alce weighed 416 kilograms. Its wheelbase was 1090 mm, and the highest gearing in this version gave a top speed of 78 kph.

Trialce

The Trialce was a quasi-Alce up front, but in the rear it had two wheels with a common axle, and it was what would later be called a trike. The propulsion system's technical specifications were similar to those of the Alce, but the chassis dimensions were of course different. The wheelbase was 1880 mm and the machine weighed 335 kilos. The rear track width was 1120 mm. The Trialce was only built until 1943 and just 1,741 were made. A special version for use by airborne troops could be broken down into two parts.

Alce	
Production Period:	1939-1945
Number produced:	6,390 + 669 (with sidecar)
Engine:	1-cyl., standing inlet valve, overhead exhaust valve
Displacement:	498 cc
Bore x Stroke:	88 x 82 mm
Compression:	4.7:1
Power output:	13.2 hp (9.7 kW) at 4,000 rpm
Mixture preparation:	Dell'Orto MC 26 F, Marelli magneto ignition
Clutch:	multi-plate wet clutch
Gearbox:	4 speeds, primary gear, chain
Frame:	steel tube with sheet metal sections
Wheelbase:	1455 mm
Front suspension:	parallelogram fork with friction damping
Rear suspension:	sprung with friction damping
Front tire:	3.50 x 19
Rear tire:	3.50 x 19
Front brake:	drum, 177 mm
Rear brake:	drum, 200 mm
Empty weight:	180 kg ready to ride
Tank capacity:	13.5 liters
Maximum speed:	90 kph

The Alce came as a solo machine, a motorcycle-sidecar combination, and as the three-wheeler. The drive train was the same in all three machines. The three-wheeler weighed an impressive 335 kilograms.

Single-Cylinders of the Postwar Period

Single-Cylinders of the Fifties and Sixties

During the war, the manufacturer delivered single-cylinder machine to the military and the changeover to postwar production was almost seamless. The features of the old Guzzis with horizontal cylinders and external flywheel, were retained by the first postwar models, with displacements of 250 and 500 cubic centimeters. The somewhat livelier Falcone soon appeared and was based on the first postwar Guzzis. It became the symbol of the sporting activities in Mandello. There were other experiments during the single-cylinder era though, such as the motorcycle-like Galletto scooter, which was built from 1954 to 1966.

The GTV and GTW were only made for a short time and in limited numbers.

This period also saw the last engine designed by Carlo Guzzi, which powered the Lodola. It initially had an overhead cam and a displacement of 175 cc, but was soon enlarged to 235 cc with pushrods. The factory built small numbers of off-road machines with this engine for the Italian trophy team in the international six-day race. Moto Guzzi also had a big Grand Prix racing team until 1957, and its designs were hardly suited for quantity production. The switch to off-road sport was almost seamless, with motorcycles whose only link to production was the Stornello model. This single (125 and 160 cc), together with the Falcone Nuovo, remained in the program until the early Seventies, when both disappeared shortly before the introduction of the Le Mans.

Carlo Guzzi himself decided on the designs of his company well into the 1950s. All of the single-cylinders were based on his ideas.

GTV (GTW)

Production Period:	1947-1948
Engine:	1-cyl., OHV/twin valves
Displacement:	498.4 cc
Bore x Stroke:	88 x 82 mm
Compression:	5.5:1
Power output:	18.9 hp at 4,300 rpm (22 / 4,500 rpm)
Mixture preparation:	Dell'Orto MC 27, Marelli magneto ignition
Clutch:	multi-plate wet clutch
Gearbox:	4 speeds
Frame:	bolted-together steel tubes with stiffening plates behind and under the engine
Wheelbase:	1400 mm
Front suspension:	trapezoid fork, hydraulic telescopic fork from late 1947
Rear suspension:	swing arm with friction damping, from late 1947 with hydraulic pistons
Front tire:	3.25 x 19
Rear tire:	3.50 x 19
Front brake:	drum
Rear brake:	drum
Empty weight:	180 kg
Tank capacity:	12 liters
Maximum speed:	110 kph (130 kph)

GTV, GTW 1947 – 48

During the three years of Italy's involvement in the Second World War, Moto Guzzi motorcycles saw action on every front. The machines still used prewar technology. After the war, the army continued to procure most of its motorcycles from Mandello, and the Superalce, built to appropriate specifications, was initially bought exclusively by the authorities. From it were later developed two twin-valve single-cylinders. The GTV and the more powerful GTW were based (like the Superalce) on a single-cylinder from 1933, but had a single exhaust port instead of the previous two. Both of these new designs retained the classic features of that design: the horizontal cylinder and exposed flywheel. Both models were produced for a brief period and in small numbers.

Astore 1949 – 53

The Astore was a developed version of the GTV. It had the 200-mm drum brakes introduced the previous year, and both the cylinder and cylinder head were made of aluminum. At the time, the Astore was considered a true GT machine, although it was almost identical to its GTV predecessors. Apart from the aluminum engine parts, the only innovation was the carburetor. The Astore retained its place as Moto Guzzi's top model for several years. It was not replaced until the introduction of the Falcone Sport and Turismo, in 1954.

Astore

Production Period:	1949-1953
Engine:	1-cyl., OHV/twin valves
Displacement:	498.4 cc
Bore x Stroke:	88 x 82 mm
Compression:	5.5:1
Power output:	18.9 hp at 4,300 rpm
Mixture preparation:	Dell'Orto MC 27F, Marelli magneto ignition
Clutch:	multi-plate wet clutch
Gearbox:	4 speeds
Frame:	bolted-together steel tubes with stiffening plates behind and under the engine
Wheelbase:	1475 mm
Front suspension:	hydraulic telescopic fork
Rear suspension:	hydraulically-damped swing arm
Front tire:	3.50 x 19
Rear tire:	3.50 x 19
Front brake:	drum, 200 mm
Rear brake:	drum
Empty weight:	180 kg
Tank capacity:	13.5 liters
Maximum speed:	120 kph

Airone 1939 – 49

The 250-cc Airone was created in 1939 and was delivered to the authorities between 1940 and 1957. It was not until the arrival of the postwar civilian model, however, that it became a commercial success. The basic version of the Airone was produced for just a short time. With its aluminum engine and telescopic fork, it had almost the same innovations as the larger Astore, which it also resembled visually, with its horizontally mounted cylinder and exterior flywheel. The motorcycle was popular on account of its low price, but buyers were also attracted by its ease of handling and low weight.

Airone	
Production Period:	1939-1949
Engine:	1-cyl., OHV/twin valves
Displacement:	247 cc
Bore x Stroke:	70 x 64 mm
Compression:	6:1
Power output:	9.5 hp at 4,800 rpm
Mixture preparation:	Dell'Orto SBF 22, Marelli magneto ignition
Clutch:	multi-plate wet clutch
Gearbox:	4 speeds
Frame:	front frame bolted together behind and under the engine
Wheelbase:	1370 mm
Front suspension:	hydraulic telescopic fork
Rear suspension:	swing arm with friction damping (hydraulic one model year)
Front tire:	3.00 x 19
Rear tire:	3.00 x 19
Front brake:	drum
Rear brake:	drum
Empty weight:	140 kg
Tank capacity:	10.5 liters
Maximum speed:	95 kph

The 250 Airone was actually a prewar design, but it only became a big success after the war.

Airone Sport 1949 – 58

A sport version of the Airone appeared in 1949. Thanks to higher compression and a new carburetor, its engine developed twelve horsepower, 2.5 more than the initial model. The Sport's engine underwent continuous development and ultimately produced 13.5 hp at 6,000 rpm. The power plant was one of Carlo Guzzi's most successful designs, but unfortunately the popularity of the Airone models was limited to Italy. The little motorcycle was unable to compete in countries like Germany or Great Britain. In England, for example, its price was equivalent to that of a Triumph 500.

Airone Sport	
Production Period:	1949-1958
Engine:	1-cyl., OHV/twin valves
Displacement:	247 cc
Bore x Stroke:	70 x 64 mm
Compression:	7:1
Power output:	12 hp at 4,800 rpm
Mixture preparation:	Dell'Orto SS1 25A, Marelli magneto ignition
Clutch:	multi-plate wet clutch
Gearbox:	4 speeds
Frame:	tubular frame
Wheelbase:	1370 mm
Front suspension:	hydraulic telescopic fork
Rear suspension:	swing arm with friction damping
Front tire:	3.00 x 19
Rear tire:	3.00 x 19
Front brake:	drum, 180 mm
Rear brake:	drum
Empty weight:	137 kg
Tank capacity:	10.5 liters
Maximum speed:	115 – 130 kph

Airone Turismo 1949 – 57

The first postwar Airone received the add-on Turismo to distinguish it from the Sport, also new in 1949. Apart from the frame, which was a simple structure made largely of pressed/cast parts, it was the same motorcycle. Beginning in 1952, the Turismo was given the frame of the Sport, and in 1954 it received a 12-hp engine. Repeated facelifts caused the Sport and Turismo to more closely resemble each other visually, causing the differences between the two models to blur more and more.

Airone Turismo	
Production Period:	1949-1957
Engine:	1-cyl., OHV/twin valves
Displacement:	247 cc
Bore x Stroke:	70 x 64 mm
Compression:	6:1
Power output:	9.5 hp at 4,800 rpm
	(from 1954 12 hp at 5,200 rpm)
Mixture preparation:	Dell'Orto SBF22, Marelli magneto ignition
Clutch:	multi-plate wet clutch
Gearbox:	4 speeds
Frame:	tubular frame, from 1952 same as the Sport
Wheelbase:	1370 mm
Front suspension:	hydraulic telescopic fork
Rear suspension:	swing arm with friction damping
Front tire:	3.00 x 19
Rear tire:	3.00 x 19
Front brake:	drum, 180 mm
Rear brake:	drum
Empty weight:	140 kg
Tank capacity:	10.5 liters
Maximum speed:	95 – 100 kph

Galletto 160 1950 – 51

The Galetto prototype, which was unveiled in Geneva in 1950, had a displacement of 150 cubic centimeters, however the first production version, deliveries of which began at the end of the year, was powered by a 160-cc engine. Carlo Guzzi himself designed a small, four-stroke engine for this model. This first model version had a much-criticized, three-speed gearbox. The machine itself was a successful blending of scooter and motorcycle. The user-friendly equipment included details such as a gas filter in front of the carburetor and a washable air filter. The spare tire could be mounted front or back, as both wheels had identical dimensions. The jack mounted on the frame simplified changing tires; the brake and drive chain remained on the single swing arm when the rear tire was removed.

The prototype of the Galetto still had a 150-cc engine, however the first production models had a 160-cc engine that delivered six horsepower.

Galletto 160	
Production Period:	1950-1951
Engine:	1-cyl., OHV/twin valves
Displacement:	159.5 cc
Bore x Stroke:	62 x 53 mm
Compression:	6:1
Power output:	6 hp at 5,200 rpm
Mixture preparation:	Dell'Orto MA18BS1, flywheel magneto
Clutch:	multi-plate wet clutch
Gearbox:	3 speeds
Frame:	pressed steel frame with tubular spine
Wheelbase:	1310 mm
Front suspension:	scooter fork
Rear suspension:	single-sided swing arm with
	horizontal shock absorber
Front tire:	2.75 x 17
Rear tire:	3.00 x 17
Front brake:	drum, 125 mm
Rear brake:	drum, 125 mm
Empty weight:	107 kg
Tank capacity:	7 liters
Maximum speed:	80 kph

Galetto 175 1952 – 53

In 1952, two years after the introduction of the Galetto, the engine was increased in size to 175 cubic centimeters. Output increased to seven horsepower and Moto Guzzi added a fourth gear. It also increased overall gearing and added a gear indicator for the shifter. These were the changes compared to the earlier model, and the rest of the scooter was the same as the well-known Galletto 160. In this form the robust general-purpose motorcycle became a best seller.

Galetto 175	
Production Period:	1952-1953
Engine:	1-cyl., OHV/twin valves
Displacement:	174.4 cc
Bore x Stroke:	65 x 53 mm
Compression:	5.6:1
Power output:	7 hp at 5,200 rpm
Mixture preparation:	Dell'Orto MA 18 BS1, flywheel magneto
	Marelli ST 119 DAS
Clutch:	multi-plate wet clutch
Gearbox:	4 speeds
Frame:	pressed steel frame with tubular spine
Wheelbase:	1310 mm
Front suspension:	scooter fork
Rear suspension:	single-sided swing arm with
	horizontal shock absorber
Front tire:	2.75 x 17
Rear tire:	3.00 x 17
Front brake:	drum, 125 mm
Rear brake:	drum, 125 mm
Empty weight:	107 kg
Tank capacity:	7 liters
Maximum speed:	80 kph

The engine of this scooter also had the typical characteristics of a Guzzi of that time: horizontal cylinder, large external flywheel.

Galletto 192 1954 – 60

Scarcely two years after the last increase in displacement, Moto Guzzi's Galletto underwent a thorough redesign. Unveiled at the beginning of 1954, the machine had a crankshaft with a longer stroke, resulting in a displacement of 192 cc and an output of 7.5 hp at 5,000 rpm. Far more important than the increase in power, however, was the new electrical system. A dynamo with starter feature not only supplied the (now larger) battery, but the ignition as well. Thanks to the modified electrical system, it was also possible to improve the headlight, with a more powerful bulb and increased diameter (150 mm). This model also had a larger, 8.5-liter fuel tank.

Galletto 192	
Production Period:	1954-1960
Engine:	1-cyl., OHV/twin valves
Displacement:	192 cc
Bore x Stroke:	65 x 58 mm
Compression:	6.4:1
Power output:	7.5 hp at 5,000 rpm
Mixture preparation:	Dell'Orto MA 19 BS1, battery ignition
Clutch:	multi-plate wet clutch
Gearbox:	4 speeds
Frame:	pressed steel frame with tubular spine
Wheelbase:	1310 mm
Front suspension:	scooter fork
Rear suspension:	single-sided swing arm with horizontal shock absorber
Front tire:	2.75 x 17
Rear tire:	3.00 x 17
Front brake:	drum, 125 mm
Rear brake:	drum, 125 mm
Empty weight:	110 kg
Tank capacity:	8.5 liters
Maximum speed:	85 kph

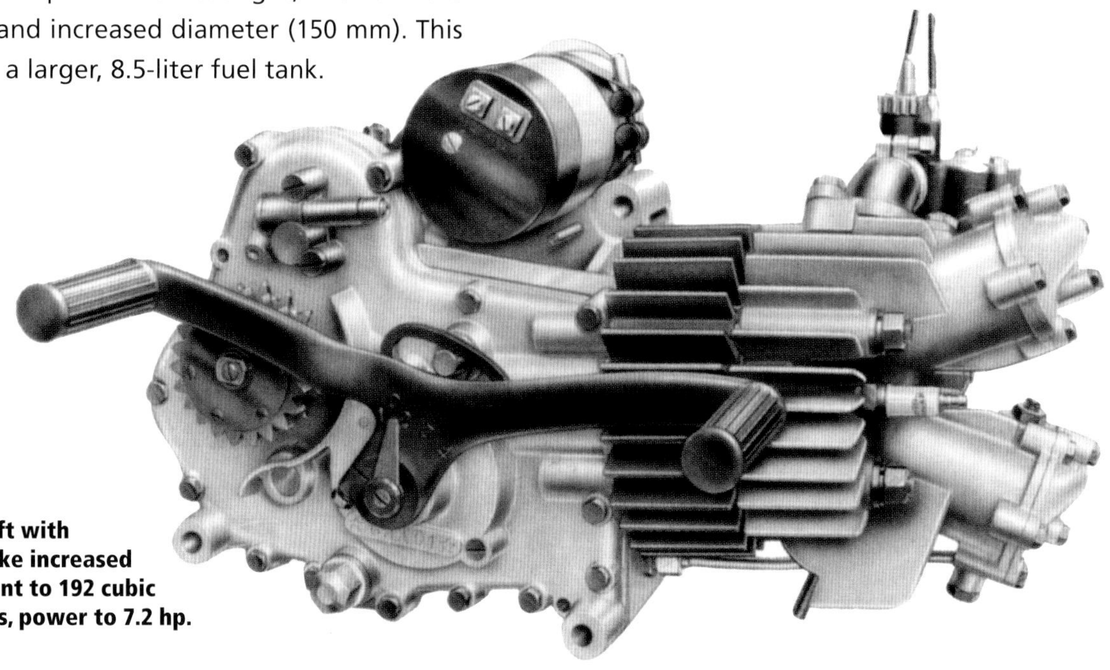

A crankshaft with longer stroke increased displacement to 192 cubic centimeters, power to 7.2 hp.

Galletto 192 Elettrico

The last Galletto series, of 1961, differed from its predecessors in having larger fenders and a larger tail light. The biggest changes, however, were once again in the electrical system. Made necessary by the electric starter, a proper alternator supplied a 12-Volt battery with 20 Amperes. The rear wheel suspension was now hydraulically damped. Thanks to higher compression, the engine produced 7.7 hp. This last Galletto remained in production until 1966, when it and several other models were removed from the program because of financial difficulties.

Galletto 192 Elettrico	
Production Period:	1960-1966
Engine:	1-cyl., OHV/twin valves
Displacement:	192 cc
Bore x Stroke:	65 x 58 mm
Compression:	7:1
Power output:	7.7 hp at 5,200 rpm
Mixture preparation:	Dell'Orto MA 19 BS1, battery ignition
Clutch:	multi-plate wet clutch
Gearbox:	4 speeds
Frame:	pressed steel frame with tubular spine
Wheelbase:	1310 mm
Front suspension:	scooter fork
Rear suspension:	single-sided swing arm with horizontal shock absorber
Front tire:	2.75 x 17
Rear tire:	3.00 x 17
Front brake:	drum, 125 mm
Rear brake:	drum, 125 mm
Empty weight:	134 kg
Tank capacity:	8.5 liters
Maximum speed:	90 kph

Postwar production: the early 1950s were the heyday of the motorcycle.

Falcone 1950 – 53

The prewar, single-cylinder concept lived on in the GTV and GTW models, and finally the Astore until 1950, when the Falcone appeared. Its roots extended back to the Condor racing machine, although it was essentially a much revised GTW. The engine itself had a much sportier layout and its 23 hp could be used with little effort. The visual-technical differences lay in the encapsulated valve mechanism, the aluminum cylinder including head, and the Dell'Orto SS racing carburetor. The new frame made the machine lower and its general lines made it look sportier. It was made for three years, until 1953, when the less powerful Turismo appeared. From then on the basic Falcone was called the Sport.

Falcone	
Production Period:	1950-1953
Engine:	1-cyl., OHV/twin valves
Displacement:	498.4 cc
Bore x Stroke:	88 x 82 mm
Compression:	6.5:1
Power output:	23 hp at 4,500 rpm
Mixture preparation:	Dell'Orto SS 29A, magneto
Clutch:	multi-plate wet clutch
Gearbox:	4 speeds
Frame:	pressed steel frame, rear section bolted together
Wheelbase:	1500 mm
Front suspension:	telescopic fork
Rear suspension:	spring assembly under engine, friction damping
Front tire:	3.25 x 19
Rear tire:	3.50 x 19
Front brake:	drum
Rear brake:	drum
Empty weight:	170 kg
Tank capacity:	17.5 liters
Maximum speed:	135 kph

The Falcone is considered the classic postwar Guzzi: it was built in various versions well into the 1960s.

Falcone Turismo 1954 – 68

In 1954, the Turismo, a less-powerful version of the Falcone, appeared on the market. Visually, it differed from the Falcone Sport in having black-painted knee panels on the tank (these had previously been chrome), a luggage rack instead of a rear seat, and no speedometer. Engine power was reduced in favor of greater torque. This was made possible by smaller valves, a smaller carburetor, and lower compression.

Falcone Turismo	
Production Period:	1954-1968
Engine:	1-cyl., OHV/twin valves
Displacement:	498.4 cc
Bore x Stroke:	88 x 82 mm
Compression:	5:1
Power output:	18 hp at 4,300 rpm
Mixture preparation:	Dell'Orto MD 27F, magneto
Clutch:	multi-plate wet clutch
Gearbox:	4 speeds
Frame:	pressed steel frame, rear section bolted together
Wheelbase:	1500 mm
Front suspension:	telescopic fork
Rear suspension:	spring assembly under engine, friction damping
Front tire:	3.50 x 19
Rear tire:	3.50 x 19
Front brake:	drum
Rear brake:	drum
Empty weight:	176 kg
Tank capacity:	17.5 liters
Maximum speed:	120 kph

Falcone Sport 1954 – 64

Following the introduction of the Turismo in 1954, the original Falcone became the Sport, retaining the original technology. Success in Italian long-distance events, such as the Milan to Taranto race, assured its sales success. Tuning measures were easily achieved with the aid of parts from the Dondolino racing machine, which increased the machine's popularity even further. A reintroduction in 1963, for example, saw the use of a new muffler without the fishtail.

Falcone Sport	
Production Period:	1950-1953
Engine:	1-cyl., OHV/twin valves
Displacement:	498.4 cc
Bore x Stroke:	88 x 82 mm
Compression:	6.5:1
Power output:	23 hp at 4,500 rpm
Mixture preparation:	Dell'Orto SS 29A, magneto
Clutch:	multi-plate wet clutch
Gearbox:	4 speeds
Frame:	pressed steel frame, rear section bolted together
Wheelbase:	1500 mm
Front suspension:	telescopic fork
Rear suspension:	spring assembly under engine, friction damping
Front tire:	3.25 x 19
Rear tire:	3.50 x 19
Front brake:	drum
Rear brake:	drum
Empty weight:	170 kg
Tank capacity:	17.5 liters
Maximum speed:	135 kph

Lodola 175 1956 – 58

When it was introduced in 1956, the 175 cc Lodola became the first Moto Guzzi four-stroke for the street to depart from the classic horizontal cylinder layout. The engine was also the last product of Carlo Guzzi, who chose a very modern layout for the times. His design even had an overhead camshaft and produced an impressive nine horsepower. The entire valve train was sprung and compensated for varying valve play. The small, light machine was a typical Italian sport bike and the initial model remained in production for two years.

Lodola 175	
Production Period:	1956-1958
Engine:	1-cyl., OHV/twin valves
Displacement:	174 cc
Bore x Stroke:	62 x 57.8 mm
Compression:	7.5:1
Power output:	9 hp at 6,000 rpm
Mixture preparation:	Dell'Orto UB 22 BS2, battery ignition
Clutch:	multi-plate wet clutch
Gearbox:	4 speeds
Frame:	Cradle type with twin down tubes and semi cantilever rear sub-frame
Wheelbase:	1314 mm
Front suspension:	telescopic fork
Rear suspension:	double swing arm, two shock absorbers
Front tire:	2.50 x 18
Rear tire:	3.00 x 17
Front brake:	drum, offset, 180 mm
Rear brake:	drum, offset, 150 mm
Empty weight:	109 kg
Tank capacity:	12 liters
Maximum speed:	110 kph

Lodola 175 Sport 1958 – 59

In 1958, the Lodola became the Sport, and to justify this name it was given more power (11 hp at 6,500 rpm) and larger, full drum brakes, which in the final series were even polished. Fuel capacity was increased to 16 liters and the tank came with a chrome racing cap. The 175-cc class was an important part of the Italian market, but was not well received in other countries. Consequently, the Lodola was sold almost exclusively south of the Alps.

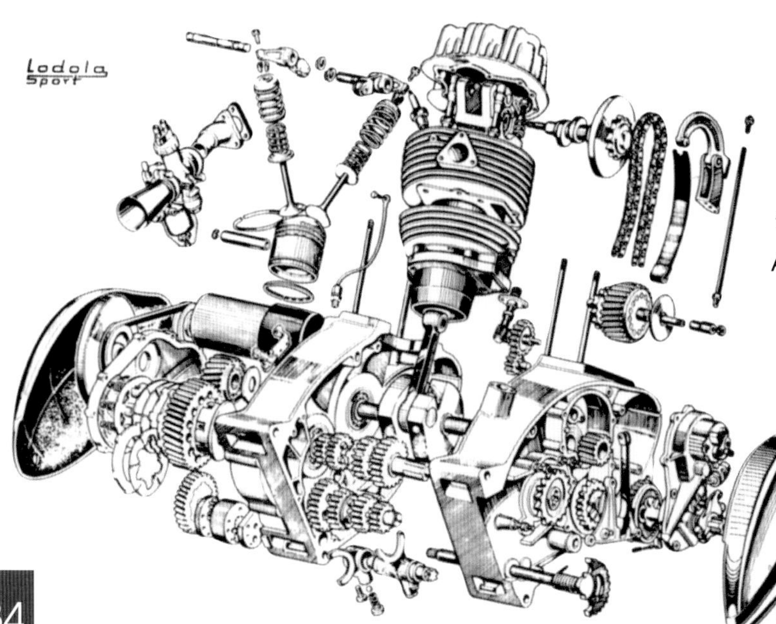

The single-cylinder engine of the Lodola was a very modern power plant with enclosed valve train and timing chain to the overhead camshaft.

Lodola 175 Sport

Production Period:	1958-1959
Engine:	1-cyl., OHC/twin valves
Displacement:	174 cc
Bore x Stroke:	62 x 57.8 mm
Compression:	9:1
Power output:	11 hp at 6,500 rpm
Mixture preparation:	Dell'Orto UB 22 BS2, battery ignition
Clutch:	multi-plate wet clutch
Gearbox:	4 speeds
Frame:	cradle type with twin down tubes
	and semi cantilever rear sub-frame
Wheelbase:	1314 mm
Front suspension:	telescopic fork
Rear suspension:	double swing arm, two shock absorbers
Front tire:	2.50 x 18
Rear tire:	3.00 x 17
Front brake:	drum, 180 mm
Rear brake:	drum, 150 mm
Empty weight:	109 kg
Tank capacity:	16 liters
Maximum speed:	115 kph

Lodola Gran Turismo 1959 – 66

When the Gran Turismo replaced the Sport, it differed from its predecessor in having an increased displacement of 235 cubic centimeters and a new valve drive. The factory eliminated the overhead cam and replaced it with conventional pushrods and rockers. The overhead cam supposedly caused problems over time, which is why the later big sister dispensed with this feature.

The 235 had no more power than the 175 Sport, but it did have improved torque. The off-road version, based on the 235 GT, did have an overhead cam and produced 14 hp. There was also an off-road version with a displacement of 247 cubic centimeters and a five-speed gearbox.

Lodola Gran Turismo

Production Period:	1959-1966
Engine:	1-cyl., OHV/twin valves
Displacement:	235 cc
Bore x Stroke:	68 x 64 mm
Compression:	7.5:1
Power output:	11 hp at 6,000 rpm
Mixture preparation:	Dell'Orto UB 22 BS, battery ignition
Clutch:	multi-plate wet clutch
Gearbox:	4 speeds
Frame:	cradle type with twin down tubes
	and semi cantilever rear sub-frame
Wheelbase:	1314 mm
Front suspension:	telescopic fork
Rear suspension:	double swing arm, two shock absorbers
Front tire:	2.50 x 18
Rear tire:	3.00 x 17
Front brake:	drum, 180 mm
Rear brake:	drum, 150 mm
Empty weight:	115 kg
Tank capacity:	16 liters
Maximum speed:	115 kph

Stornello 125 Turismo 1960 – 68

The Stornello appeared in 1960 as a mass-produced item. The small, pushrod engine with flat combustion chamber and parallel valves, had a low power output, but the motorcycle gained great popularity on account of its looks (and price) and remained in production for fifteen years. The valve layout forced the relocation of the carburetor to the left outside, while the exhaust manifold moved to the right. When, in the second model year (1961), the 125 Sport was introduced, the base Stornello was renamed the Turismo and at the same time was fitted with a larger carburetor.

Stornello 125 Turismo	
Production Period:	1960-1968
Engine:	1-cyl., OHV/twin valves
Displacement:	123.1 cc
Bore x Stroke:	52 x 58 mm
Compression:	8:1
Power output:	7 hp at 7,200 rpm
Mixture preparation:	Dell'Orto ME 18 BS, flywheel magneto
Clutch:	multi-plate wet clutch
Gearbox:	4 speeds
Frame:	cradle type, open bottom
Wheelbase:	1250 mm
Front suspension:	telescopic fork
Rear suspension:	double swing arm
Front tire:	2.50 x 17
Rear tire:	2.75 x 17
Front brake:	drum
Rear brake:	drum
Empty weight:	92 kg
Tank capacity:	12.5 liters
Maximum speed:	100 kph

Stornello Sport 1960 – 68

The Stornello Sport appeared at the end of 1961, two years after the first Stornello was unveiled. A modified combustion chamber shape and a change in the valve angles resulted in an increase in performance from the small engine to 8.5 hp. Visually, it followed the typical Italian school with a nicely formed tank, sports seat, aluminum rims, and small bars. Both versions of this first Stornello were ultimately replaced by the Stornello Nuovo in 1968.

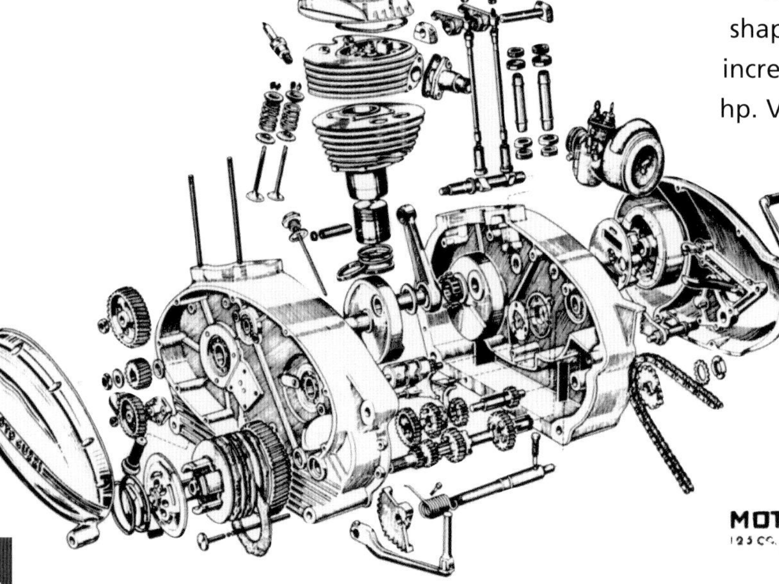

In contrast to the Lodola, the valves in the engine of the Stornello were controlled by pushrods.

Stornello Regolarita 125 1966

Moto Guzzi earned a great reputation in Italy by successfully participating in the International Six Days Trials, with the Lodola in the 175 and 250 classes and modified Stornellos in the 125 class. Then, the company produced a real factory replica, the Regolarita 125, for 1966. This model could be ordered direct from the dealer, nevertheless it is now a rare and much sought after motorcycle.

Stornello Sport

Production Period:	1960-1968
Engine:	1-cyl., OHV/twin valves
Displacement:	123.1 cc
Bore x Stroke:	52 x 58 mm
Compression:	9.8:1
Power output:	8.5 hp at 7,500 rpm
Mixture preparation:	Dell'Orto ME 18 BS, flywheel magneto
Clutch:	multi-plate wet clutch
Gearbox:	4 speeds
Frame:	cradle type, open bottom
Wheelbase:	1250 mm
Front suspension:	telescopic fork
Rear suspension:	double swing arm
Front tire:	2.50 x 17
Rear tire:	2.75 x 17
Front brake:	drum
Rear brake:	drum
Empty weight:	92 kg
Tank capacity:	14.5 liters
Maximum speed:	110 kph

Stornello Regolarita 125

Production Period:	1966
Engine:	1-cyl., OHV/twin valves
Displacement:	123.1 cc
Bore x Stroke:	52 x 58 mm
Compression:	11.4:1
Power output:	10.5 hp at 8,000 rpm
Mixture preparation:	Dell'Orto UB 22 BS2, battery ignition
Clutch:	multi-plate wet clutch
Gearbox:	4 speeds
Frame:	cradle type, open bottom
Wheelbase:	1250 mm
Front suspension:	telescopic fork
Rear suspension:	double swing arm
Front tire:	2.50 x 19
Rear tire:	3.00 x 19
Front brake:	drum, 180 mm
Rear brake:	drum, 150 mm
Empty weight:	95 kg
Tank capacity:	not known
Maximum speed:	100 kph

Stornello 125 Scrambler America (Sport)	
Production Period:	1967-1969
Engine:	1-cyl., OHV/twin valves
Displacement:	123.1 cc
Bore x Stroke:	52 x 58 mm
Compression:	9.8:1
Power output:	12 hp
Mixture preparation:	Dell'Orto UB 20 B, battery ignition
Clutch:	multi-plate wet clutch
Gearbox:	4 speeds
Frame:	cradle type, open bottom
Wheelbase:	1250 mm
Front suspension:	telescopic fork
Rear suspension:	double swing arm
Front tire:	2.50 x 17 (2,75 x 17)
Rear tire:	2.75 x 17 (3.00 x 17)
Front brake:	drum
Rear brake:	drum
Empty weight:	93 kg (95kg)
Tank capacity:	12.5 liters
Maximum speed:	110 kph (100 kph)

Stornello 125 Scrambler America, Sport America 1967 – 69

These two models were technically identical, but had a new look and replaced the Stornello and Stornello Sport models in 1967. With the exception of the seat, most components came from the two earlier models: the tank from the base model and the fenders from the Sport, for example. The Scrambler America, however, had a fatter rear tire and a high-mounted exhaust. The official performance figures were somewhat more optimistic than before, however the technical specifications of the engine and the combustion chamber shape were the same as those of the predecessors, which makes this performance increase rather questionable.

Stornello 125 Nuovo 1970 – 75

Along with the 160 Stornello, the small sister was updated in the 1971 model year. The final Stornello generation was influenced technically and visually by the new V7 series and was available mainly in white with red trim. The biggest technical innovation, however, was its five-speed gearbox. The external appearance of the engine had also changed, but–apart from the inclined valves – the insides had not changed much. For a short time there was also a Scrambler version.

Stornello 125 Nuovo

Production Period:	1970-1975
Engine:	1-cyl., OHV/twin valves
Displacement:	123.1 cc
Bore x Stroke:	52 x 58 mm
Compression:	9.8:1
Power output:	12 hp
Mixture preparation:	Dell'Orto VHB 22 BS, flywheel magneto
Clutch:	multi-plate wet clutch
Gearbox:	5 speeds
Frame:	cradle type, open bottom
Wheelbase:	1250 mm
Front suspension:	telescopic fork
Rear suspension:	double swing arm
Front tire:	2.50 x 17
Rear tire:	2.75 x 17
Front brake:	drum
Rear brake:	drum
Empty weight:	100 kg (95 kg)
Tank capacity:	12 liters
Maximum speed:	110 kph

Stornello 160 Nuovo 1968 – 74

The 160 Stornello, introduced in 1968, was in principle nothing more than a 125 bored out by an additional 58 mm, and otherwise was identical to the smaller version. It was the first Moto Guzzi to receive the new alternating current generator as well as a somewhat larger front drum brake. The design updating process led, in 1971, to a machine with a completely new look, the Stornello Nuovo. Apart from the difference in displacement, it was identical to the Nuovo 125.

Stornello 160 Nuovo

Production Period:	1968-1974
Engine:	1-cyl., OHV/twin valves
Displacement:	153.2 cc
Bore x Stroke:	58 x 58 mm
Compression:	9:1
Power output:	13.8 hp
Mixture preparation:	Dell'Orto UB 20 B, flywheel magneto
Clutch:	multi-plate wet clutch
Gearbox:	4 speeds (5 speeds)
Frame:	cradle type, open bottom
Wheelbase:	1250 mm
Front suspension:	telescopic fork
Rear suspension:	double swing arm
Front tire:	2.50 x 17
Rear tire:	2.75 x 17
Front brake:	drum, 157 mm
Rear brake:	drum
Empty weight:	107 kg
Tank capacity:	12 liters
Maximum speed:	117 kph

Falcone Nuovo 1971 – 76

The last civilian Falcone was officially delivered in 1967. From then on the only remaining version of this tradition-rich machine was the one built for the authorities. Faithful Guzzi fans were not satisfied with this and demanded a big single. And they finally got one. In the first two production years (1969-70) it was only available as a machine for the authorities, but in 1971 it again appeared in civilian guise. The new engine had wet lubrication, a large oil pan, and looked very tidied-up. Rated power was 26 hp; the cradle type frame shared many features with those of the later V7 Sport and the Le Mans. In 1974, the military version became available to regular customers as the Sahara. The Falcone variants finally disappeared from the catalogue for good in late 1976.

Falcone Nuovo

Production Period:	1971-1976
Engine:	1-cyl., OHV/twin valves
Displacement:	498.4 cc
Bore x Stroke:	88 x 82 mm
Compression:	6.8:1
Power output:	26.2 hp at 4,800 rpm
Mixture preparation:	Dell'Orto VHB 29A, battery ignition
Clutch:	multi-plate wet clutch
Gearbox:	4 speeds
Frame:	cradle type frame of steel tube
Wheelbase:	1450 mm
Front suspension:	telescopic fork
Rear suspension:	double swing arm
Front tire:	3.25 x 18
Rear tire:	3.50 x 18
Front brake:	Duplex drum
Rear brake:	drum
Empty weight:	214 kg
Tank capacity:	18 liters
Maximum speed:	128 kph

Brochure for the Falcone Nuovo: note the enclosed flywheel. The Nuova was initially offered only in a version for the authorities, and it was not until 1971 that it became available to civilian customers.

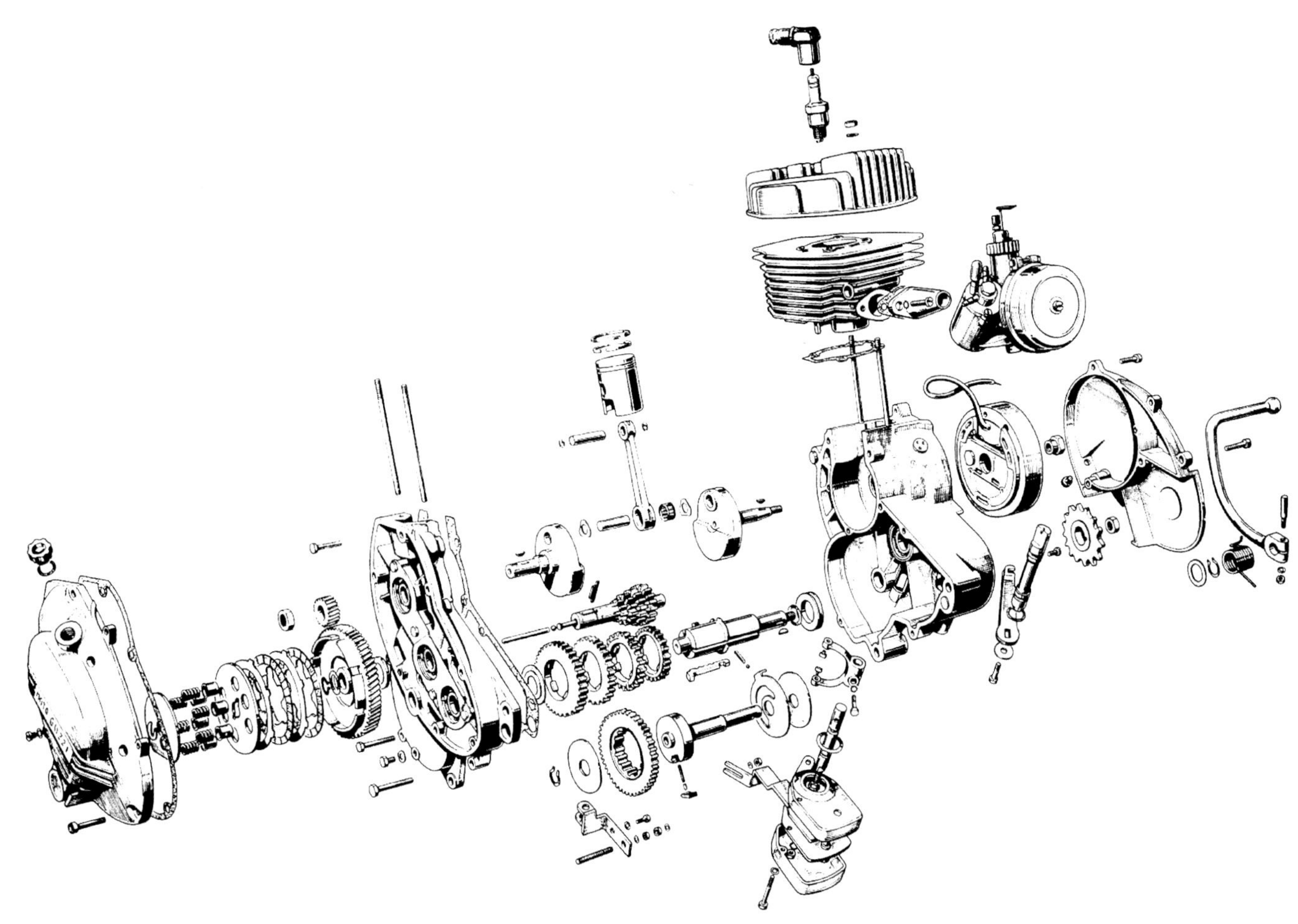

Two-Stroke Variants and Four-Strokes of the de Tomaso Period

From 1946 until 1982, there was always at least one two-stroke model in Moto Guzzi's product line. Several of these were failures, while others were often desperate attempts to derive market advantages from the small motorcycles. The first in the series, the Motoleggera, was a big hit, however, and was part of the class of motorcycles that made Italy mobile in the postwar period. The line of small motorcycles continued in a series through the Cardellino (1954-1965) to the Dingo (1963-1975). The variants of the final model, however, were too numerous to be listed here in their entirety.

Between 1946 and 1982 Moto Guzzi always offered at least one two-stroke model. While they might not seem like typical Guzzis today, they helped ensure the brand's survival.

Motoleggera 65 1946 – 54

In 1946, Moto Guzzi had no experience with two-strokes, but despite this it scored a direct hit the first time around. While the 65-cc rotary valve induction single only produced two horsepower at 5,000 rpm, the motorcycle was capable of more than 50 kph. As designed by Guzzi, the frame was not laid out for two-man operation, but many owners ignored this flaw and mounted an extra seat or large cargo carriers. The motorcycle's suspension consisted of a trapezoid fork up front and two horizontally hinged springs in the rear. The frame itself consisted of a single, diagonally placed tube extending from the steering head to the rear wheel swing arm behind the engine. The Motoleggera enjoyed tremendous popularity and underwent few changes between 1946 and 1954. These included the introduction of a horn in 1948.

Motoleggera 65	
Production Period:	1946-1954
Engine:	single-cylinder two-stroke, rotary valve induction
Displacement:	64 cc
Bore x Stroke:	42 x 46 mm
Compression:	5.5:1
Power output:	2 hp at 5,000 rpm
Mixture preparation:	Dell'Orto MA 13, flywheel magneto
Clutch:	multi-plate wet clutch
Gearbox:	3 speeds, manual
Frame:	central tube frame
Wheelbase:	1200 mm
Front suspension:	trapezoid fork
Rear suspension:	rigid
Front tire:	26 x 1¾ (bicycle type)
Rear tire:	26 x 1¾ (bicycle type)
Front brake:	drum
Rear brake:	drum
Empty weight:	45 kg
Tank capacity:	6.5 liters
Maximum speed:	50 kph

The Motoleggera was an immediate success, even though its tiny engine produced just two horsepower.

Cardellino 1954 – 65

When it was introduced at the end of 1953, the Cardellino was no more than a modernized Motoleggera. It was capable of carrying a heavier load, had a more stable frame tail, and a much sturdier swing arm. Full drum brakes and an undamped telescopic fork followed in 1956. Later, but the same year, the engine was increased in size to 73 cubic centimeters. Modern times came in 1958 with the Lusso. Sporty lines, sport handlebars, double seat and friction damping for the hindquarters were its distinguishing features. The Nuovo Cardellino was the everyday model, but mechanically it was almost identical to the Lusso. In both models the engine, with its square layout (46 x 46 mm), produced 2.6 hp. The final version of 1961 had a full swing arm in the rear, with two hydraulically damped shock absorbers. In the last three production years, engine displacement was increased to 83 cc (48 x 46 mm), resulting in a power output of 2.9 hp at 5,200 rpm.

Cardellino	
Production Period:	1954-1965
Engine:	single-cylinder two-stroke, rotary valve induction
Displacement:	64 cc, 73 cc, 83 cc
Bore x Stroke:	42 x 46 mm, 45 x 46 mm, 48 x 46 mm
Compression:	5.5:1
Power output:	2 hp at 5,000 rpm. 2.6 hp at
	5,200 rpm, 2.9 hp at 5,200 rpm
Mixture preparation:	Dell'Orto MU 14 B2 (B3), flywheel magneto
Clutch:	multi-plate wet clutch
Gearbox:	3 speeds, manual
Frame:	central tube frame
Wheelbase:	1200 mm
Front suspension:	trapezoid fork, from 1956
	undamped telescopic fork
Rear suspension:	horizontal springs with friction damping,
	from 1962 full swing arm with two shock absorbers
Front tire:	2.25 x 20
Rear tire:	2.25 x 20
Front brake:	drum
Rear brake:	drum
Empty weight:	55 kg, final model 59 kg
Tank capacity:	6.5 liters
Maximum speed:	55 - 65 kph

Unlike the Motoleggera, the Cardellino had a stable rear frame capable of supporting two persons. Engine power rose to 2.6 hp.

Dingo 1963 – 76

In 1963, the Dingo Turismo and Sport models replaced Cardellino and company. Both had pressed steel frames, three-speed gearboxes, and a 48.9-cc engine producing 1.7 hp. A tubular frame followed in 1967, by which time the line consisted of GT, Cross, and Sport versions. The biggest innovation, however, was a four-speed gearbox. A fourth member of the group later appeared as the Mofa 50 Monomarcia ,with automatic transmission and pressed steel frame. The final Dingo was the 62T, which had a larger 62 cc engine and a top speed of 85 kph.

Dingo	
Production Period:	1963-1976
Engine:	single-cylinder two-stroke
Displacement:	48.9 cc (62 cc)
Bore x Stroke:	38.5 x 42 mm (43.5 x 42 mm)
Compression:	7.5:1
Power output:	1.4 hp at 4,800 rpm (1.5 hp at 5,000 rpm)
Mixture preparation:	Dell'Orto SHA 14.9, flywheel magneto
Clutch:	multi-plate wet clutch
Gearbox:	3 speeds (from 1967 4 speeds in the
	Dingo GT, Nuovo Cross and Super Sport)
Frame:	from 1967 tubular frame, previously pressed steel
Wheelbase:	1130 mm
Front suspension:	telescopic fork
Rear suspension:	full swing arm with two shock absorbers
Front tire:	2.00 x 18 (Cross 2.50 x 17, MM 2.50 x 16)
Rear tire:	2.00 x 18 (Cross 2.50 x 17, MM 2.25 x 16)
Front brake:	drum
Rear brake:	drum
Empty weight:	48 kg (approx., all models)
Tank capacity:	6.5 liters
Maximum speed:	40 kph

The Dingo models replaced the earlier two-strokes in 1963.

Zigolo 1953 – 66

The Zigolo (Sparrow) was unveiled in Milan in April 1953. It was the first motorcycle with a fully enclosed frame, which was accepted by the customers. Ensconced within it was a 98-cc slide valve engine that was good for a top speed of about 75 kph. The frame was similar to that of the Motoleggera and Cardellino. In the rear, the swing arm was centrally sprung against a rubber pad, assisted by Guzzi's familiar friction damping. An undamped telescopic fork was used up front. The luxury model (Lusso) was introduced in 1954. It had a twin seat, 17-inch wheels, and a two-tone finish. The 6.8-hp Sport appeared at the same time; the base model became the Turismo. By 1957, only the Lusso remained in the program, and in 1958 it received full hub brakes and a new fork. The final version, which was built between 1960 and 1966, had a displacement of 110 cc. The fork was hydraulically damped, as were the double swing arm's two modern shock absorbers.

Zigolo	
Production Period:	1953-1966
Engine:	single-cylinder two-stroke, rotary valve induction
Displacement:	98 cc (110.3 cc)
Bore x Stroke:	50 x 50 mm (52 x 52 mm)
Compression:	6:1 (7.5:1)
Power output:	4 hp at 5,200 rpm (98 Sport 6.8 hp, 110 4.8 hp)
Mixture preparation:	Dell'Orto MAF 15 BI (from MkII 1957 MAF 18 BI), flywheel magneto
Clutch:	multi-plate wet clutch
Gearbox:	3 speeds
Frame:	central tube frame
Wheelbase:	1240 mm
Front suspension:	undamped telescopic fork (damped telescopic fork)
Rear suspension:	swing arm with horizontal springs and friction damping (double swing arm with two shock absorbers)
Front tire:	2.50 x 19, 2.50 x 17
Rear tire:	2.50 x 19, 2.50 x 17 (2.75 x 17)
Front brake:	drum
Rear brake:	drum
Empty weight:	75 kg (78 kg)
Tank capacity:	13.5 liters
Maximum speed:	75 kph

Zigolo means "sparrow" in English; with its faired chassis, the machine was completely in style in the 1950s.

Trotter / Chiu 1966 – 73

The Trotter moped was unveiled when the Parodi family placed the factory under the custody of the federal authorities (which then formed SEIMM). It was hoped that profitable numbers could be produced, utilizing capacities to the full. Initially equipped with a 40.8 cc two-stroke with automatic and 1.2 hp, in its third year the moped received a new engine with horizontal cylinder and 49 cc. Various versions, with and without rear wheel suspension and various gearboxes, were produced, before the Trotter was forced to give way to the Chiu (Robin) in November 1973. The technical concept was the same, only the look was more modern. The Chiu also had a telescopic fork. The moped experiment ended at the end of the 1970s.

Trotter

Production Period:	1966-1973
Engine:	single-cylinder two-stroke
Displacement:	40.8 cc until 1969, (48.9 cc)
Bore x Stroke:	37 x 38 mm (38.5 x 42 mm)
Compression:	7.5:1
Power output:	1.2 hp at 5,000 rpm (1.5 hp at 5,000 rpm)
Mixture preparation:	Dell'Orto SHA 14.9 (14.12)
Clutch:	automatic
Gearbox:	2 speeds, manual
Frame:	pressed steel frame
Wheelbase:	1035 mm
Front suspension:	short turn fork
Rear suspension:	rigid (MkII from 1970 swing arm/shock absorbers)
Front tire:	2.00 x 16
Rear tire:	2.00 x 16
Front brake:	drum
Rear brake:	drum
Empty weight:	35 kg (37 kg)
Tank capacity:	2.5 liters
Maximum speed:	35 kph

Chiu

Production Period:	1974-1976
Engine:	single-cylinder two-stroke
Displacement:	49 cc
Bore x Stroke:	40 x 39 mm
Compression:	8.5:1
Power output:	1.5 hp at 4,400 rpm
Mixture preparation:	Dell'Orto SHA 14.9
Clutch:	automatic, in oil bath
Gearbox:	single speed
Frame:	stamped sheet metal
Wheelbase:	1130 mm
Front suspension:	telescopic fork, two shock absorbers
Rear suspension:	shock absorbers
Front tire:	2.25 x 16
Rear tire:	2.25 x 16
Front brake:	drum
Rear brake:	drum
Empty weight:	48 kg
Tank capacity:	3.3 liters
Maximum speed:	40 kph

The Trotter and Chiu were two mopeds with two-stroke engines made by Moto Guzzi. They remained in the program until the 1970s.

Cross 50 / Nibbio 1974 – 82

Moto Guzzi unveiled two new small motorcycles in Milan in November 1973. Technically identical, the Cross and Nibbio were designed for different purposes and were aimed at the youth market south of the Alps. The machines actually came from Benelli and were created in the early days after the takeover by Alejandro de Tomaso. The attempt to expand the model range downwards failed, however, and the Cross was to be the last Moto Guzzi two-stroke, the others having been abandoned in 1979. The Cross was modernized several times and in the end – 1982 – it looked like a proper Enduro, even if it had an output of just 1.1 hp.

Cross 50 / Nibbio	
Production Period:	1974-1982 (1975-1976)
Engine:	single-cylinder two-stroke (Benelli)
Displacement:	49 cc
Bore x Stroke:	40 x 39 mm
Compression:	8:1
Power output:	1.5 hp at 3,750 rpm
Mixture preparation:	Dell'Orto SHA 14.12
Clutch:	multi-plate wet clutch
Gearbox:	5 speeds
Frame:	tubular frame
Wheelbase:	1210 mm
Front suspension:	hydraulically-damped telescopic fork
Rear suspension:	swing arm with two shock absorbers
Front tire:	2.50 x 19 (2.50 x 18)
Rear tire:	3.00 x 17 (2.50 x 18)
Front brake:	drum
Rear brake:	drum
Empty weight:	81 kg
Tank capacity:	9.5 liters
Maximum speed:	35 kph

The Nibbio shown here was basically a Benelli at heart. The Cross 50 and the Nibbio were created at the start of the de Tomaso era.

Called the Furghino, this mini truck had the two-stroke engine of the Dingo.

Magnum 1976 – 79

Unveiled in 1975, the Magnum was also a Benelli with Guzzi stickers, another mini-bike in its line with high handlebars and stylish colors. Its production ended in 1980.

Magnum	
Production Period:	1976-1979
Engine:	single-cylinder two-stroke (Benelli)
Displacement:	49 cc
Bore x Stroke:	40 x 39 mm
Compression:	8.2:1
Power output:	1.2 hp at 5,400 rpm
Mixture preparation:	Dell'Orto SHA 14.9, flywheel magneto
Clutch:	multi-plate wet clutch
Gearbox:	5 speeds, foot shifter
Frame:	stamped steel frame
Wheelbase:	1040 mm
Front suspension:	telescopic fork
Rear suspension:	hydraulically-damped shock absorbers
Front tire:	4.00 x 10
Rear tire:	4.00 x 10
Front brake:	drum
Rear brake:	drum
Empty weight:	58 kg
Tank capacity:	3 liters
Maximum speed:	40 kph

125 TT, 125 Turismo 1974 – 81

At the beginning of the 1970s the Guzzi model line was lacking a cheap model. When de Tomaso took over, Moto Guzzi got access to several Benelli two-strokes. While the Tuttoterreno was based on an older Benelli design, it was nevertheless a joint project between two manufacturers. The TT was unveiled in 1974 and the Turismo followed one year later. It was the same motorcycle, but with a front disc brake and different tires. Other minor details, such as the tank and seat, also emphasized that it was a street bike.

125 TT (Turismo)	
Production Period:	1974-1981
Engine:	single-cylinder two-stroke, air cooled
Displacement:	120.6 cc
Bore x Stroke:	56 x 49 mm
Compression:	9.9:1
Power output:	11.5 hp at 6,700 rpm
Mixture preparation:	Dell'Orto VHB 22 SS, flywheel magneto
Clutch:	multi-plate wet clutch
Gearbox:	5 speeds
Frame:	tubular steel frame
Wheelbase:	1300 mm
Front suspension:	telescopic fork
Rear suspension:	double swing arm, two shock absorbers
Front tire:	2.50 x 21 (2.50 x 18)
Rear tire:	3.50 x 18 (2.75 x 18)
Front brake:	drum (disc)
Rear brake:	drum
Empty weight:	105 kg (fueled)
Tank capacity:	8.5 liters
Maximum speed:	85 kph (100 kph)

250 TS 1974 – 82

The 250 TS was unveiled in 1973 as one of the first joint projects with Benelli. The only difference from its Benelli role model was the introduction of aluminum cylinders with chromed sleeves. The 250 TS did not enter the market until 1974, however. One year later the duplex drum brake of the first model (of which more than 4,500 were made) gave way to a front disc brake. These two series were also fitted with an electronic ignition.

250 TS	
Production Period:	1974-1982
Engine:	two-cylinder two-stroke, air cooled
Displacement:	231.4 cc
Bore x Stroke:	56 x 47 mm
Compression:	9.7:1
Power output:	24.5 hp at 7,570 rpm
Mixture preparation:	2 x Dell'Orto VHB 25, contact/electronic
Clutch:	multi-plate wet clutch
Gearbox:	5 speeds
Frame:	tubular steel frame
Wheelbase:	1330 mm
Front suspension:	telescopic fork
Rear suspension:	double swing arm, two shock absorbers
Front tire:	3.00 x 18
Rear tire:	3.25 x 18
Front brake:	drum/disc
Rear brake:	drum
Empty weight:	137 kg (fueled)
Tank capacity:	17 liters
Maximum speed:	130 kph (100 kph)

Another Benelli in disguise: the 250 TS came with chromed aluminum cylinders and produced a lively 25 horsepower.

125 TT, BX, 125 C 1985

The new Guzzi-Benelli1 125 appeared at the beginning of the 1980s. With reed valves, separate lubrication, balance shaft and liquid cooling, it was modern in every respect. The TT was first offered for sale in 1985. After two production years the cooling vanes on the cylinder, which were in fact superfluous, disappeared. A successor with the radiator on the right side and exhaust pipe on the left was still offered in the 1990s as the 125 BX. The engine was more or less unchanged, however. Simultaneous with the 125 TT, in 1985, the custom variants appeared with identical power plants. On the "Custom," however, the engine was not painted black. The suspension and wheels were designed for street use. Its lines were reminiscent of the 125 Turismo from the 1970s, and only the large radiator changed its outward appearance. Instrumentation also included a tachometer. Bags and a windscreen could be purchased from the manufacturer as accessories.

125 TT, BX, 125 C	
Production Period:	1985
Engine:	single-cylinder two-stroke, liquid cooled
Displacement:	123 cc
Bore x Stroke:	56 x 50 mm
Compression:	11.5:1
Power output:	16.5 hp at 7,000 rpm
Mixture preparation:	Dell'Orto PHBL 25 BS, electronic ignition
Clutch:	multi-plate wet clutch
Gearbox:	6 speeds
Frame:	tubular steel frame
Wheelbase:	1380 mm
Front suspension:	telescopic fork, 35 mm Marzocchi
Rear suspension:	central shock absorber
Front tire:	2.75 x 21 (80/100 x 16)
Rear tire:	4.10 x 18 (3.50 H 18)
Front brake:	disc, 260 mm
Rear brake:	drum, 125 mm
Empty weight:	110 kg (fueled)
Tank capacity:	11.5 liters (11 liters)
Maximum speed:	110 kph (115 kph)

The 125 TT really looked like the big Enduros, and a cruiser variant was produced with the same drive train.

254 1977 – 81

In the shadow of several four-cylinder and six-cylinder models by Benelli, this small quarter-liter machine was also offered with the Guzzi emblem during the de Tomaso era. Its radical appearance was probably not to everyone's taste, consequently while the 254 remained in the program for three years, just a thousand were sold. The scanty frame made it necessary for the engine to bear part of the load. The whole thing was cloaked in plenty of thermoplastic, virtually a shell with quick-release fasteners. All of the instruments were placed in the tank fairing, a most unpractical location.

254	
Production Period:	1977-1981
Engine:	four-cylinder OHC four-stroke
Displacement:	231 cc
Bore x Stroke:	44 x 38 mm
Compression:	11.5:1
Power output:	27.8 hp at 10,500 rpm
Mixture preparation:	4 x Dell'Orto PHBG 18 B, points
Clutch:	multi-plate wet clutch
Gearbox:	5 speeds
Frame:	open tubular frame
Wheelbase:	1270 mm
Front suspension:	telescopic fork
Rear suspension:	double swing arm, two shock absorbers
Front tire:	2.75 x 18
Rear tire:	3.00 x 18
Front brake:	disc
Rear brake:	drum
Empty weight:	126 kg (fueled)
Tank capacity:	10 liters
Maximum speed:	138 kph

A Honda engine in a Benelli chassis: the 254 could be described that way. It was not particularly successful.

350 GTS 1974 – 79

The de Tomaso organization originally wanted to present the newly-designed four-cylinder in two models: a 500-cc version for Benelli and a 350-cc one for Moto Guzzi. This strict division later blurred somewhat, as Benelli got its own 350. The 350 GTS Guzzi, on the other hand, was supplemented by the somewhat faster 400 GTS after one production year. Both were supposed to challenge the Japanese, and the engine design, at least, was reminiscent of the competition from the Far East, in particular the Honda CB 500. Like the 250 TS, in its first production year the 350 GTS had a duplex drum front brake, after which it was replaced by a disc brake.

350 GTS	
Production Period:	1974-1979
Engine:	four-cylinder OHC, air cooled
Displacement:	345.5 cc
Bore x Stroke:	50 x 44 mm
Compression:	10.2:1
Power output:	31 hp at 9,200 rpm
Mixture preparation:	4 x Dell'Orto VHB 20 D, points
Clutch:	multi-plate wet clutch
Gearbox:	5 speeds
Frame:	tubular steel frame
Wheelbase:	1370 mm
Front suspension:	telescopic fork
Rear suspension:	double swing arm, two shock absorbers
Front tire:	3.00 x 18
Rear tire:	3.50 x 18
Front brake:	drum/disc
Rear brake:	drum
Empty weight:	198 kg (fueled)
Tank capacity:	17 liters
Maximum speed:	150 kph

At first glance this could be mistaken for a small four-cylinder Honda. Actually a Benelli, this Moto Guzzi also closely resembled its Japanese inspiration.

400 GTS 1975 – 79

When the 400 GTS arrived in 1975, it had a front disc brake from the beginning. Its design features, like the design itself, it shared with the 350 GTS. The increased displacement was the result of lengthening the stroke, and that resulted in a power increase of almost ten horsepower, according to its documentation 40 hp at 9,000 rpm. It was built alongside the smaller GTS 350 until 1979.

400 GTS	
Production Period:	1975-1979
Engine:	four-cylinder OHC, air cooled
Displacement:	397 cc
Bore x Stroke:	50 x 50.6 mm
Compression:	10.2:1
Power output:	40 hp at 9,000 rpm
Mixture preparation:	4 x Dell'Orto VHB 20 D, points
Clutch:	multi-plate wet clutch
Gearbox:	5 speeds
Frame:	tubular steel frame
Wheelbase:	1370 mm
Front suspension:	telescopic fork
Rear suspension:	double swing arm, two shock absorbers
Front tire:	3.00 x 18
Rear tire:	3.50 x 18
Front brake:	drum/disc
Rear brake:	drum
Empty weight:	198 kg (fueled)
Tank capacity:	17 liters
Maximum speed:	170 kph

The 400 differed from the smaller 350 mainly in having slightly more displacement and a front disc brake.

125 2C 4T 1979 – 81

The 125 2C 4T was created from the 254, and its engine was essentially a halved four-cylinder. The chassis was also similar to that of its larger cousin, with the difference that the instruments were located on the upper fork bridge and not, as on the 254, in the tank fairing. The electrics, suspension, and body were adopted almost unchanged from the larger four-cylinder. The high-revving engine needed rpm just to get moving, however. Almost unknown in Germany, the 125 2C 4T was produced in 1980 and 1981.

125 2C 4T	
Production Period:	1979-1981
Engine:	two-cylinder OHC four-stroke
Displacement:	123.6 cc
Bore x Stroke:	45.5 x 38 mm
Compression:	10.65:1
Power output:	16 hp at 10,600 rpm
Mixture preparation:	2 x Dell'Orto PHBG 20 B, points
Clutch:	multi-plate wet clutch
Gearbox:	5 speeds
Frame:	tubular frame, open below
Wheelbase:	1290 mm
Front suspension:	telescopic fork
Rear suspension:	double swing arm, two shock absorbers
Front tire:	2.75 x 18
Rear tire:	3.00 x 18
Front brake:	disc
Rear brake:	drum
Empty weight:	110 kg (fueled)
Tank capacity:	8.5 liters
Maximum speed:	130 kph

Looks like the 254, but has a 125-cc engine with two cylinders. The 125 2C 4T no longer had the instruments on the tank, however.

Creation of a Legend

The Requirements: What The New Guzzi Must Be Capable Of

The year is 1963. Moto Guzzi is making uninspiring motorcycles like the Stornello, the Falcone, the Lodola, and the Dingo with its 50-cc two-stroke engine. Honestly, none of the products from this product line could knock a motorcyclist's socks off or make his jaw drop. But for many years, the Italian police and civilian authorities had relied on the proven, seemingly indestructible Falcone. Orders from the authorities provided Moto Guzzi with a not inconsiderable source of income. It is still the same today, by the way. But by then the Falcone had become very long in the tooth. Chugging along leisurely on their single-cylinders, the police could only watch the growing volume of ever faster traffic passing them by. The police needed a new motorcycle.

The officials in the Roman ministries now found it highly unfair to simply hand over the contract for the design of a more-powerful successor to Moto Guzzi.

Carcano, Cantoni and Todero designing the V7. The power plant produced by the young engineers would set the direction for the company's future.

Author Jan Leek and "his" V7. The Swedish journalist rode this Guzzi through the Orient in the 1970s, and in the summer of 2006 he was reunited with the machine in Sweden.

After all, the other Italian motorcycle makers were having just as hard a time of it. Consequently, the police and military authorities issued tenders for the design of a new official motorcycle to all the manufacturers in the land – it was a sort of contest.

The list of requirements looked like this: the new machine had to be considerably more powerful than the Falcone, in any case faster. Its power supply had to be designed so that all of the other electrically-powered equipment – blue lights, sirens, radios – could be supplied. It also had to be easily maintained by mechanics who were not particularly well trained, its servicing requirements had to be minimal, its down time during regular maintenance short. Furthermore, it had to be capable of running for at least 100,000 kilometers without the need for replacement of vital components – pistons and cylinders, for example. Even more – to the extent possible, the engines should not have to be opened up prior to achieving that mileage. That was a list of requirements that was not so easy to meet. What motorcyclist of that era would travel far from home and garage without an extensive onboard tool kit?

The Concept Phase: This Is What the Machine Could Look Like

Carcano and Todero began seriously studying the police motorcycle project in early 1963 – more precisely in May of that year. They reached agreement on the concept quite quickly. It would have the twin-cylinder, four-stroke V engine that Carcano practically already had lying in his desk drawer. The power plant would be installed longitudinally, and the four-speed transmission with intervening dry clutch flange-mounted on the rear, automobile style. A Cardan shaft would provide the logical final element in the transmission of power to the rear wheel.

The machine was to have about forty-five horsepower, making it about twice as powerful as the Falcone then in police service. Both designers believed that they could easily achieve this performance with a piston displacement of about 700 cubic centimeters. And the cylinder angle was to be ninety degrees. This configuration promised to minimize vibration without having to use a complicated and expensive balance shaft. The engine would have pushrod-operated valves, which significantly reduced construction costs. Adjusting valve play was no problem, even for unpracticed mechanics, for once the valve cover was removed the valves were exposed to the screwdriver as if on a serving tray. An alternator producing about 300 Watts and a correspondingly large 32-Ah battery was believed adequate to supply all consumers.

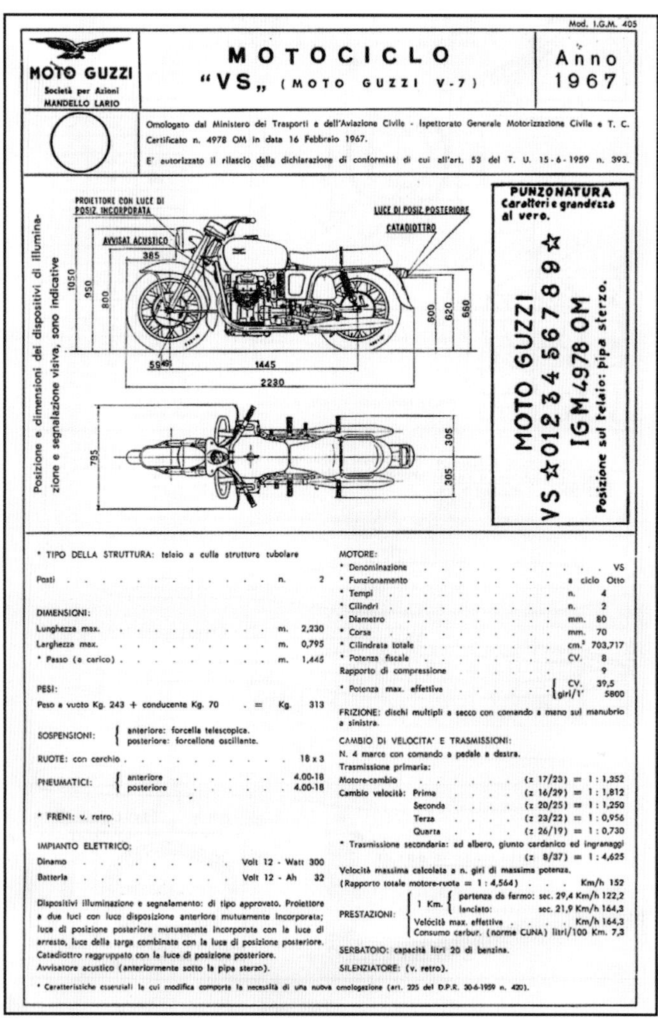

Mod. I.G.M. 405

MOTO GUZZI
Società per Azioni
MANDELLO LARIO

MOTOCICLO
"VS" (MOTO GUZZI V-7)

Anno 1967

Omologato dal Ministero dei Trasporti e dell'Aviazione Civile - Ispettorato Generale Motorizzazione Civile e T. C.
Certificato n. 4978 OM in data 16 Febbraio 1967.
E' autorizzato il rilascio della dichiarazione di conformità di cui all'art. 53 del T. U. 15-6-1959 n. 393.

PUNZONATURA
Caratteri e grandezza al vero.
MOTO GUZZI
VS ☆0123456789☆
IGM 4978 OM
Posizione sul telaio: pipa sterzo.

* TIPO DELLA STRUTTURA: telaio a culla struttura tubolare

Posti . . . n. 2

DIMENSIONI:
Lunghezza max. . . . m. 2,230
Larghezza max. . . . m. 0,795
* Passo (a carico) . . . m. 1,445

PESI:
Peso a vuoto Kg. 243 + conducente Kg. 70 . = Kg. 313

SOSPENSIONI: anteriore: forcella telescopica. posteriore: forcellone oscillante.

RUOTE: con cerchio . . . 18 x 3

PNEUMATICI: anteriore . . . 4.00-18; posteriore . . . 4.00-18

* FRENI: v. retro.

IMPIANTO ELETTRICO:
Dinamo . . . Volt 12 - Watt 300
Batteria . . . Volt 12 - Ah 32

Dispositivi illuminazione e segnalamento: di tipo approvato. Proiettore a due luci con luce disposizione anteriore mutuamente incorporata; luce di posizione posteriore mutuamente incorporata con la luce di arresto, luce della targa combinata con la luce di posizione posteriore. Catadiottro raggruppato con la luce di posizione posteriore. Avvisatore acustico (anteriormente sotto la pipa sterzo).

MOTORE:
* Denominazione . . . VS
* Funzionamento . . . a ciclo Otto
* Tempi . . . n. 4
* Cilindri . . . n. 2
* Diametro . . . mm. 80
* Corsa . . . mm. 70
* Cilindrata totale . . . cm.³ 703,717
* Potenza fiscale . . . CV. 8
Rapporto di compressione . . . 9
* Potenza max. effettiva . . . CV. 39,5 giri/1' 5800

FRIZIONE: dischi multipli a secco con comando a mano sul manubrio a sinistra.

CAMBIO DI VELOCITA' E TRASMISSIONI:
N. 4 marce con comando a pedale a destra.
Trasmissione primaria:
Motore-cambio . . . (z 17/23) = 1 : 1,352
Cambio velocità: Prima . . . (z 16/29) = 1 : 1,812
Seconda . . . (z 20/25) = 1 : 1,250
Terza . . . (z 23/22) = 1 : 0,956
Quarta . . . (z 26/19) = 1 : 0,730
* Trasmissione secondaria: ad albero, giunto cardanico ed ingranaggi (z 8/37) = 1 : 4,625
Velocità massima calcolata a n. giri di massima potenza.
(Rapporto totale motore-ruota = 1 : 4,564) . . . Km/h 152

PRESTAZIONI:
1 Km. partenza da fermo: sec. 29,4 Km/h 122,2
1 Km. lanciato: sec. 21,9 Km/h 164,3
Velócità max. effettiva . . . Km/h 164,3
Consumo carbur. (norme CUNA) litri/100 Km. 7,3

SERBATOIO: capacità litri 20 di benzina.

SILENZIATORE: (v. retro).

* Caratteristiche essenziali le cui modifica comporta la necessità di una nuova omologazione (art. 225 del D.P.R. 30-6-1959 n. 420).

The V7's approval document. The specification for the first version states that output was 39.5 hp. The machine weighed 243 kilograms dry.

On 28 May 1963, Todero put the first 1:5 sketch to paper; at the bottom right hand corner of the drawing was, "*Studio Motociclo per Servizione di Polizia.*" This first draft contained no dimensions, but the study was carried out with Todero's usual meticulousness. And, if one had taken a ruler and measured and calculated the values for the wheel base and castor, for example, one would have come up with the same measurements found on the first V 7 – 1445 millimeters wheel base and just under sixty millimeters castor. Even the fairing, the muffler, the taillight, the fuel tank, indeed even the tank filler cap were similar in detail to the parts later used. The first design did, however, envisage a frame consisting of straight sections of tube welded together. This design later proved considerably too expensive. This first design also addressed the problem of the cylinders extending into the driver's leg area. The solo seat – we are after all still talking about a police motorcycle – was positioned rather far to the rear, and the handlebars were swept back accordingly. Behind the rider's seat was a plate for mounting a radio.

Carcano and Todero spent all of 1963 on the concept and design of the machine, and at the beginning of 1964 the drawings were sent over to the prototype construction shop. Then, in the winter of 1964-65, the first machines rolled through the gray factory door onto the winding roads around the Lago di Como. At the end of 1965, a year of testing, the first machine, in civilian street clothes, became the star of the 39th Milan Motorcycle Show.

The Falcone Nuovo (in the background) was already clearly dated when the new big Guzzi appeared on the market in 1967. Both of the machines illustrated here are former police motorcycles restored by Günter Flincker-Kuhlmann.

It seemed clear from the beginning that there was not only going to be an official version of this motorcycle. The contract from the Roman ministries was going to help Moto Guzzi develop a new market for big motorcycles. For by then, one thing could already be foreseen: the motorcycle's days as a cheap means of transportation were already over. For the majority of Western Europeans the times of hardship after the Second World War were over – there was a car parked at the door. What remained for many was the dream of the long-past, fifty-cubic-centimeter years: the dream of a big motorcycle. At best, a pounding Norton, like the one the neighbor across the street had had ten years ago, or perhaps a BMW Boxer, like the one always parked in front of the small movie theater in the suburbs – yes, the one parked beside the small gray Zündapp.

The Competition: The V7 Is Awarded the Contract

In 1966, the Italian police and military authorities launched the above-described competition among the country's motorcycle manufacturers. Taking part, in addition to Moto Guzzi, were Benelli, Ducati, Gilera and Laverda. A BMW with full swing-arm suspension, an R 69, which was in service with countless police units around the globe, acted as a sort of reference motorcycle.

Ducati dropped out of the competition at the very outset – its machine simply wasn't ready yet. The first prototype of the police Ducati was finally rolled out in 1967 – too late. The remaining three competitors – Benelli, Gilera and Laverda – all entered parallel twins. The Gilera and Laverda had 500-cc engines, the Benelli a 650. The rear wheels of all three twins were chain-driven. Ultimately, four motorcycles – plus the BMW reference machine – stood ready to take part in the competition.

Nothing came of the threatened 100,000 kilometer test distance. In any case, the Guzzi returned from the police trials with 31,000 kilometers on its odometer. The test riders were very satisfied with the seat. In the company's own trials, riders put another 55,000 kilometers on the machine around Lake Comer. The motorcycle thus had 86,000 kilometers on it before its creators went over its insides with calipers and micrometer screw gauges. The results were encouraging: the cylinders and pistons did not need to be changed, the crankshafts and connecting-rod bearings were as good as new, the gears were all still in order – only its appearance had suffered somewhat.

As a final aid to decision making, the authorities held a sort of "nuts and bolts contest." The four competitors – again including the BMW – were parked side by side in a garage. Regular police mechanics then had to carry out a series of tasks on the motorcycles. An overseer stood by with a stopwatch. Each mechanic had to set the valves, change the points and reset the ignition, check the alternator – important because of the many electrical accessories – install and remove the tires, and finally tension the chain.

The mechanic responsible for the Guzzi was able to gain a slight advantage in almost every single operation. He was able to get at the valves and ignition more quickly than his colleagues on the other machines, because of the shaft drive the tire change posed fewer problems, and of course the Guzzi man was able to sit out the "tension change" part of the test.

The results of this practical competition and the wear values measured in the factory in Mandello finally tipped the scales: the Moto Guzzi V 7 was the new machine for the Italian police – the *Polizia Stradale*, the *Polizia Urbana* and the *Carabinieri*. The military also wanted the Guzzi. Carcano and Todero had done it – the V 7 was going into production. The *Corazzieri*, the Italian president's bodyguards, received the first fifty machines.

The Technology of the V7

The Development and the Inside of a Legend

"First make it and then see." Giulio Cesare Carcano must have been thinking along those lines when he began designing a V-twin engine at the end of the 1950s. Perhaps he was just bored, or did he simply find designing the Stornello – with its 125-cc four-stroke, a bread-and-butter design with twin overhead valves – not enough of a challenge? After all, a few years earlier he had put something much more demanding on its wheels: the legendary eight-cylinder racer. Who can say for sure? One thing is clear, however: at the start of the concept phase there was no concrete purpose for Carcano's twin-cylinder.

Why did Carcano not simply design a motorcycle for his twin-cylinder? Well, at that time the motorcycle was almost on its deathbed. In the Federal Republic of Germany, for example, registrations of new motorcycles had dropped by fifty percent from 1957 to 1958, and this downward trend continued in 1959. And the phenomenon wasn't confined to Germany. The clocks were also about to strike twelve in good old England and sunny Italy. Only a few crazy people still appeared to believe that the motorized two-wheeler might still have a future and yet avoid the grim reaper. And in this period of deep depression, designing a big motorcycle was simply out of the question.

And so Carcano was more than grateful when the opportunity came to adapt his V-engine for the 500-cc Fiat automobile. That was, after all, better than nothing. Two versions – a 500 and a 650 – were tested. The "hottest" variant with twin carburetors produced all of 34 hp. But the tiny car could only dream of such abundant power. Fiat let the project die at the last minute.

Not long afterwards, a vehicle did enter production with Carcano's V-twin: the "3 x 3" three-wheeled vehicle. This motorized mule was supposed to replace the stubborn animals still used by the Italian mountain troops. The three-wheeler was obviously no great success, as the mules are still in service today. Carcano designed a 750-cc version of his V-engine to power this curious vehicle. It had two crankshafts beneath the cylinder-V, pushrod-operated valves, dry sump lubrication, a 26 mm carburetor, and fan cooling. Twenty horsepower drove the three wheels of the all-terrain vehicle. About 400 examples left the assembly line between 1960 and 1963.

1963 – the concept phase of the new police motorcycle begins. At last, Carcano can do what he has been dreaming about for years: build a motorcycle with "his" V-twin. For this purpose, he and Todero completely redesigned the twin-cylinder. It was a completely new engine that only shared its basic concept with its two predecessors in the Fiat prototypes and military three-wheeler.

Everything along the wall: the V engine was once supposed to power this bizarre vehicle.

Its two designers probably could never have dreamt that this engine – its essential features unchanged – would still be doing its duty reliably almost fifty years later. One can, however, accept the long design time as an indication of the genius of the design. The engine was simple – so simple that it is almost comparable to a simple two-stroke. And yet the basic design was so suitable for development that the engine is still being built today – as said, fifty years later – with more than twice its original power. And it still has the same crankshaft. Okay, the stroke has become longer, and up front there is a cone for the alternator rotor. But that is all. The crankshaft main bearing and the basic dimensions of the shaft have remained unchanged since the first 700-cc V7. The Dr. John's replicas with twin valves and Le Mans IV housing, still run with the old V7 Sport crankshaft. And they show themselves equal to the brute power of the four-valve racing machines – a full 128 hp. That is surely proof of the design's solidity.

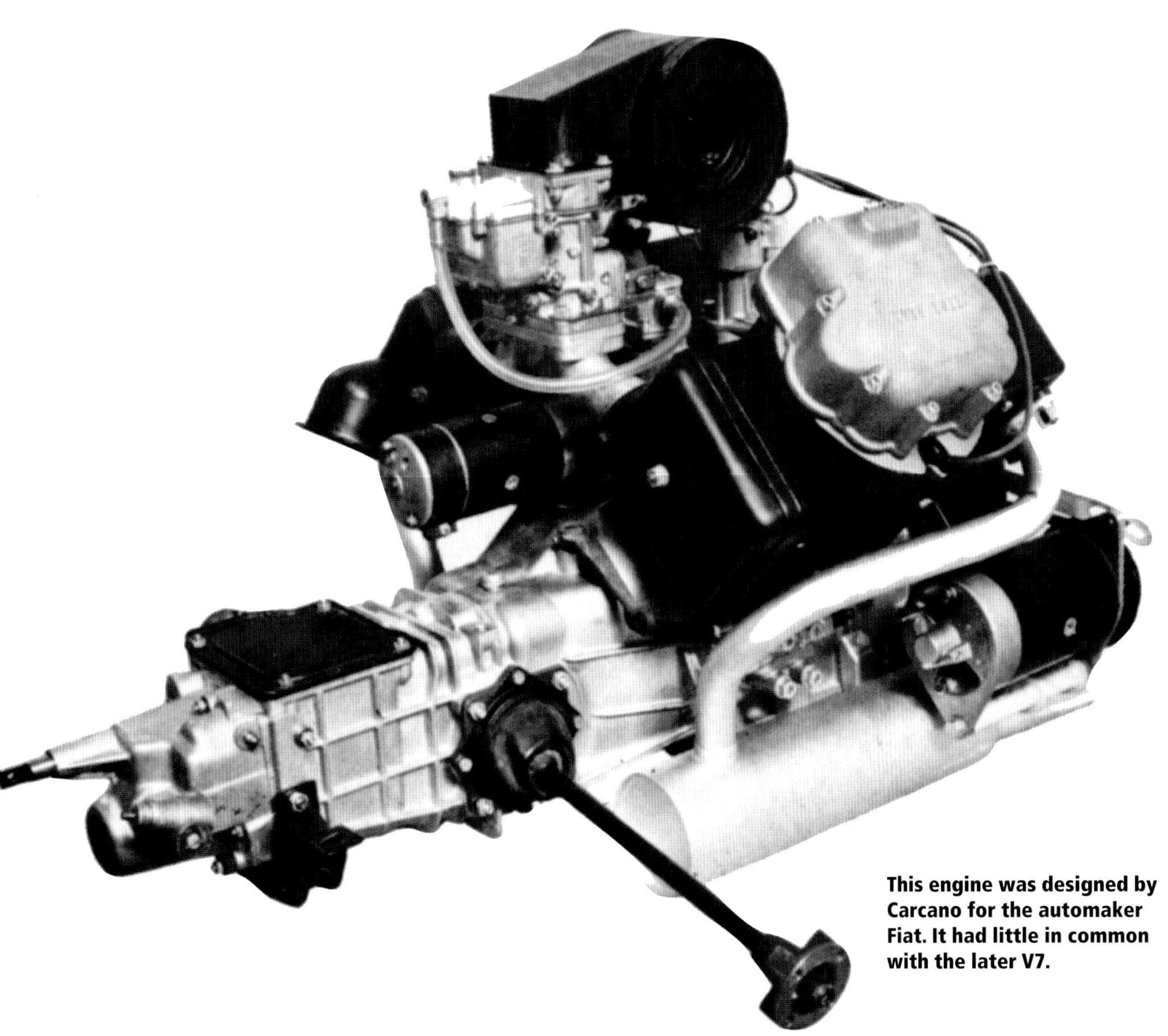

This engine was designed by Carcano for the automaker Fiat. It had little in common with the later V7.

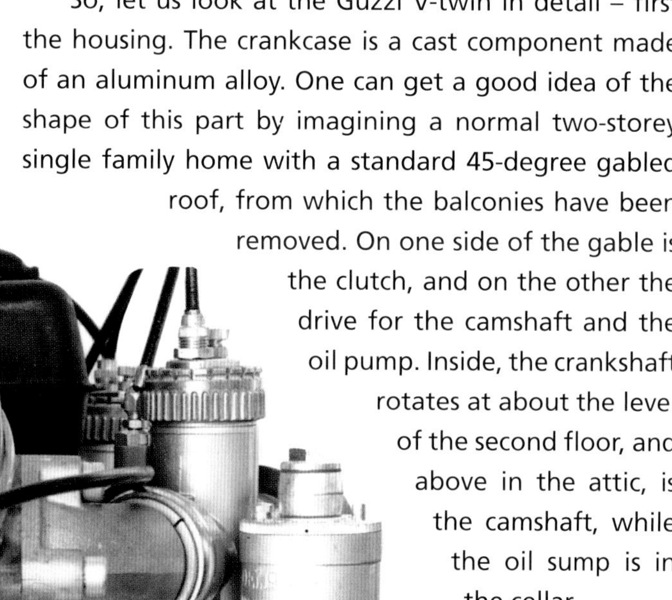

So, let us look at the Guzzi V-twin in detail – first the housing. The crankcase is a cast component made of an aluminum alloy. One can get a good idea of the shape of this part by imagining a normal two-storey single family home with a standard 45-degree gabled roof, from which the balconies have been removed. On one side of the gable is the clutch, and on the other the drive for the camshaft and the oil pump. Inside, the crankshaft rotates at about the level of the second floor, and above in the attic, is the camshaft, while the oil sump is in the cellar.

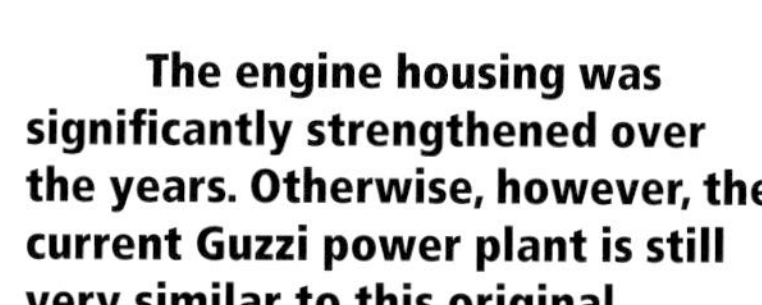

The engine housing was significantly strengthened over the years. Otherwise, however, the current Guzzi power plant is still very similar to this original.

The two cylinders and the heads are up on the roof. The crankshaft is a rather heavy steel design – two sturdy crank arms, a crank pin, 70 mm stroke – and turns in two slide bearings. One is housed in the front gable wall of the case and the larger in the rear wall. The bearings rest firmly in their corresponding bearing shields. The diameter of the crankshaft's front bearing pin is supposed to be between 37.975 and 37.959 mm, that of the rear bearing pin 53.970 to 53.931 mm.

The front slide bearing must have a diameter of 38.000 to 38.016 mm, the rear 54.000 to 54.019 mm. Bearing play is thus between 0.025 and 0.057 mm on the timing gear side and between 0.030 and 0.068 mm on the clutch side. For the case of damage or excessive wear, there are four undersize bearings in 0.2-mm springs for both sides.

A defective crankshaft can thus be adjusted a maximum of four times. During adjustment, attention must be paid to the transition radii of the bearing pins on the crank arms, otherwise failure of the shaft is inevitable.

In the center of the crankshaft, between the two crank arms, the two connecting rods sit on a common crank pin.

The connecting rods are separable at their bottom ends and mounted in slide bearings. In each of the lower connecting rod eyes are two bearing shells made of an aluminum-tin alloy. The diameter of the crankshaft crank pin is supposed to be between 44.013 and 44.033 mm. The corresponding connecting rod bearing shells are between 1.534 and 1.543 mm thick. Bearing play is supposed to be between 0.011 and 0.061 mm. Here again, there are four oversize bearing shells in 0.254-mm springs, in case of damage. The bearing for the piston pin at the upper end of the 560-gram connecting rod is pressed in. The diameter of this slide bearing is supposed to be between 22.020 and 22.041 mm, bearing play 0.014 to 0.040 mm. The piston pins are between 22.021 and 22.006 mm thick.

Now, we turn to the attic of our house. As indicated earlier, the camshaft turns at the very top, under the roof. It also rotates in two slide bearings. Here, however, there are no separate bearing shells, the shaft turns directly in the aluminum of the engine case. The rear camshaft bearing is supposed to measure between 32.025 and 32.064 mm, the front 47.025 to 47.064 mm.

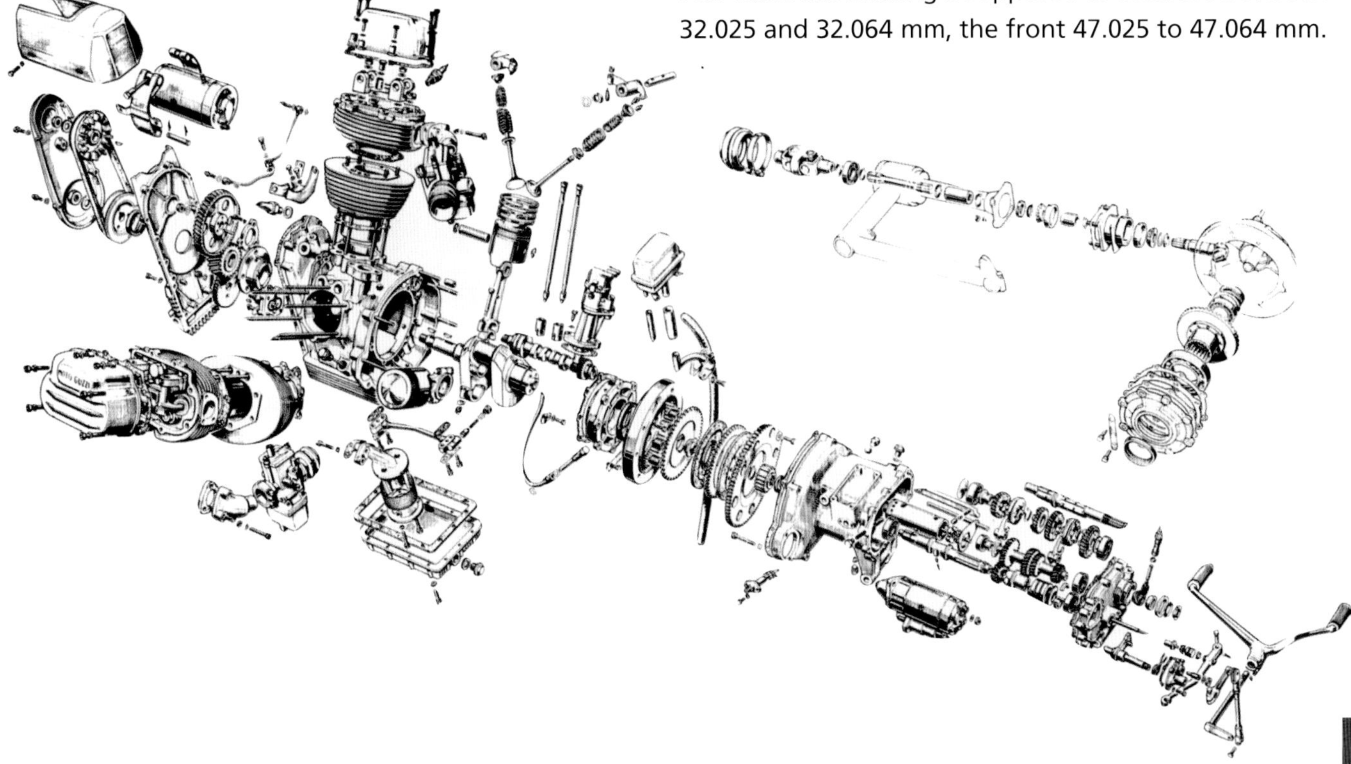

The shaft itself is supposed to measure between 31.975 and 32.000 mm at the rear and between 46.975 and 47.000 mm at the front.

A damaged camshaft bearing results in an engine casing ready for the scrapheap. There are no oversize bearings here. There are four lobes on the shaft. Seen from behind, they are responsible for the right outlet, left outlet, right intake, and left intake valves. The port timings – measured at 0.5 mm checking clearance – are: intake open 24 degrees before top dead center, closed 58 degrees after bottom dead center, outlet open 58 degrees before bottom dead center, closed 22 degrees after top dead center. This shaft was used until the 850 GT and was gear-driven from the crankshaft.

In the roof of the engine casing, there are four holes directly above the camshaft nodes that hold the tappet rod cups. These measure 22 mm in diameter and move up and down right in the aluminum of the casing. If the mating surfaces become worn, there is a way to repair them. Oversize tappet rods are available – 0.05 and 0.10 mm larger.

If we continue our observations in a logical direction, upwards, we climb onto the roof. Carcano and Todero decided to use chromed cylinders. At the time this decision was little understood, but such a design precluded repairs in the event of premature wear or damage to the cylinder mating surfaces. On the other hand, one must bear in mind that both had to take the requirements of the Italian police and military into consideration. And they both demanded a mileage of 100,000 kilometers without having to change vital components – which certainly included pistons and cylinders. And as today's coating methods for cylinder mating surfaces were unknown at the beginning of the 1960s, the two designers were forced to choose chromed mating surfaces. For the otherwise standard cast, cylinder liners wore much too quickly and would require attention before the 100,000 kilometer mark was reached. The Guzzi men had already amassed experience with chromed cylinder linings: beginning in 1958, the small Nuovo Cardellino powered by a 73 cc two-stroke engine had an aluminum cylinder with hard, chrome-plated mating surfaces.

The two V7 cylinders are also cast from an aluminum alloy. Six stud bolts attach the two cylinders – together with the heads – to the crankcase. Moto Guzzi makes the V7 cylinder in three different sizes: the bore of the Class A cylinder has to be between 80 and 80.006 mm, that of the Class B 80.006 to 80.012 mm, and the Class C 80.012 to 80.018 mm. The pistons are, of course, also divided into respective classes: the diameter of the Class A piston is between 79.952 and 79.958 mm, that of the Class B 79.958 to 79.964 mm, and that of the Class C 79.964 to 79.970 mm. The pistons and cylinders always have to come from the same class. Piston play is thus between 0.042 and 0.054 mm.

Four piston rings are used, with a hemispherical dome without milled pockets for the valves. Above, directly beneath the top land, sit two compression rings. One oil scraper ring is placed over, and another under, the piston pins. The pistons are made by Borgo, the cylinders by Gilardoni.

Let us look farther upwards – to the two cylinder heads. They are also cast from light metal with lavish ribbing, which increases the cooling surface. The combustion chambers are hemispherical, the valves are suspended obliquely in the cylinder head, at 35 degrees to the vertical. In the V7, the inlet valve head measures 38.5 mm, the outlet valve head 34.5 mm. The valve stems are 8 mm thick. The valve seats consist of a special, cast iron alloy, the inlet valve seating surface is milled at about 60 degrees and that of the outlet valve at about 45 degrees. The valve guides can be replaced in event of wear. The V7 uses simple valve springs. They are 48 mm long in a relaxed state and 37 mm long installed. The closing pressure is 33 kg when the valve is closed. As usual, the spring plate is held by small gussets.

Atop each cylinder head is a rocker arm bearing block, which is held in place by four or six head bolts. The two remaining standing bolts are shorter and hold the cylinder head directly. The rocker arm bearing block is made of steel. It accepts both rocker arm shafts, which are held by a No.6 screw. They measure between 14.983 and 14.994 mm in diameter. The rocker arms are also made of steel, however the valve surfaces – to the rocker arm shaft – are made of a bronze alloy. The inside diameter is between 15.032 and 15.059 mm. Two shafts run through the cylinder and cylinder head, through which the two aluminum pushrods can be inserted into the tappet cups. Adjusting screws with spherical ends are found in a hemispherical recess at the upper end of the pushrods. Valve play is measured between the valve stem and the rocker arm and is adjusted with the help of the adjusting screws. A No.11 lock nut secures the adjusting screw.

Up on the cylinder heads sit rather high aluminum valve covers with engraved Moto Guzzi lettering. They are held in place by eight hexagon screws. In between is a thin paper gasket. Similar paper seals are found between the engine case and cylinders. The head gasket is a sandwich design made of metal and paper. There are also six O rings on each side – two under the cylinder and four under the rocker arm block.

Despite its generous dimensions, the V7 proved to be a motorcycle with excellent handling and cornering capabilities.

Let us now turn, once again, to the front gable. On the forward end of the crankshaft sits a helical cut gear made of chrome-nickel steel, which drives the camshaft above and the oil pump below. This gear pump – with straight-teeth gears by the way – circulates the oil from the three-liter oil sump, forces the oil simultaneously into both crankshaft main bearings – avoiding the otherwise usual drop in pressure within the shaft, through the crankshaft, and into both connecting rod bearings. There the oil comes out and the rotating shaft hurls it against the cylinder walls. The oil destined for the two camshaft bearings is also forced upwards inside the crankcase, while the cylinder heads are supplied by external lines. An overpressure valve inside the oil sump reduces operating pressure to 2.5 to 3.0 kp/cm^2. In front of the left cylinder there is an oil pressure switch, which activates a warning lamp on the control panel if oil pressure is too low. The circulation system also includes an oil separator. It is intended to vent excess pressure in the crankcase without allowing the oil to be ejected.

Let us remain at the front end for a moment. An aluminum cover seals the front of the engine casing. On the projecting end of the crankshaft there is a V-belt pulley. Atop the crankcase, between the cylinders, sits the 300-Watt alternator, which is driven by V-belts. The upper belt pulley is designed as a quasi fan, blowing cool air onto the stressed generator. Belt tension is adjusted with the help of the bottom pulley. Spacers between the two halves of the pulley are narrowed or widened, depending on whether the tension is too great or insufficient. The alternator itself produces 300 Watts – at a voltage of 12 Volts – once 2,400 rpm is reached. An electro-mechanical regulator limits the voltage to a maximum value of about 14 Volts.

If we take a look back on the roof of the house, we can take a few steps farther to the rear end. There, a kind of cast chimney projects upwards between the two cylinders at an angle of 45 degrees. If one looks into this chimney, below one can see the rear end of the camshaft. At that point the shaft has a spiral bevel. The distributor is found at the top of this shaft. A long shaft, which has a helical cut gear at the bottom end, extends into the chimney and drives the ignition distributor.

The distributor itself comes from Marelli and is also used in the 500 Fiat. It has just a single pair of points, and therefore also just a single lobe on the camshaft. Logically, there is also only one ignition coil, also made by Marelli. Inside the distributor, under the contact plate, is a centrifugal distributor. It regulates pre-ignition from static 10 degrees to 38 degrees – which is reached at 1,800 rpm – before top dead center. The ignition timing itself is set by twisting the entire distributor. Corresponding ignition markings are found on the bottom pulley on the front of the engine.

In conclusion, let us turn to the rear end of the engine. The end of the crankshaft peeks from the rear bearing shield. A heavy steel flywheel is attached to the crankshaft with the help of six bolts. Inside this flywheel is the double-disc dry clutch. It consists of eight springs seated in housings inside the flywheel, an externally-geared pressure plate with a pickup for the mushroom-shaped pressure piece, with whose help the two plates are later disengaged, followed by two friction discs separated by an externally-geared intermediate disc. At the end, there is the heavy steel starter ring, which is attached by eight screws to the flywheel. This clutch unit weighs almost nine kilos – a truly impressive gyrating mass.

The whole thing is set in motion by an electric starter. Carcano and Todero never envisaged a kick starter. To ensure the necessary reliability, they turned to a component that had already proved itself in millions of cars. Marelli provided the same electric starter used in various Fiats. The technical stats for this small – by motorcycle standards – electric motor are impressive. The Marelli component produces 0.7 hp, reaches 3,500 rpm under load, and in that state has a power consumption of 100 Amperes. To give just one example of the performance of the V7's electrical system: provided that the starter doesn't melt from the heat, using the starter alone one can ride more than a kilometer and a half in fifth gear before the capacity of the huge, 30-Amp battery is completely exhausted!

V7 1967 – 69

"In any case, we were lucky to catch one of the test riders on his daily trip over the winding shore road of Lake Como near the factory." These lines were written in the winter of 1964-65 by the Italian motorcycle journalist Carlo Perelli, who had caught one of the Moto Guzzi test riders during a brief siesta on one of the narrow roads around the Lago di Como. He wrote about a sensation: "Moto Guzzi is Building Buffaloes," appeared in bold letters over his article in issue 5/65 of *The Motorcycle*. "Of course, no one – not even at Moto Guzzi – can yet say if and when it will become available." How right Perelli was to be. It would, in fact, be two years before the first production machines with the big V engine would be released for sale.

Whether it is particularly clever for a manufacturer to present a new model numerous times, change it, present it again, fuel expectations, disappoint, and then fuel expectations again, remains to be seen. In any case, the new Moto Guzzi V7, as it was already called at its first presentation, was shown to an amazed public for the first time at the Milan motorcycle show in November 1965. One year later, it was again in the public spotlight. But the machine, which was admired at the International Bicycle and Motorcycle Show in Cologne (IMFA) in the autumn of 1966, was still not a production motorcycle. Not until 16 February 1967, did the Italian Ministry of Transport and Civil Aviation

The big new Guzzi received high praise in the first tests by motorcycle magazines. The fat machine was the dream of motorcycle riders at that time.

complete type-testing of the *Motociclo V7* (Moto Guzzi V7), as the machine was called in the heading of the certification document. Only then could series production begin.

In Germany, however, the V7's story began much earlier; to be more precise, with one of the pre-production display machines, which was shown at the Cologne IFMA in autumn 1966. The handful of editors then on the staff of *Das Motorrad* (The Motorcycle), including Ernst "Klacks" Leverkus, quickly took the powerful machine into their hearts. After all, it appeared to be the fulfillment of a dream, for the men around Klacks Leverkus had longed dreamed – the dream of buffalos.

A "buffalo" suggests what type of motorcycle they suspected lay behind the name. But let us listen briefly to the words of Klacks Leverkus, who on the occasion of his first test ride on the new Guzzi, in the autumn of 1966, summarized his expectations of such a buffalo: "Motorcycles with displacements greater than 500cc should not only be improved with respect to the performance of their engines, but also with respect to their lifespan. In 1966, the question of whether a motorcycle requires repairs after 5,000 or not until 50,000 kilometers is a very important factor to all enthusiasts of this class, especially in our country, where one doesn't just drive such machines from one café to the next. But one also doesn't want to be a wallflower in general traffic, which is becoming ever faster, and this requires 40, 50, 60 or even more horsepower."

Motorcycle colleagues of the 2000 and later age group may argue that all of this sounds quite modest. 50,000 kilometers without repairs couldn't really be a problem? And 50 or 60 horsepower, what was that? Yes, in today's world of 150-hp engines, of two-year warranties and a dense network of garages, Klacks Leverkus' wishes may in fact sound modest. Yet, if we encounter a beautifully-restored old timer from that generation at a vintage race, in a museum, or less frequently at a motorcycle meet, we forget all too quickly that the shiny paint and glittering chrome conceals, in most cases, a highly unreliable mechanical system that three decades ago was capable of infuriating entire hosts of motorcycle riders. A small sample? Klacks Leverkus said, "Shall I list everything that went wrong just among our close circle of friends on the ride to the Elephant Meet in 64? A Harley FLH 74, with just 15,000 kilometers on it, threw a connecting rod because it touched a crank web because of faulty assembly; the right cylinder of an R 69 S flew into the sidecar, on another a rocker arm broke; a BMW R 60 had three seized pistons; an R 69 had a defect in the rear wheel drive; an almost new Norton 650 SS had a primary chain break; an older Horex Imperator suddenly began literally drinking oil!"

And it was then that the new Guzzi V7 burst onto the scene. "When I saw this whopper of a motorcycle, it was clear that I would have no peace until the V7 was in my hands. Moto Guzzi gave me the display machine from the stand in Cologne, where perhaps many still thought that it was a prepared one-off showpiece. But they charged the battery, topped up the gas and oil, and off I went." Klacks was the first journalist permitted to ride the new Moto Guzzi. Initial reserve turned into enthusiasm: "We were prepared for cross-shaking and vibration, for wobbling when reducing or applying throttle, for instability when braking. The shaking was there, specifically at the moment of opening the throttle from idle, but as soon as the centrifugal masses were properly moving the engine ran smoothly."

Let us once again kneel before the V7 – exactly as Klacks Leverkus probably did at the IFMA in 1966. At first, the powerful engine, with its two towering cylinders left and right of the tank, get all the attention. Its stroke of 70 millimeters and a bore of 80 millimeters result in a displacement of exactly 703.7 cubic centimeters. Compression is 9:1. Two Dell'Orto rotary valve carburetors with separate float chambers and 29 millimeter passages supply the two fat pots with fresh gas, which they sniff through a large fine paper filter. Performance figures vary widely, which is simply due to the different measuring practices used at that time. Moto Guzzi quotes a power rating

The first Guzzi with the now legendary V-twin engine was an extremely reliable motorcycle, quite unlike most motorcycles of its day.

V7

Production Period:	1967-1969
Engine:	V-twin OHV/2 V
Displacement:	703.7cc
Bore x Stroke:	80 x 70 mm
Compression:	9:1
Power output:	42 hp at 6,400 rpm
Mixture preparation:	2 Dell'Orto SSI 29 DS (D), points
Clutch:	double plate
Gearbox:	4 speeds
Frame:	steel tube
Wheelbase:	1445 mm
Front suspension:	telescopic fork
Rear suspension:	double swing arm, 2 shock absorbers
Front tire:	4.00 x 18
Rear tire:	4.00 x 18
Front brake:	Duplex drum, 220 mm
Rear brake:	drum, 220 mm
Empty weight:	243 kg
Tank capacity:	20 liters
Maximum speed:	164 kph

of a modest 39.5 CV (Cavalli) at 5,800 rpm for the V7. This value, measured using the CUNA standard common in Italy, was measured without air filter and muffler. The V engine had to carry even less during a performance measurement according to the American SAE standard. In addition to the air filter and muffler, the oil pump, alternator, and flywheel were allowed to be removed. This resulted in the oft-quoted 50 SAE horsepower. Measured using the now-standard DIN standard, with all components and sound-dampening installed, the 700cc variant produces 42 hp at 6,400 rpm.

The foot shifter is on the right side of the machine. The four-speed gearbox shifts in the reverse order – compared to what we are now used to – with first gear at the top and the rest below. The 700 V7 has a relatively short gear ratio: inside the gearbox is a 17/23 primary gear set, in the rear wheel drive an 8/37 floating bevel gear set. At 5,800 rpm – rated power using the CUNA standard – the machine achieves 152 kph.

The engine-gearbox unit is bolted to the steel tube frame in three places: from beneath on the engine case, and beneath and above the gearbox. The frame consists of a central upper tube, which supports the steering head at the top and extends downwards to a cross-tube under the seat, and two curved tubes which are bolted to the engine in front and the gearbox in the rear. These two cradle tubes arc to the rear over the swing arm pivot, bracket the above-mentioned cross-tube, against which the single upper tube is braced, and in a loop form the frame tail. The steering head is also braced by an open-top tube which runs along beneath the upper tube and is also generously stiffened by gussets. The steering head tube itself has an outer diameter of 58 millimeters, while the bearing seat measures 52 millimeters.

The rear wheel swing arms are each guided by a single tapered roller bearing on each side. The swing arms are fixed in position by two sturdy steel bolts that are inserted from the outside and screwed almost through the frame. They are braced against the frame tail by two shock absorbers. The spring preload of these two shock absorbers can be adjusted to three settings. The pre-production machine that Klacks Leverkus rode still lacked this feature.

The front wheel is guided by a hydraulically-damped telescopic fork with a travel of 120 millimeters. The straight tubes have a diameter of 34.7 millimeters. The suspension springs are not inside the fork legs, as on modern bikes, instead they are outside and are protected against the effects of weather by a thin-walled, steel sheet tube. The fork crowns are very widely spaced – 90 millimeters.

The V7 has a wheelbase of 1445 millimeters, which was sufficiently long for the conditions of the day. The steering angle is 62 degrees, the front wheel castor 59.5 millimeters. With its 20-liter tank empty, the machine weighs 243 kg and rides on 18-inch Borrani valanced rims with a rim width of 2.15 inches front and back. The same tires are installed on both wheels: 4.00 x 18 Pirellis with pronounced lug tread. Braking is achieved by means of mechanically-activated 220-mm drum brakes front and rear. The drum on the front wheel is a duplex design, while that on the rear wheel is a simplex brake.

The most important components of the electrical system were described in the previous chapter. The big 32-Ah battery – the largest installed in a motorcycle at that time – is located above the gearbox, sharing space with the flat, air filter box. The instrument cluster on the upper fork bridge is dominated by the large speedometer. V7 riders have to do without a tachometer. There are four warning lights inside the speedometer: parking light indicator, charging indicator light, neutral indicator, oil pressure light. The Bilux bulb in the headlight has 45/40 Watts, the two-filament bulb in the tail light 5/20 Watts, and the four warning lights and the instrument panel lighting each 5 Watts. The V7 does not have turn signals. The ignition switch is located on the upper fork bridge directly under the speedometer. It has a parking light position, in which the parking light lights up when the key is removed. The V7 is normally started using the ignition key and starter – just like an automobile. There are also models with a separate starter button, as we know them today, at the end of the right handlebar. Unfortunately, in this version, the designers neglected to provide a switching relay between the starter button and the ignition relay. As a result, during every engine start the full switching current for the ignition relay flows through the pushbutton and an undersized wire. If the engine fails to start immediately and the starter runs longer than usual, the pushbutton and holder can sometimes melt like snow in the sun.

The V7 was initially offered in two color variations. The fuel tank, side covers, the two tool boxes left and right of the rear wheel, and the two elegantly-shaped fenders were painted either red or silver. The tank also had silver sides, and the frame, the fork legs, and the headlight housing were black. The two cylinders are each protected against damage in a crash or tip-over by a chrome roll-bar. The seat is very long and sufficiently wide; the handlebars are swept far to the rear. Because of the two projecting cylinders in the leg area, overall the seating position is unusually far to the rear. Long before the V7 entered service, this seating arrangement provoked much discussion, even open skepticism. The editor-in-chief of *Das Motorrad*, Siegfried Rauch, devoted all of two sentences to this problem following a brief demonstration of the new Guzzi by Carlo Perelli, in the spring of 1965. "The new Guzzi buffalo shows very clearly, though, where this engine arrangement in a motorcycle can be disadvantageous ... Guzzi also had no other choice but to position the rider unusually far to the rear, because of the huge cylinders of the 700 engine! It remains to be seen whether this displacement will have negative effects during actual riding."

The few lines that our friend Klacks Leverkus dedicated to the seating position and the two cheeky cylinders after his initial test-drive of the V7 show how insignificant the apparent disadvantage is in normal use: "As rider up front or passenger on the second half of the seat, one actually sits comfortably, for the seat length offers plenty of room. Because the

V-twin's two cylinders project to the side, the rider sits farther back than usual. The legs are comfortably angled, touching no part of the engine. This also requires somewhat longer handlebars, but they are in no way unsporting or unattractive."

By the standards of the day, the performance of the new Guzzi was very good. Klacks Leverkus's test machine reached a top speed of about 160 kph, but he was more enthusiastic about its enormous torque. Precisely this conveys the casual confidence that V7 owners so value in their machines. Klacks: "During these rides, I didn't simply ride hectically and nervously, pursued by a thousand flashes – I rode like a man of the house, confident and calm; I didn't shift much, I simply bestrode the land that way."

The motorcycle's relatively high weight also failed to diminish the enjoyment of the big Guzzi. "Tight turns are no problem; one gets around very well, even taking corners brilliantly. On the Nürburgring, I initially had the feeling of performing aerobatics in a heavy bomber – impossible to achieve fast times. But the results (with a tachograph) showed lap times as good as thirteen minutes." On the present-day north loop, which has been shortened to about two kilometers, that would be equivalent to a time of 11 minutes 30 seconds – with just 40 horsepower and a weight of almost 250 kilograms on a much more uneven track and less than outstanding tires. A respectable performance!

The famous Hamburg to Vienna ride with the first V7 has gone down in history: average speed over almost 1400 kilometers was just under 100 kph.

Importer Fritz Röth brought the machine across the Alps to us. From Hammelbach, where the importer was based, it cost 4,800 Deutschmarks. That was surely not excessive given the remarkable reliability that the machine displayed. The legendary Hamburg to Vienna ride by Erwin Müller, on his own V7, is just one of the many examples of the indestructibility of the new Guzzi. On 27 November 1967 – precisely at midnight – Müller set off from Stillhorn for Vienna. The weather was about what one could expect at that time of year. It snowed and stormed. Fourteen hours, eleven minutes, and 1383 kilometers later Erwin arrived in Vienna – rider and Guzzi in good health. His average speed had been 100 kph!

Klacks' test machine also had to travel a few more kilometers, not unusual for a motorcycle trial. After 20,000 kilometers of testing, the machine was taken apart and the engine opened. This revealed components in almost new condition – crankshaft, connecting rods, pistons, cylinders all with almost no signs of wear. The men around Klacks Leverkus attributed this to the generous size of all components, especially the crankshaft and its bearings.

Moto Guzzi carried out its first model update in 1968. The motorcycle was given a new starter and different carburetors. Instead of the Dell'Ortos with external float chambers (SSI), the company's VHB carbs with central float chamber were installed. A small step was added to the rear end of the seat, to provide the passenger with a little support during acceleration. Also new was a white paint finish, in which the machine was now delivered exclusively. Umberto Todero also looked after the issue of use with a sidecar, for in Germany, in particular, the V7 was enjoying increased popularity among three-wheel artists. Finally, beginning in 1968, the 700 was given a shorter final drive ratio of 7/37 – instead of 8/37 – teeth on the bevel and crown gears, a matching mechanical speedometer drive, and fork crowns that reduced castor.

The V7 ended its civilian life in July 1969, when the new V7 Special entered production. But the "old" V7 lived on in its various versions for the authorities – and after all it had been designed for that customer base – until 1976.

Let us hear from Klacks Leverkus once again: "There I sat on the 27-percent steep ramp of the Nürburgring. I had shifted into first gear, clutch engaged, foot on the brake so the thing didn't roll backwards. Then I turned the ignition key – vroom, the dinosaur was running. A little more gas, perhaps a quarter twist, and I let out the clutch. Above, they had of course opened the gate, but by the time I reached it I was already in second gear. Up the ramp and out onto the track – boy, what a bluebottle. All that remains is to take it into the mountains on vacation and make 500 kilometers a day. We'll see if I can get enough of it."

V7 Special 1969 – 71

The V7 Special was the last design by Giulio Cesare Carcano. When SEIMM took over Moto Guzzi, the gifted designer left the company to which he had given so many fantastic designs. Carcano never again worked with motorcycles. Instead he turned all his creative powers to his second great passion, sailing yachts. Carcano's successor was Lino Tonti. The engineer from Romagna – the area around Forli and Ravenna – began his career in the motorcycle field with Benelli. After a few years, he moved to Aermacchi, Bianchi and Gilera. Several more or less successful racing machines were created under his leadership. Just remember the notorious Linto, a 500cc twin-cylinder, four-stroke racer whose engine was basically a combination of two Aermacchi 250cc single-cylinders. The motorcycle was supposed to enable less well-off private riders to keep pace with the fastest in the class. In capable hands, the

The V7 Special was the first variant of the V7 produced by Moto Guzzi. The Special had 50 cubic centimeters more displacement.

V7 Special

Production Period:	1969-1971
Engine:	V-twin OHV/2 V
Displacement:	757.5cc
Bore x Stroke:	83 x 70 mm
Compression:	9:1
Power output:	51 hp at 6,500 rpm
Mixture preparation:	2 Dell'Orto VHB 29, points
Clutch:	double plate
Gearbox:	4 speeds
Frame:	steel tube
Wheelbase:	1470 mm
Front suspension:	telescopic fork
Rear suspension:	double swing arm, 2 shock absorbers
Front tire:	4.00 x 18
Rear tire:	4.00 x 18
Front brake:	Duplex drum, 220 mm
Rear brake:	drum, 220 mm
Empty weight:	246 kg
Tank capacity:	22.5 liters
Maximum speed:	172 kph

Lintos were fast; much more often, however, they were sidelined by some sort of malfunction.

Why tell this story here? Well, Lino Tonti obviously had racing in his blood, but struggling with a mass of iron like the V7, which had just 40 horsepower and weighed all of 240 kilos, did not fit well into Tonti's concept of racing. And with such a stable suspension and brakes that were not overtaxed – why not a little more performance? Tonti was surely expressing what was in the hearts of many V7 riders, for they had just one complaint about the buffalo from Mandello – "it could have a little more 'oomph.'"

"Tonti would have preferred to tune the engine conventionally – a sharper camshaft, a pair of bigger carburetors, something along those lines," recalled Umberto Todero. "But we Guzzi old timers and the company management were finally able to convince him that improved performance should come from increasing the displacement. Anything else would have contradicted the philosophy of the V7 as a long-distance machine with stamina. We therefore increased the bore to 83 millimeters. Together with the unchanged stroke of 70 millimeters, that resulted in a displacement of exactly 757.5 cubic centimeters." The pistons and cylinders of the 750 variants – with hard-chrome mating surfaces as before – were grouped in three size classes. Class A pistons measured between 83.000 and 83.006 mm, Class B pistons between 83.006 and 83.012 mm, and Class C pistons between 83.012 and 83.018 mm in diameter. As before, the pistons had two compression and two oil control rings, although all four were now seated above the piston pin.

At the same time, Tonti also increased the diameter of the valves. Remember: on the V7 the disc of the inlet valve measured 38.5 mm, that of the exhaust valve 34.5 mm. The V7 Special, as the new machine was called, was fitted with 36-mm inlet and

41-mm exhaust valves, and double valve springs. The camshaft remained untouched. The 29 VHB Dell'Orto carbs of the final V7 model were also retained. The crankcase was strengthened by the addition of another rib below the cylinder. The crank web became slightly heavier to compensate for the slight increase in piston weight. All of these measures resulted in a significant increase in power: the Special put out 51 hp at 6,500 rpm, and maximum torque rose to 58 Nm (42.7 ft-lb) at 5,000 rpm.

The gearbox was almost completely redesigned: the primary gear ratio and all four gears became shorter, however the ratio of the secondary drive at the rear wheel was lengthened. The result of this was that all gears turned faster, which in turn reduced the loads on the teeth flanks. This reduction seemed a good idea to the men around Tonti, given the increase in engine performance. The basic design of the gearbox remained unchanged, however. As with the last V7s, customers could choose to have the shifter installed on either the right or left side.

The V7 Special was also given a tachometer, something V7 owners still had to do without. The Special also differed from its predecessor in having a larger, 22.5-liter tank, new side covers with integral air filter box, revised tank design, and slightly-modified suspension geometry with increased castor (88.2 mm) and wheel base (1470 mm). Overall weight rose by three kilos to 246 kg. Otherwise, the differences from the "normal" V7 were minimal. Nevertheless, the Special received a new model code in front of its chassis number. With the new letter combination "VM" – instead of "VS" as on the V7 – the creators of the V7 Special stated clearly: "This is a new motorcycle, not an updated model!" Nevertheless, there was just one shop manual for the two models and this would later also include the 850 GT.

There was little difference in handling between the two V7 models. The new Special was clearly a little faster – top speed of 172 kph, eight kph better than the proven V7. Because of the taller final ratio, however, there was no corresponding improvement in acceleration. During official type trials on 28 July 1969, the Special was almost two seconds slower in the 1000-meter sprint than the lower-powered V7. But what difference did that make? Overall, the Special made a much more powerful impression and simply appeared superior to its predecessor.

The motorcycle retained its character, however. What had Klacks Leverkus written about "his" test machine? "It is perfect for long distances because of the toughness of its engine, the comfortable and fatigue-proof seating position for rider and passenger, the suspension and loading capacity, and the ability to cruise for hours on the highway at about 150 kph." But this Guzzi also had to struggle with its image of an unwieldy heap of iron. Klacks countered, "It is simply not true that the V7 is a 'straightaway' machine! After all, in 10,000 kilometers we scratched up a pair of mufflers, the roll bars and the stands in the curves. It is clear, of course, that one can be quicker on a 120-kg machine, but the point is that the V7 can do much more than many suspect."

One thing was certain though. While the euphoria over the new Guzzis was still perceptible, the selection of words in the test reports was already much more sober, the return to critical realism palpable. For the big Guzzis were not truly all-rounders nor were they indestructible. It was true that the basic design was absolutely reliable and the engine and suspension generously dimensioned. But as is so often the case with Italian motorcycles, a feel for details was missing. Installation of the electrical wiring was sometimes slipshod, consequently many machines broke down with damage to their electrical system. As well, balancing of the crank mechanism sometimes left something to be desired. Vibration caused screws to back out, electrical wires broke.

Even the *Motorrad* long-distance machine was not spared such problems. "A frayed wiring harness caused a short circuit and resulted in a complete rewiring; the Italian SAFA battery was replaced with a German Varta (with 38 Ah!) after a plate shook loose; the dipstick on the oil pan screw plug fell off; the alternator mount shook loose several times; the clamping nut for the left exhaust pipe unscrewed itself several times; a number of times we had to tighten the nuts on the oil lines to the cylinder heads. Finally a brake shoe retaining spring on the rear wheel broke because of scuffing."

The motorcycle riders of that era were used to worse, however. A few degrees less spark advance helped the V7 Special's engine run more smoothly – top speed barely suffered as a result – Bosch silicon spark plugs, interference suppressed ignition wires and a covered distributor protected the ignition electrics against water ingress and the effects of salt. Tonti and his design staff were also not idle. In later production models they improved the clutch friction plates – resulting in a more controllable clutch – strengthened the alternator mount, and once again reworked the crankshaft balancing.

Once again Jan Leek on his former V7 Special. The machine has now been in use for more than three decades, not unusual for the big road burner.

On 27 September 1969, three V7 Specials began a Hamburg – Vienna autobahn marathon similar to the one Erwin Müller had undertaken almost exactly two years earlier. Erwin again took part, riding a privately-owned Special. The second solo machine was ridden by Hugo Schmitz from Bad Ems, and a V7 Special with sidecar was ridden by Guzzi importer Fritz Röth from Hammelbach. All three machines already had several thousand kilometers on them. This time, it was to be a 24-hour ride from Hamburg to Vienna and back – provided the machines and their riders managed to hold out. Fritz Röth's sidecar motorcycle made it 1700 kilometers before an irreparable tank crack (vibration!) brought his trip to an end. Hugo Schmitz and Sozia Jeannie covered exactly 2766 kilometers – equivalent to Hamburg to Vienna and back plus a few hundred kilometers back to the Rhön area. Erwin Müller even made it several hundred kilometers farther to Würzburg. Both solo machines averaged more than 120 kph – factoring in the stops. It was an almost unbelievable physical feat by the crews and proof of the big Guzzi's reliability. The English specialist press subsequently awarded the twin-cylinders from Mandello the nickname "road burner."

The V7 Special was made until December 1971. For the export market to America, there was the somewhat better-equipped V7 Ambassador – with red metallic paint, a different headlight, and chrome instruments and otherwise identical technology. As well, at the end of 1971, a number of machines were built with the equipment later featured by the V7 California 850.

V7 GT 850 cc. 1972 – 74

The last model with the proven V7 chassis, the new V7 – GT 850 cc, as the machine was officially titled, began leaving the assembly line in December 1971. This 850 ended the era of the big "road burner," and several details showed what the future would bring – namely, an 850 cubic-centimeter engine and a five-speed gearbox.

Actually the V7 and the Special were fast enough. The international press had never complained about inadequate performance. Nevertheless, those in Mandello became convinced that the people wanted the big Guzzis to have a little more oomph. The 850 GT – unlike the contemporary V7 Sport – was supposed to be a pure touring model and therefore a tuned 750 engine was out of the question. Torque was the watchword, and it could best be produced by increasing displacement. With a bore-stroke ratio of 83 to 70 millimeters, the 750 variants were decidedly short-stroke. Further boring out of the engine was absolutely out of the question for both Tonti and Todero.

They therefore decided to design a new crankshaft with a stroke of 78 millimeters. The bearing measurements and the shaft length remained unchanged, however, keeping design costs within limits. At the same time, they employed the modified crankcase built for the V7 Special with its significantly more lavish ribbing.

The cylinder linings were hard-chromed as before, the 83-mm pistons were divided into the same size classes as had been the case in the Special. Unlike those of the V7 and the Special, the pistons had three rings instead of four, an oil control ring, and two compression rings. As well, the base of the piston was almost flat and lacked the high dome of the two previous models. As before, 22-mm piston pins were used.

A bore of 83 millimeters and a stroke of 78 millimeters produced a displacement of exactly 844.05 cubic centimeters. Compression was 9:1, on the same level as the V7 and V7 Special. The camshaft and carburetors of the two older models were also used. Performance was 55 DIN hp at 6,100 rpm, just four horsepower more than the 750 model, but it was the big twin's torque that profited most from the increase in displacement. Compared to that of the Special, it rose an impressive 30 to 90 Nm (66.38 ft-lb). In view of this tremendous value, it is almost impossible to understand why this Guzzi

The last variant of the V7 series was this 850. The bigger displacement was achieved by increasing the stroke by eight millimeters.

V7 GT 850 cc	
Production Period:	1972-1974
Engine:	V-twin OHV/2 V
Displacement:	844.05cc
Bore x Stroke:	83 x 78 mm
Compression:	9:1
Power output:	55 hp at 6,100 rpm
Mixture preparation:	2 Dell'Orto VHB 29, points
Clutch:	double plate
Gearbox:	5 speeds
Frame:	steel tube
Wheelbase:	1470 mm
Front suspension:	telescopic fork
Rear suspension:	double swing arm, 2 shock absorbers
Front tire:	4.00 x 18
Rear tire:	4.00 x 18
Front brake:	duplex drum, 220 mm; from Nov. 1973, 300 mm disc
Rear brake:	drum, 220 mm
Empty weight:	249 kg
Tank capacity:	22.5 liters
Maximum speed:	174 kph

was equipped with a five-speed gearbox. Tonti had designed a five-speed gearbox for the V7 Sport, which was built alongside this 850, and the 750 sport engine of that model needed it. The 850 tourer was given the extra gear for reasons of rationalization. The basic design of the gear train remained largely unchanged, although of course there was another pair of gears on the intermediate shaft and drive shaft, immediately next to those of the first gear. The sequence of gear pairs from front to back was: fourth, third, second, first, fifth gears. Unlike those of the first four gears, the fifth gear's idler turned on the intermediate shaft, while its partner on the drive shaft was rigidly connected to this. The arrangement was reversed for the first four gears. The reason for this arrangement was simple: there wasn't room on the driveshaft for another driver gear, for the transmission unit could not be longer than the four-speed box, otherwise they would have had to change the chassis. And so the driver gear for fifth gear was located on the intermediate shaft. With the gearshift drum – which of course received an additional fifth hole for the retaining pin and a third nut for the additional shift fork – in the appropriate position, this driver wheel established traction between the gear and intermediate shaft. All of the transmission gears are helical. Compared to that of the Special, the chassis of this first 850 was absolutely unchanged. Wheelbase, steer angle, castor – all of these values were exactly the same as those for the 750. On the other hand, overall weight rose slightly. The clearly reinforced crankcase and gearbox housings and the new crankshaft were responsible for the extra three kilos.

The machine completed Italian type testing on 15 December 1971, and was given the identification code "VP" in front of the chassis number. The 850 could be bought from importer Fritz Röth for 7,165 Deutschmarks. Amazingly, the machine was certified with the duplex drum brake of the Special. It was delivered – at least in Germany – with a double duplex on the front wheel, although the diameter was the same as the single drum of the 750.

This brake system received much criticism from owners. In the first place, properly adjusting the double duplex was unbelievably complicated, and second, its performance wasn't that great. The simple drum brakes of the Special or the V7 were certainly not inferior. On the contrary – the braking control provided by the simple duplex was considerably better. The double duplex, on the other hand, often functioned according to the "all or nothing" principle. In autumn 1973, Moto Guzzi introduced the front single-disc brake as standard. The gray cast iron brake disc sat on the right side of the spoked front wheel. The large disc measured 300 mm in diameter. A Brembo 2-pot caliper gripped the unperforated disc. The hydraulic unit with 16-mm piston, also provided by Brembo, was located on the end of the right handlebar. With the help of this system and capable support from the rear 220-mm drum brake, the motorcycle, which weighed just under 250 kg, was somewhat easier to control.

Performance of the more powerful twin was more satisfactory. A quote from a test report in *Motorrad*: "One feels a tremendous pull when accelerating at maximum rpm and when shifting from third to fourth gear, almost giving the impression of a barrel roll [gyroscopic effect]. One has to take care not to be too brutal coming out of corners, if the many kilos are to behave." Yes, unlike the two older models, on this 850 the rider clearly feels the tremendous backdriving torque of the twin-cylinder, for which the huge gyrating masses and the generous torque are responsible.

The chassis of the 850 – exactly like its two predecessor models – is trimmed for handling. The relatively short wheelbase, the short castor (88 mm), and the low center of gravity help give this whopper of a motorcycle unexpectedly good handling. The Guzzi pays for this agile handling at speeds in excess of 150 kph. For there, the rider now and then needs a rather big heart if he wants to get the machine to its maximum speed – just under 180 kph. The rider has to "make himself small" to minimize wobbling.

Moto Guzzi built two versions of the 850 – the V 850 GT and the V7 California 850. The two machines differed only in their equipment packages. While the only visual difference between the V 850 GT and the Special was the former's dark paint, the California received an upswept, black and white seat, a windscreen, footboards for the rider, roll bars, luggage carrier, and two bags. It is simple to tell the two versions apart from their serial numbers: the standard version has a combination of two numbers and two letters, while the California models are numbered from 11.111.

In conclusion, let us once again read the words that Klacks Leverkus found for this Guzzi: "Once one works things out with the 850 Guzzi, then one has a road burner in the truest sense of the word. It begins exerting its charm when covering long distances. It is a big, fast touring machine – somewhere between a Harley and a BMW."

The California differed from the standard GT only in its equipment. The Cali models can easily be identified by their chassis numbers. They were numbered consecutively from 11.111.

V7 Sport 1972 – 74

Let us turn the page back to 1968. Moto Guzzi has been out of motorcycle racing for five years – at least it has not had a factory race team. The last victory by the Guzzi team had been at the International Six Days Trials in Czechoslovakia in 1962, when it won the Silver Vase in the motocross event. But Lino Tonti's heart belonged to road racing – he had no interest in motocross bikes. As well, he considered motorcycle racing to be an excellent advertising tool. The company lacked the financial means for a return to the Grand Prix scene, however. One must not forget that, despite the success of the V7 series, Moto Guzzi was still fighting for its survival at that time. Because of this, the best it could hope for was to become involved in the production racing scene. Only, the V7 really wasn't a particularly sporty machine.

Tonti found a way out of the dilemma. At that time, there were a few, rather old, world speed records. The Moto Guzzi team broke both of these in June and October 1969 – with the heavy, non-sporty V7. The story of these two record rides is very important for Moto Guzzi. For with these records in his pocket, from then on Tonti got on the nerves of company management. The big V-twin engine undoubtedly had sporting potential, but it needed a new, modern chassis. This would give the entire series a second leg to stand on. Finally, the president of SEIMM Donato Cattanio, the general manager Romolo De Stefani, and, most importantly, the new head of product development Dr. Giorgio Araldi heard his pleas. Tonti was given the green light to develop a new sporty chassis.

Tonti's criticisms focused on the great overall height of the V-twin engine. This necessitated large, wide, and consequently unstable frame loops. He

The V7 Sport of 1972 still presents itself as the classic Italian sport bike. Moto Guzzi absolutely copied its lines from the V7 Special unveiled in Milan.

imagined a significantly lower and much more stable chassis, but designing one around the V7 Special's power plant was no easy task. The two large, towering cylinders were not responsible for the great height of the engine. No, it was largely the alternator, which was located up in the cylinder V. Tonti transplanted the alternator onto the forward crankshaft stub. This required some redesign, however, and he added a cone that housed the alternator rotor. The alternator itself came from Bosch, bore a new designation G1(R)14 V13 A19, and now produced 182 Watts – instead of the 300 Watts on the touring models. The new alternator, of course, made necessary a new control box cover. The crankcase itself was covered with a network of stiffening ribs. Incidentally, on the cases used today, one can still find the cast-on bearing blocks for the "old" alternator between the cylinders.

There was also much that was new inside the engine. Most striking was the changed bore-stroke ratio. Compared to the 750 Special, Tonti reduced the bore by half a millimeter. Why? Well, the Special had a displacement of exactly 757.5 cubic centimeters, and piston displacement for production machines and Formula 750 racing was restricted to under 750 cubic centimeters. And the new machine was intended in part, to participate in those classes. As usual, the cylinders and pistons were made in three size classes: Class A pistons measured between 82.500 and 82.506 mm, Class B 82.506 to 82.512 mm, and Class C 82.512 to 82,518 mm. Displacement was exactly 748.4 cubic centimeters. Moving up and down inside the cylinder tubes were high-domed, four-ring pistons. Compression was 9.8:1, significantly higher than on the Special.

At the same time, they designed a new camshaft with clearly sharper port timings, the sportiest shaft ever used in a production Guzzi. The port timings: inlet opens 40 degrees before top dead center, closes at 70 degrees after bottom dead center, outlet opens 63 degrees before bottom dead center, closes 29 degrees after top dead center. The valves were the same size as those of the Special – 36 mm on the outlet, 41 mm at the inlet. Larger 30-mm Dell'Orto VHB carburetors supplied mixture to the combustion chambers. As on the Special, twin valve springs closed the valves. This combination produced 62 hp at 7,250 rpm. It did not reach its maximum torque of about 65 Nm (47.94 ft-lb) until 6,250 rpm – a true sporting power plant therefore.

The clutch remained unchanged from that of the Special. The gearbox, however, was new. We already described the five-speed gearbox in detail in the chapter on the V 850 GT. It was originally designed for the sport Guzzi, however. Because of the expected narrower power band, Tonti believed that the new

V7 Sport

Production Period:	1972-1974
Engine:	V-twin OHV/2 V
Displacement:	748.4cc
Bore x Stroke:	82.5 x 70 mm
Compression:	9.8:1
Power output:	62 hp at 7.250 rpm
Mixture preparation:	2 Dell'Orto VHB 30, points
Clutch:	double plate
Gearbox:	5 speeds
Frame:	steel tube, removable cradle braces
Wheelbase:	1470 mm
Front suspension:	telescopic fork
Rear suspension:	double swing arm, 2 shock absorbers
Front tire:	3.25 x 18
Rear tire:	3.50 x 18
Front brake:	double duplex, 220 mm
Rear brake:	drum, 220 mm
Empty weight:	225 kg
Tank capacity:	22.5 liters
Maximum speed:	206 kph

engine could make good use of an additional fifth gear. Inside, however, was the "short," 16/22 primary drive of the Special – as the 850 had a 17/21 gear set. The fifth gear and the final drive (8/85) of the sport model, however, were geared noticeably longer. The shifter could be located on the left or right.

The V7 Sport's real innovation, however, was not its more powerful engine – after all, that was part of a fast sport machine – but rather its new frame design. And one must concede one thing to Tonti, even if his working style pulled Umberto Todero to pieces – his new design for the V7 chassis was one of the finest creations in the history of motorcycles. But, maybe it was the tight design and financial constraints that the designer with the avant-garde ideas was subjected to while designing the sport chassis that resulted in his work becoming a great design. The fixed length of the entire drive train – crankshaft, transmission, driveshaft – alone placed tangible limits on Tonti's creativity.

Straight tube is stronger than curved – Tonti followed this maxim in almost every detail in designing the new frame. Only the two removable cradle braces – which play a relatively minor role in the frame's stability – are slightly curved. Two tubes extend in an absolutely straight line from the bottom of the steering head to behind the seat. A central frame tube braces the top of the steering head and ends roughly at the rear end of the tank at a welded cross piece. The engine is wedged just beneath the two straight upper tubes. The fit is so tight that the cradle beams had to be made removable: both of them, by the way, and not just the left as entire legions of writers have claimed for the past two decades. Triangular braces on both sides of the frame support the swing arm pivot. The engine is held by a bolt that passes through a hole in the new control box cover. The gearbox is attached to the cradle braces, also by a bolt, and also above by the battery base plate. Cross tubes above and below the swing arm pivot provide additional strength.

The swing arm is unchanged from that of the touring models. Up front, however, is a telescopic fork developed and made in-house, with a suspension travel of 120 millimeters and a most unconventional damping system. Unlike normal telescopic forks, where the oil in the cylinder is squeezed through small holes in the damping unit during compression and decompression and whose viscosity has a significant influence on the fork's damping qualities, Moto Guzzi used encapsulated damping cartridges, as seen in steering dampers, for example. They sit up top, right under the sealing caps. The oil in the Guzzi forks is for lubrication only and has no influence on damping.

The V7 Sport had to get by with drum brakes. Up front, however, was a double duplex brake with ventilation slots, like the one later used on the V 850 GT. Spoked wheels with Borrani valanced rims were used front and back. The rear rim is 2.15 inches wide, the front just 1.85 inches. A Michelin 3.25 tire is mounted on the front rim, a 3.50 Michelin on the back.

The V7 Sport made its debut in July 1971 – and as was only fitting for a sport bike, at a race. Moto Guzzi sent the newcomer to the starting line of a 500-kilometer race that took place at the legendary racetrack in the royal park north of Milan and was advertised for production machines. Raimondo Riva from Lecco – ten kilometers south of Mandello del Lario – rode the graceful machine to a third place finish. There was great enthusiasm in the factory, and it became even greater when, a few days later, a few well-known riders – including Mike "the Bike" Hailwood – were given the opportunity to test the Sport. They gave the new chassis full marks.

Of course, the customers on the other side of the Alps soon heard of this success. Carlo Perelli was again responsible for distributing the new motorcycle. "In Mandello they're definitely planning to build 100 machines this year!"

In fact, the Sport had already undergone Italian type testing on 10 March 1971 – without it the machine would not have been permitted to race in Monza three months later. It is difficult to say with certainty exactly how many 1971 V 7 Sports were built, but Umberto Todero estimates the number at about 200. All of these machines were assembled by hand in the experimental department. The frame was made of cheap but light chrome-molybdenum steel and was painted fire-red, while the tank and the tiny triangular side panels were champagne color. The small fenders were chromed and the rear fender folded upwards to facilitate tire changes. The machine weighed 225 kg and drew rave reviews from motorcycle riders around the globe – a dream in aluminum, chrome, green, red, and black. The gooseneck handlebars could be placed in almost any desired position, while the tachometer was mechanically-driven and finally gave an accurate indication.

The outstanding performance of the Sport models convinced test riders from the outset. Klacks Leverkus: "If one revved up the engine to between 5,000 and 6,000 rpm and then let out the clutch in first gear, the 200-kilo bike sped away like a cannonball – we measured a time of under five seconds to accelerate from 0 to 100 kph. In normal driving, the bike accelerates so quickly between 120 and 160 kph as to bring tears to the eyes of a theoretical competitor. That is what makes it such a great riding experience." The Sport was genuinely capable of 200 kph. A longer 9/37 final gearing was available from the manufacturer, with which – given a light and low-drag rider – a top speed in excess of 210 kph was easily achieved. A shorter 8/37 gear set could be ordered for racing use.

The new suspension also received high praise: "The Guzzi can be ridden unexpectedly aggressively through tight and fast turns, in S-turns it is a joy to throw the machine from one side to the other. We can only be filled with praise for this suspension. We even rode this bolt of lightning through the first snow – albeit at no more than 150 kph."

As stated, about 200 examples of this exclusive racer left the experimental department in Mandello, far short of the number required to meet demand. Production of the standard V 7 Sport did not begin until 1972, but this second version lacked some of the flair of the first 200 examples. The frame was made of poorer-quality steel – chrome-molybdenum steel was too expensive in the long run – and it was painted black instead of red. The tank and side covers could be had in the previous green or in red. The ignition and valve train were slightly modified.

Many owners, after having waited so eagerly for their Sports, were a little disappointed by the '72 and '73 version. While the suspension met all their expectations, performance often suffered compared to the handmade versions of the previous year, which had garnered such attention from the press.

Many examples, in fact, ran faster in fourth gear than in fifth. The true enthusiast was bothered little by this. All that mattered was that the big Guzzis finally had a competitive suspension, with which, on our roads, one could literally blow away the Japanese competition.

The V 7 Sport came off the production lines in Mandello del Lario until the end of 1973. In Germany, it initially cost just under 8,000 *Deutschmarks*, but the price later rose to almost 9,000. Exactly 879 examples were built. In February 1974, perhaps the most beautiful of all Guzzis was replaced by the 750 S.

750 S 1974 – 75

The 750 S appeared in February 1974, as successor to the V7 Sport. The close relationship between these two Guzzis is documented by their chassis numbers. The Sport's numbers begin with the abbreviation VK, those of the 750 S with VK 1. The new machine didn't even undergo new type testing. The type approval – issued on 13 February 1974 – was based on that of the Sport.

Nevertheless, there were a few innovations. A timing chain with three sprockets and a tensioner now powered the camshaft and oil pump. The gearing previously used was simply too costly. This design has since been used in all production Guzzis with the big V-twin. Otherwise the engine remained untouched. Pistons, cylinders, camshaft, carburetor – all of these components were identical to those of the sport. Performance was also unchanged.

Nevertheless, there was once again a new gear ratio. The primary ratio was taller (17/21) and the individual gears were identical to those of the V 850 GT. As the Sport's gearbox was actually perfectly graduated – though the S gearing was available on the Sport as an option – rationalization must have been behind this change. The foot shift lever was now fitted exclusively on the left side.

The second important innovation was also obvious to the consumer at first glance: the double duplex front brake was replaced by a double disc brake. The two discs, which were made by Brembo, measured 300 mm in diameter. The Italian manufacturer also supplied the hydraulic cylinder with a 16-mm piston.

All of the other changes on the 750 S were cosmetic. Like those of the last Sport models, the frame was painted black. The side covers had become larger. The motorcycle was only available in the base color black, however red, orange or green stripes were available on the tank and side covers. The seat was flatter and now had a mighty hump on the end – as a result of which there was only room for 1 ½ people on the Guzzi. But the Sport wasn't a true two-seat motorcycle either. The two Lafranconi pipes were finished in black instead of shiny chrome. The three shark gills on the beveled ends of the Lafranconis were retained.

On the road, the handling of the two bikes with the new lower, sportier chassis was almost identical. The disc brake system did, however, allow the machine to finally achieve braking performance befitting its status. This was only true in dry conditions, however, for in the wet the system hesitated for a long second before finally gripping.

The company claimed a maximum speed of 206 kph for the S and the Sport – a figure that the machine could in fact only reach under optimal conditions. 1,059 examples of the Type VK 1 were built in Mandello. Then, at the start of 1975, production of the 750 S was halted in favor of the 750 S3.

750 S

Production Period:	Feb.1974 - Jan.1975
Engine:	V-twin OHV/2 V
Displacement:	748.4cc
Bore x Stroke:	82.5 x 70 mm
Compression:	9.8:1
Power output:	62 hp at 7.250 rpm
Mixture preparation:	Dell'Orto VHB 29, battery ignition, points
Clutch:	double plate
Gearbox:	5 speeds
Frame:	steel tube, removable cradle braces
Wheelbase:	1470 mm
Front suspension:	telescopic fork
Rear suspension:	double swing arm, 2 shock absorbers
Front tire:	3.25H18
Rear tire:	3.50H18
Front brake:	double disc, 300 mm
Rear brake:	drum, 220 mm
Empty weight:	225 kg
Tank capacity:	22.5 liters
Maximum speed:	206 kph

750 S3 1975 – 76

In the spring of 1975, precisely on 7 April, the responsible Italian authorities approved the third edition of the sporty 750 Moto Guzzi – half a year before the first 850 Le Mans caused the hearts of Guzzi fans to beat a few beats faster. The S3 followed precisely in the footsteps of the already legendary V7 Sport, whose countless racing victories had helped solidify its reputation.

If one looks in the S3's family tree for its direct predecessor, however, one discovers that the blue blood of a sporty thoroughbred no longer flows in the oil system. Rather, the Guzzi technicians infused a healthy dose of the bourgeois blood of the T models into the veins of this last 750cc sport model.

Let us take a close look at the S3's power plant. The crank mechanism, cylinders, pistons, and cylinder heads are the same as those of the 750 S. Compression is still a sporty 9.8:1. Beneath the crankcase cover, however, turns a much tamer camshaft, similar to the one used in the T models. Sweet port timings? Inlet opens 20 degrees before top dead center, closes 52 degrees after bottom dead center, outlet opens 52 degrees before bottom dead center, closes 20 degrees after top dead center. As before, 30-mm Dell'Ortos supply the combustion chambers with mixture. They draw air from a sort of air filter box, but the actual filter element is missing.

There are modifications to be found in the bottom of our crankcase, however; no longer is a simple sieve filter responsible for filtering impurities from the oil circulation system. Instead, there is now an auto-type oil filter in the oil pan. The oil pump now has helical gears and delivers an impressive 500 liters per second. Operating oil pressure is 4.2 Bar. Mounting of the exhaust manifold on the cylinder head is new: no longer do they rely on large union nuts – which are so fond of vibrating loose – rather, they attach the new manifold with the help of an aluminum cast ring held by two 8-mm bolts. Visually, this assembly differs from its predecessor mainly in somewhat lower valve covers. The S3 is also recognizable by its side covers, taken from the 850 T3 tourer.

The electrical system – including starter and alternator – is entirely made by Bosch. Unlike the 750 S, the S3 has turn signals front and rear. Surprisingly, not much was done with the gearbox, although there is again a new final ratio. The 7/33 plate-bevel gear pairing of the S3 would remain the standard ratio for all of the "big Guzzis" in the future.

All of these changes did not produce an increase in performance. As before, the sporty 750 delivered 62 DIN hp to the fat crankshaft at 6,900 rpm. Maximum torque rose to 54 Nm (39.82 ft/lb) at 5,500 rpm. This was about ten units less than could be measured on the V7 Sport. The significantly more baffled exhaust system was largely responsible for this weakness in the mid-rpm range. For the first time, noise limits demanded their tribute.

The running gear held much more that was new, and not just in the chassis itself – which was unchanged from that of the famous 750 S, again reflected in the almost identical abbreviation VK 2 for the chassis number – but in the brake system. On the S3 – and the 850 T3 made at the same time – Moto Guzzi used a rear disc brake for the first time. But they didn't simply leave it at changing from drum to disc, which incidentally made it necessary to redesign the shaft housing. No, a lot of brainwork went into the S3's brake system, for – like all subsequent "big" Guzzis, the machine had a so-called "integral brake system."

Umberto Todero recalled the development of the system. "We began experimenting with such systems on the Grand Prix racing machines in the early 1950s. But hydraulic operating systems did not then exist. And tuning such a system, with the front and rear brakes operated by a single lever, was scarcely possible with cables and horizontal bars alone. Friction losses inside the many Bowden cables were enormous. A lot of force was required to pull the brakes. Nevertheless, in 1953 Lorenzetti won the 500cc class at Hockenheim with such a system."

750 S3

Production Period:	1975-1976
Engine:	V-twin OHV/2 V
Displacement:	748.4cc
Bore x Stroke:	82.5 x 70 mm
Compression:	9.8:1
Power output:	62 hp at 6,900 rpm
Mixture preparation:	Dell'Orto VHB 30, battery ignition, points
Clutch:	double plate
Gearbox:	5 speeds
Frame:	steel tube, removable cradle braces
Wheelbase:	1470 mm
Front suspension:	telescopic fork
Rear suspension:	double swing arm, 2 shock absorbers
Front tire:	3.25H18
Rear tire:	3.50H18
Front brake:	double disc, 300 mm
Rear brake:	integral brake, disc, 242 mm
Empty weight:	230 kg
Tank capacity:	22.5 liters
Maximum speed:	206 kph

Lino Tonti began similar experiments with the drum-braked V7 at the end of 1967, beginning of 1968. Once again, problems with the mechanical transfer of forces proved unsolvable. Not until the end of 1973 did Umberto Todero, together with the brake specialists at Brembo, produce a prototype with a hydraulically-operated integral braking system which performed satisfactorily. "That required a big, big studio," continued the veteran engineer. What he meant was a great deal of thought and testing. "The main problem was to ensure that, under all circumstances and on all surfaces, the rear wheel locked before the front wheel during maximum braking. The TÜV in Hanover, which was handling approval in Germany, was largely responsible for this requirement." Todero solved the problem with the help of a pressure control valve, different size brake discs, and different disc pads.

And this is how the whole thing functions: the main brake cylinder is located beneath the right side cover. From there a pressure line leads to the pressure control valve, which is attached to the left side of the frame in front of the rear tire. From there pressure is applied to the rear and the front left brake calipers. If one applies the foot brake, the motorcycle is slowed by these two brake discs. The brake lever on the right side of the handlebars only operates the right front disc and is only used to support the integral braking system. "Actually, we wanted to incorporate it into the system. But the German approval law required two independent brake systems for the front and rear wheels. I would have preferred to develop a system in which both wheels were braked by the hand brake lever."

In practice, however, the system worked well, as described in the following excerpt from a *Motorrad* test report on the 750 S3: "What this type of brake system makes possible in late braking was clearly demonstrated when our youngest writer, who is not known for his reckless riding style, played his little game for several laps with trained Yamaha race riders on the small track in Hockenheim. How he completely outbraked the Yamahas on a machine that was twice as heavy deserves a chapter of its own." Inexperienced riders, in particular, benefited from the trouble-free system.

Physics could not be tricked, even by the integral brakes, as the Guzzi would have had the Guzzi-inclined customer base believe. The braking distance was no shorter than with a conventionally controlled system operated by a skilled rider. But to evaluate what was possible – for many riders the integral system made this easier. "Whether the brakes are hot or cold – the values are consistently between 9 and 9.7 meters per second squared. During braking the chassis remains so steady that one could brake 'free-handed.'"

The chassis, largely unchanged from that of the 750 S, was also able to hold its own against the improved products from the Far East. Even more, "Safely and confidently, after a very few kilometers one gets the feeling that he has beneath him a vehicle which, in the interaction of all important components, is not simply a stroke of luck. The tuning of all of the chassis properties has been so masterfully achieved that it will not be surprising if the competition comes up with similar designs."

Although the chassis of the last "big" 750 Guzzi received high praise, its engine came in for some harsh criticism from some quarters. The power and torque curves showed a sharp drop between 3,500 and 4,500 rpm, which was largely blamed on the baffled exhaust system. The S3 pulled very hard below this, and only unwillingly in the above-mentioned range, and it wasn't until 5,000 rpm was reached that it went like the much-hackneyed cannonball.

The S3 remained in production until 1976 and exactly 927 were built. The fast, 230-kilo machine was imported into Germany by Mobylette, located in Brackwede near Bielefeld. It cost 9,650 Deutschmark.

"Machines combining a hint of the past with the signs of the new age are being created beneath the bronze statue of the legendary Guzzi test rider Omobono Tenni in Mandello," wrote Peter Limmert at the conclusion of his S3 test. But the time of the 700 and 750 Guzzis had run out. The future belonged to the 850s.

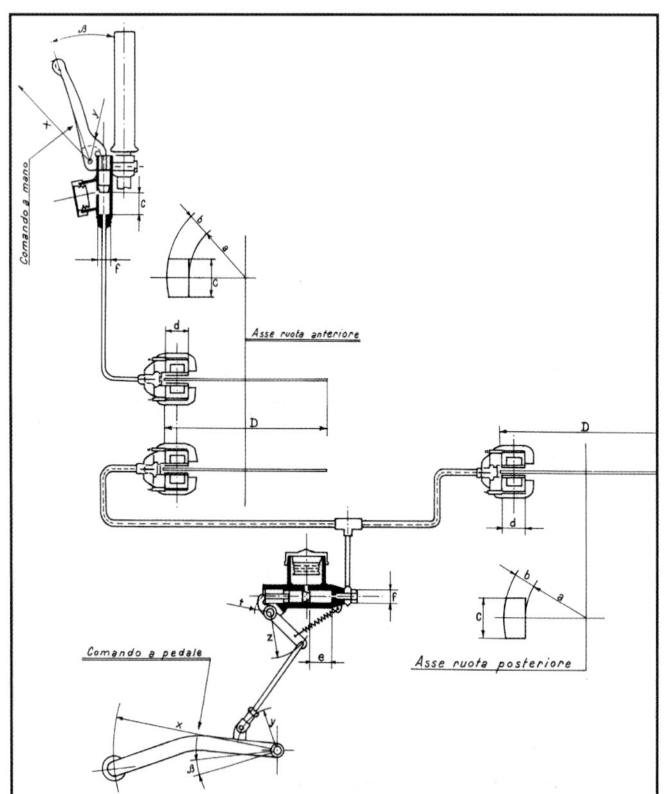

Moto Guzzi was the first manufacturer to introduce an integral braking system, in which the front and rear brakes work together, on a production motorcycle.

1000S 1990 – 93

"Machines combining a hint of the past with the signs of the new age." This sentence, by Peter Limmert, took on a whole new meaning almost fifteen years later. For almost a decade and a half after production of the last sport model, the 750 S3, had been stopped, the S Class experienced a rebirth – and the 1000 S captured the hearts of Guzzi fans. The design of this machine goes back to the initiative of the German Guzzi importer. He first became involved in the matter of product planning at the keel laying of the Mille GT in Mandello. The success of this touring motorcycle encouraged the men from Bielefeld, around manager Eberhard Just, to ask for the design of a classic, unfaired sport bike in the style of the old V7 Sport. Just argued that a market existed for such a motorcycle. Many Guzzi riders – at least in Germany – preferred a motorcycle with classic, sporty lines. This was demonstrated by the many fans who converted their Le Mans models, stripping them to the bare metal, as did the hefty increase in price for good quality used Le Mans I or S3 models.

In Mandello the men from Bielefeld found themselves preaching to the converted, and in the end the German importer scored a bull's eye with his conception of the Mille GT. A proven base machine already existed in the Le Mans V, and all the other necessary parts – tank, side covers, instruments – were sleeping in one spare parts shelf or another. In the spring of 1989, the prototype was in the factory buildings of the Deutschen Motobecane in Bielefeld. The decision to actually build the classic sport bike was not reached, however, until after A&G became Motobecane's successor as German importer of Moto Guzzi motorcycles.

Technically, the 1000 S was, in fact, based on the Le Mans V. This is documented by the unchanged abbreviation before the chassis number. The numbers of the Le Mans IV and V also began with VV. The 1000 S is identified as a Le Mans model on its approval sheet – interesting, no? It differs from its faired colleague only in its bolt-on parts – tank, seat, handlebars, instruments, roll bar, lights, turn signals.

1000 S	
Production Period:	1990-1993
Engine:	V-twin OHV/2 V
Displacement:	948cc
Bore x Stroke:	88 x 78 mm
Compression:	9.8:1
Power output:	81 hp at 7,400 rpm
Mixture preparation:	Dell'Orto PHM 40, points
Clutch:	double plate
Gearbox:	5 speeds
Frame:	steel tube, removable cradle braces
Wheelbase:	1485 mm
Front suspension:	telescopic fork
Rear suspension:	double swing arm, 2 shock absorbers
Front tire:	100/90V18
Rear tire:	120/90V18
Front brake:	double disc, 270 mm
Rear brake:	disc, 270 mm
Empty weight:	240 kg
Tank capacity:	22.5 liters
Maximum speed:	210 kph

A look at the technology shows not much had happened, even after fifteen years. Okay, there was a new crankcase with increased staybolt distance, angular cylinders with nikasil-coated mating surfaces, cylinder heads with larger valves (inlet 47 mm, outlet 40 mm), and aluminum rocker lever blocks, huge 40 mm Dell'Orto PHM carburetors with accelerator pumps, an oil pan with spacer ring, and an exhaust system with presilencer. But basically it is still the same engine. A bore of 88 mm and a stroke of 78 mm result in a displacement of exactly 949 cubic centimeters. Compression ratio is 9.8:1. The gain in performance is impressive, however; the big V-twin delivers 81 hp at 7,400 rpm to the twin-plate dry clutch. The transmission ratios in the gearbox and final drive are exactly those of the old S3.

The more modern engine revs significantly higher, but the 1000 S is not significantly faster than its 750 precursor. The top speed of 203 kph recorded by *Motorrad* magazine's writer was significantly slower than the 210 kph claimed by the manufacturer. And, like the S3, the 1000 S is also weak in the lower rpm range. The reasons were similar: much tighter noise and emission regulations at the beginning of the 1990s forced the Guzzi technicians to use an extremely weak carburetor jetting for the lower and mid-rpm range. Because of this, at low rpm the mixture forms inadequately in the huge carburetors, resulting in annoying carburetor splashing until 4,000 rpm is reached. The only solution is the illegal installation of larger idler jets.

The chassis of the 1000 S was better received. It was not adapted from the Le Mans entirely unchanged. The only difference, however, was the absence of the Le Mans' upswept rear frame tubes. Of course spoked wheels were no longer standard, as they still were on the late 750 variants. As an alternative to the installed 18-inch five-spoke cast wheels, the German importer A&G offered a version with classic spoked wheels of the same size.

The Bitubo 40-mm fork, with adjustable spring tension and rebound damping, and the two Koni shock absorbers with three adjustable spring tension settings and four adjustable rebound damping settings, were also used on the Le Mans. The fork reacts sensitively but can also plunge a little deep during braking. For if one presses hard on the pedal – the 1000 S of course still has the integral braking system – it slams so far forward that the steering damper makes a dent in the front Nirosta steel fender. With the least spring tension and hardest rebound damping setting, the rear end is extremely well coordinated.

The chassis of this Guzzi also has the almost classic characteristics of the big Mandello bomber. Directional stability is such that one tends to get the impression that the handlebars are welded to the frame. Nevertheless, the big 240-kilo 1000 S possesses amazing handling, far better than one would expect from such a big bike – a consequence of its low center of gravity.

As before, the big Guzzis set records in one point: fuel consumption. The machine tested by the editors of *Motorrad* magazine delivered a rate of four liters per 100 kilometers (70.6 mpg). Even at full throttle on the autobahn, the 1000 hardly burned more than seven liters per 100 kilometers (40.35 mpg). Incidentally, since 1990, all of the big Guzzis have been able to use 98 octane unleaded Super Plus. The only requirement is the use of harder valve seats. The possibility of being able to use unleaded fuel was a condition for Guzzi's first step towards more environmentally-friendly motorcycles – the catalytic converter. Since the IMFA 1990 the 1000 S – like many other models with the "big" engine – has come with an unregulated three-way catalytic converter. It is located inside the large presilencer under the gearbox. The 1000 S pays, however, with the loss of ten horsepower. For it was decidedly too expensive for the Moto Guzzi management to develop many different more powerful catalytic converter engines for its diverse models – California III, 1000 SP III, Mille GT, 1000 S. Consequently, since January 1991, all of these machines have been available only with the 71-hp power plant of the SP III. This small performance loss did not, however, affect the enjoyment of riding the classic 1000s. In fact the somewhat less powerful engine with the 36-mm carburetors, is considered clearly more harmonious.

And so, even in the future, the 1000 S remained what Peter Limmert had so elegantly attested – even without knowing it – fifteen years earlier: a machine that combined a hint of the past with the signs of the new age.

850 T 1974 – 75

"In all riding situations the Guzzi runs like clockwork; this chassis responds to riding over the notorious grooves on the autobahn, even at high speed – or even in sharp autobahn curves – with nothing at all!" Colleague Franz-Josef Schermer was visibly impressed by his test machine. It was 1975 and Schermer had climbed onto a Moto Guzzi 850 T. And fifteen years ago something that scarcely receives mention today – faultless high-speed behavior on the autobahn – unleashed a wave of enthusiasm from the motorcycle tester. In fact many, many machines from that era left something to be desired in this respect. Something else about the new Italian also impressed Schermer: "On twisting mountain roads the 850 T demonstrated handling such as we have only become used to in smaller machines; the heaving from one curve to another is gone in the new Guzzi! Riding through passes on this 850 T is a special experience."

One must grant Lino Tonti one thing: his redesign of the V7 chassis when the keel of the V7 Sport was laid is one of the best designs in the history of motorcycles. We remember that Tonti transplanted

The 850 T was Moto Guzzi's first touring bike based on the Tonti chassis. With just one disc brake, the relatively fast machine was relatively weakly equipped.

the bulky alternator to the front crankshaft stump, used a new, somewhat lower distributor and jammed the massive V-twin engine so tightly beneath the two upper frame tubes that the two bottom tubes had to be taken off to remove it.

The machine no longer had anything in common with the "old" V7 heavyweights – it was an Italian sport machine par excellence. Handling was no longer comparable to that of the touring model. The sport models were easy to control and agile in corners. And yet – these Guzzis also exuded the flair of an indestructible endurance runner that felt at home over long distances.

What could be more logical than to give the Guzzi touring models this great chassis too? In fact the chassis of the 850 T, about which colleague Franz-Josef Schermer raved at the outset, differed only in details from that of the V7 Sport. Let's have a closer look at the 850 T.

850 T	
Production Period:	1974-1975
Engine:	V-twin OHV/2 V
Displacement:	844.05 cc
Bore x Stroke:	83 x 78 mm
Compression:	9.5:1
Power output:	57 hp at 6,500 rpm
Mixture preparation:	Dell'Orto VHB 30, points
Clutch:	double plate
Gearbox:	5 speeds
Frame:	steel tube, removable cradle braces
Wheelbase:	1470 mm
Front suspension:	telescopic fork
Rear suspension:	double swing arm, 2 shock absorbers
Front tire:	3.50H18
Rear tire:	4.10H18
Front brake:	disc, 300 mm
Rear brake:	disc, 220 mm
Empty weight:	235 kg
Tank capacity:	25 liters
Maximum speed:	184 kph

As installed in the 850 T, the Guzzi twin-cylinder has a bore of 83 mm and a stroke of 78 mm, resulting in a displacement of 844.05 cubic centimeters. Basically it is the same engine that powered the predecessor model, the 850 GT. The cylinder liners are hard-chromed as before, and the pistons are divided into the same size classes (A, B and C) as the Special. The two pistons have three rings – an oil scraper ring and two compression rings – instead of the four previously used by the V7, the Special and the Sport. Also, the piston crown is almost flat, lacking the high dome of the earlier 750 models. At 9.5:1, compression is higher than that of the 850 GT. The older model's camshaft was retained. Port timings with 1.5 millimeters checking clearance: inlet opens 20 degrees before top dead center, closes 52 degrees after bottom dead center, outlet opens 52 degrees before bottom dead center, and closes at 20 degrees after top dead center – these are called symmetrical port timings. Valve play is set at a standard 22 hundredths on all four valves. But that is how it was from the start of the series. The diameter of the two Dell'Orto carburetors with square slide, however, grew by one unit to 30 millimeters. At 57 DIN horsepower at 6,500 rpm, output was only two horsepower greater than that of the earlier 850 model. Maximum torque of just over 60 Nm (44.25 ft-lb) was achieved at 5,500 rpm.

Most 850 Ts had to get by with the oil strainer of the original V7. Only the very final models were equipped with the auto-type filter of the 750 S3 and the 850 T3 that followed in the oil sump.

The clutch and gearbox were also the same as those of the GT. The gear ratios were also identical – the primary drive, all five gears and the final gear ratio. The 850 T used an 8/37 gear ratio, but the two gears of the fifth gear were changed while retaining the same gear ratio. A 28/21 gear set was used instead of a 24/18. The shift lever was installed only on the left.

Now we come to the chassis: Tonti took the frame and suspension elements from the Sport models almost unchanged. But while the 750 S sport version, which was built alongside the 850 T, had two disc brakes on the front wheel, the T, like the 850 GT, had to get by with a Brembo single disc. Both models had a double-cam drum brake in the rear.

The slim tank of the sport models was replaced by a massive 25-liter unit. The handlebars are relatively wide and upswept. A long, flat seat provides sufficient space for two people, and a chrome bar forms the end of the seat. The side covers are made of stainless steel, while the two Lafranconi mufflers with the characteristic middle seam point straight backwards. Behind the side covers are two lockable tool boxes. The motorcycle has both center and side stands.

The electrical system had to undergo extensive modifications compared to the 850 GT. That the alternator turns on the crankshaft stump and "only" produces 180 Watts is clear, but the battery still contains 32 Ampere hours. The switches on the handlebars have been significantly improved, and four indicator lights – for neutral, oil pressure, battery charge indicator, and high beam – keep the rider informed. The T also has front and rear turn signals. The 850 T could be had in one of three colors: red, green, or brown. The latter version was never available in Germany.

The machine completed its Italian type testing on 3 November, 1973. It was assigned chassis numbers beginning with the abbreviation VC. Within a year and a half – before production startup of the 850 T3 – 2,682 machines left the production line in Mandello. This was an astonishing figure given the motorcycle's brief production life. It should also be born in mind that the Italian authorities continued to place their trust in the proven V7, consequently there was no "production enhancing" police version of the T.

The lines written by *Motorrad* tester Schermer, which appear at the beginning of this chapter, reflect the enthusiasm with which the handling of this first offspring of a new generation of Guzzi touring bikes was greeted. But the 850 power plant also earned good marks. "Lively, functions well thermically and mechanically, oil consumption within limits at 0.9 liters per 1000 kilometers." The *Motorrad* tester was not the only one baffled by the absence of an air filter – the two carburetors drew their fresh air unfiltered and undamped from a common box in the frame triangle, just like the 750 S3.

And while it seemed there was only bright sunshine when it came to the chassis, the brake system came in for considerable criticism. Once again, a quote from Franz-Josef Schermer: "Each morning surface rust had formed on the grey cast iron brake disc, which must have acted like sandpaper on the brake pads; at first the effectiveness of the very vicious and tricky rear wheel brake only dropped in the wet, but then continuously to the zero point." The brakes were the Achilles heel of the 850 T. They were hardly able to hold back the motorcycle, which weighed 235 kilos and was capable of more than 180 kph. Guzzi soon offered a kit that enabled owners to convert to the double disc system of the 750 S.

Mobylette of Brackweise imported the touring Guzzi into Germany. It cost 8,090 Deutschmark. Apart from the second brake disc for the front wheel, the importer also offered a windscreen, a luggage carrier and matching bags as accessories.

850 T3 1975 – 80

Minor criticism of the braking system had so far run through the entire history of the V7. Tired of the grousing, in 1975 Moto Guzzi introduced its patented integral braking system, previously described in the chapter on the S3, in the 850 T3. With this system the foot pedal activated both the rear and the left front discs. A hydraulic valve provided optimal pressure distribution between the front and rear wheels. The system ensured that the rear wheel locked first in any driving situation, on any surface, and with any load. Operated by the hand lever, the right front disc served only as an "emergency brake." Incidentally, Guzzi patent 1977 won an ADAC prize for two-wheeled safety. The T3 – or *Ti tre* – got its name from this three-disc braking system. There was no T2. The first motorcycles began leaving the production Line in March 1975.

Apart from the brake system the T3 differed little from the preceding model. Apart from minor details – the side and valve covers, for example – it retained the same lines, with the bulky 25-liter tank, the long, slim exhaust system, and long, comfortable seat. T3 chassis numbers began with the abbreviation VD, the 850 T numbers with VC. Engine performance differed only slightly: the vehicle's papers now claimed 59 hp. The rpm level rose a little, with the upper limit now 6,900 rpm. The final gear ratio was a little shorter (7/33). Nevertheless, maximum speed rose to 187 kph. The T3 obviously had the oil system introduced in the final T models, with the automobile-type oil filter in the oil sump. As well, the Guzzi engineers finally gave the tourer a paper air filter. The chromed cylinder mating surfaces were surely grateful for this.

Apart from the brake system, there is little new to be found in the 850 T3's chassis. The handlebars are a little higher, the headlight housing is painted black instead of being chromed – that is basically it. The machine was delivered in black, green, and again red.

The *Ti tre* was to turn out to be a real stroke of luck for Moto Guzzi. It is difficult to say exactly how many examples were built, for the T3 California and the 850 T4 had the same model code in front of the chassis number. But it was far in excess of 10,000 motorcycles in any case. More than 1,200 T3s – including Californias – were registered in Germany in July 1990. And this number only includes those with a general operating permit (ABE). It does not take into account all the motorcycles imported from Italy or elsewhere in recent years – ex police motorcycles, for example – and registered individually without ABE.

Franz-Josef Schermer was also fascinated by the 850 T3. The following is from his test report in *Motorrad*: "One hell of an engine with two cylinders, arranged in a V at an angle of 90 degrees and mounted transversely, sitting powerful in the frame. It sniffs its air deeply and unmistakably from the small air filter and through the two Dell'Orto carburetors. Sniffs – that is perhaps exactly the right expression for the unusual engine sound. At idle, the irregular

850 T3

Production Period:	1975-1980
Engine:	V-twin OHV/2 V
Displacement:	844.05 cc
Bore x Stroke:	83 x 78 mm
Compression:	9.5:1
Power output:	59 hp at 6,900 rpm
Mixture preparation:	Dell'Orto VHB 30, points
Clutch:	double plate
Gearbox:	5 speeds
Frame:	steel tube, removable cradle braces
Wheelbase:	1470 mm
Front suspension:	telescopic fork
Rear suspension:	double swing arm, 2 shock absorbers
Front tire:	3.50H18
Rear tire:	4.10H18
Front brake:	dual disc, 300 mm
Rear brake:	disc, 242 mm
Empty weight:	242 kg
Tank capacity:	24 liters
Maximum speed:	187 kph

ignition timing creates an unsettled sniffing sound, accompanied by soft tacking of the valves, which are controlled by an overhead cam and pushrods."

Exactly two years after it appeared on the market – after more than 5,000 had been built – Tonti and company approved a proper facelift. This was so thorough that the machine had to undergo new type testing by the Italian authorities. Since then it has officially been called the 850 T3-SP and there is a reason for this. The small 850 inherited numerous parts from the V1000 SP, which was built at the same time. First to catch the eye were the cast light metal wheels, which were similar in design to those of the 850 Le Mans and the previously named SP. Also adopted from it were the more generously upholstered seat, which rose towards the rear, and the then stylish rectangular tail light. Also worthy of mention are the restyled exhaust system, which was clearly upswept, and the brake pedal taken from the Le Mans. Amazingly, these changes resulted in a drop in weight, from 242 to 238 kilos. A few grams must have been added by the distasteful black plastic cover that replaced the polished aluminum cover and shielded the alternator against moisture and stones.

But as straightforward as it appears here, one cannot draw a line between the different T3 versions, for the Italians simply installed the parts that were on hand. It is possible, therefore, to discover a T3-SP which, despite its approval papers, still has the "old" straight exhaust pipes. One shouldn't look at everything so dogmatically, but a clear stop can be made at 1980. For that was when the career of the *Ti tre* officially came to an end. The next model was logically called the 850 T4. But the Italians didn't want to make it that simple for the harried author: the T3 continued to be built in small numbers alongside the T4 for another one or two years. And why not? Perhaps there weren't enough fairings on hand, or ...?

850 T4 — 1980 – 83

The 850 T4, the final stage in the development life of the "round engine tourer," made its debut in April 1980. It differed from the S3 even less than the latter had from its predecessors. This is documented by the again unchanged model code VD in the chassis number. The striking difference is the large handlebar fairing taken from the V1000 SP. Instead of the beautiful spoked wheels, light metal cast wheels – like those on T3 models delivered after 1979 – were used. The somewhat more generously upholstered seat also came from the V1000 SP.

850 T4	
Production Period:	1980-1983
Engine:	V-twin OHV/2 V
Displacement:	844.05 cc
Bore x Stroke:	83 x 78 mm
Compression:	9.5:1
Power output:	59 hp at 6,900 rpm
Mixture preparation:	Dell'Orto VHB 30, points
Clutch:	double plate
Gearbox:	5 speeds
Frame:	steel tube, removable cradle braces
Wheelbase:	1480 mm
Front suspension:	telescopic fork
Rear suspension:	double swing arm, 2 shock absorbers
Front tire:	3.50H18
Rear tire:	4.25/85H18
Front brake:	dual disc, 300 mm
Rear brake:	disc, 242 mm
Empty weight:	254 kg
Tank capacity:	24 liters
Maximum speed:	173 kph

The exhaust system, however, was entirely new. It was not as sharply upswept as that of the final T3s and was also completely round and thus lacked the characteristic center seam of earlier T models. This system provided improved torque in the middle rpm range.

While engine performance did not change compared to the T3 – 59 hp at 6,900 rpm – there was an innovation, and an important one, inside the cylinders. The cylinder mating surfaces were no longer hard chromed, and beginning in the spring of 1980 they were nigusil-coated. The coating is similar to the German nikasil method, in which nickel and silicon are applied to the mating surfaces electrolytically. This makes the liner surfaces extremely durable. With these pots there is no need for a breaking-in period – at least for the cylinders and pistons. The coating was applied by Moto Guzzi itself and not by cylinder manufacturer Gilardoni. The three-ring pistons were again available in three different classes, A, B and C. Class A pistons measured between 82.968 and 82.974 mm, Class B pistons between 82.974 and 82.989 mm, and Class C pistons between 82.980 and 82.986 mm.

The huge handlebar fairing – structurally identical to the upper part of the SP fairing – gave the machine its unmistakable look. But the plastic fairing was not to everyone's taste. PS tester Paul Simsa initially favored removing it: "Not all riders like the front fairing, called a shield, and some will decide to remove it as quickly as possible. I would leave it. The shield is perfectly formed. It shields the rider's upper body while allowing him to easily see over the windscreen. A rider in jeans caught in the rain can get home with relatively dry pants at 60 kph. The projecting cylinders help, but it is mainly the shield, whose shape and outline are perfectly developed for practical use."

While the look of the big fairing takes some getting used to, its effectiveness is undisputable. Having its own wind tunnel certainly paid off for Moto Guzzi. "We could only work in the wind tunnel at night however. The 300 hp electric motor, which drove the propeller since the development of the SP models, required so much power that all of the circuit breakers would trip if it was used during the day – when production was at its peak. By the way, it's still that way today," related Todero. During normal use the only negative was the motorcycle's sensitivity to wind at speeds in excess of 130 kph. The fairing reacted very nervously to sudden crosswind gusts. Paul Simsa: "Autobahn speed limit plus ten percent – that's how to tour comfortably on the T4. There is little difference riding two up, and even heavy bags don't make this motorcycle unstable."

Guzzis are often criticized for poor workmanship. Sloppily installed electrics, loose switches, peeling paint, dim warning lights, stone age instruments – these are the most common points of criticism. The mentality and the demands of riders were changing – one could sense that quite clearly in such comments. Fifteen years ago there simply were no "perfect" motorcycles; occasional side-of-the-road work and much reworking in detail were simply part of being a motorcyclist. But the steadily improving quality of the machines – especially those from the Far East – caused the demands riders made of their machines to grow. Also, by the beginning of the 1980s the motorcycle was much more than a simple means of transportation. More and more, it had developed into a hobby device. Minor faults were no longer acceptable. They had to work – *basta*! The Italians – including in Mandello – were generally slow in keeping up with this trend. Either they didn't take particularly seriously the importance that quality of workmanship had on the buying habits of motorcycle riders, or they simply couldn't jump over their own proverbial *Dolce-far-niente* shadows – the casual Italian way of looking at things. To this day, Guzzi still lags behind the rest of the market in this area of development, even though the company has made numerous strides in this direction.

While testing the 850 T4, Paul Simsa did note several positives: "The slider for the turn signal switch is a stupid thing. There is no blinker indicator to show that the signal light is flashing when undesired. But at last, indicator lights that can be seen: miracles take a little longer at Guzzi, but the T4 proves that they definitely happen."

The 850 T4 remained in the program until 1983. The new 850 engine with the angular cylinders had been around since 1981, but the rectangular era in the touring models did not begin until 1983.

850 T5 1983 – 88

When it appeared in 1983, the 850 T5 marked a definite step in development of the T models. This was apparent from the external shape of the cylinders. They were no longer nice and round, but instead were angular like those of the contemporary California II and Le Mans II. The engine also came from them. The only differences from the Le Mans were the slightly smaller valves and the 30 mm instead of 36 mm carburetors. With 67 horsepower at 6,900 rpm, the rectangular engine clearly surpassed the performance of the "round ones."

The crackle and pop styling of the 1980s: the optics of the T5 did not please the Guzzi fans at all; nevertheless, it was a good motorcycle that enjoyed some popularity among sidecar users.

The T5 also meant a departure from the "form follows function styling" that the design department had cherished and cultivated. The de Tomaso design bureau in Modena was responsible for designing the shape of the T5. Stylish 16-inch wheels and plenty of bright plastic documented the approximation of Japanese styling. The whole story is more amazing as we know that Alejandro de Tomaso was not exactly a friend of Japanese motorcycle design. Why he then insisted – in the face of opposition from the traditionalists in Mandello – that Turin designer Giulio Moselli and his staff in Modena come up with a new shape that clearly bore Far Eastern accents, remains a mystery. Today the whole thing looks like a sort of test of strength between Modena and Mandello, from which de Tomaso initially emerged as winner.

It was a pyrrhic victory, however – for time was to show that the tastes of the Guzzi clientele were still a little different than the rest of the motorcycle world. In the long run, the traditionalists were right. Models like the 1000 S and Mille GT prove it.

Perhaps – no, quite certainly even, the new styling was one of the reasons why the T5 was a flop. While more than a thousand T3 models remain on the roads in Germany today, just 460 T5s had sold by 1988. An upgrading of the design in 1985 – 18-inch rear wheel

Sixteen-inch front wheels were modern in the 1980s. While they improved the T5's handling, the small wheels contributed nothing to steering precision.

and new windscreen – helped but little. The "Five" was and remains a shelf-sitter. Most Guzzi riders who decided on a T5 are, however, quite happy with their equipment.

Let us look at the machine in detail. A detailed description of the new angular engine will be found later, in the chapter on the Le Mans III, but here are some basic details: the T5 engine was something of a mix of Le Mans and California II components. The underbody, cylinders, and pistons come from the sport model, the heads and mixture preparation from the "Cali." The two Dell'Ortos still measure 30 millimeters in diameter, but have a rotary slide and therefore a new abbreviation – VHBT. The gearbox is identical to that of the familiar T models. All of the gear ratios are the same as those of the T4.

The whole thing is mounted in the by now familiar twin-tube frame with the two removable cradle tubes. There is something new in the rear, however. The swing arms – from the Le Mans III – have clearly become longer and larger, increasing the wheelbase to 1505 millimeters. One doesn't need to tell sailors and motorcycle riders that "length runs." The wheelbase was lengthened mainly to improve directional stability. For reasons of style – and because there were supposedly better tires for the smaller rims – the new tourer had to get by with 16-inch wheels. The smaller tires did, however, have poorer directional stability characteristics. Hence the longer wheelbase. About two and a half centimeters made the difference.

And there began the vicious circle that was to bring the T5 such sharp criticism. A lower center of gravity and fatter tires – 110/90 in front and 130/90 in the rear – required a steeper angle of lean at the same cornering speed. But because of the reduced ground clearance – caused by the smaller wheels – this was not possible. The foot pegs touched the asphalt rather quickly.

Thanks to the 16-inch wheels there was also light and shade in the motorcycle's handling. Peter Limmert wrote in *Motorrad*: "The steady, convincing tracking characteristics remain, inherited from the T3 and T4. A decisive point has been added: the 850 T5 is easier to get off a straight line while staying under control. The T5 is, thus, much more maneuverable than its predecessors; it reacts to the slightest steering correction, weight shifts too, more willingly, one could almost say weightlessly. In return, the T5, like other 16-inch machines, must always be held on course, for the short castor angle and the small wheels create a certain sensibility in the front wheel control, although it never degenerates into unrest."

850 T5

Production Period:	1983-1988
Engine:	V-twin OHV/2 V
Displacement:	844.05 cc
Bore x Stroke:	83 x 78 mm
Compression:	9.5:1
Power output:	67 hp at 6,900 rpm
Mixture preparation:	Dell'Orto VHBT30, points
Clutch:	double plate
Gearbox:	5 speeds
Frame:	steel tube, removable cradle braces
Wheelbase:	1505 mm
Front suspension:	telescopic fork
Rear suspension:	double swing arm, 2 shock absorbers
Front tire:	100/90H16
Rear tire:	130/90H16
Front brake:	dual disc, 270 mm
Rear brake:	disc, 270 mm
Empty weight:	243 kg
Tank capacity:	22.5 liters
Maximum speed:	198 kph

Then in 1985 the Guzzi people took this criticism to heart and undertook a number of update measures; the most important was the switch to a larger 18-inch rear wheel and a smaller fairing windscreen. Neither of these measures did anything to improve the machine's handling, however. Reiner H. Nitschke wrote in *Tourenfahrer* magazine: "The T5 doesn't find its own line in corners and constantly wants to be guided. As well, it runs in long striations and allows itself to be put off stride by them."

In Mandello they still maintain that the press had been hard on the T5. True, Reiner H. Nitschke's judgment sounded harsh: "But those in Mandello should not continue falling into the sleep of the just and believing that they can remain up-to-date by giving yesterday's technology a few optical retouches." It was clear, however, that in the opinion of the clientele the 850 T5 couldn't even compete with the older model Guzzis – neither in handling nor appearance. Motorcycles are often bought with the heart – form is often more important than technology.

Brochure for the 850 T5: the machine depicted here was one of the early versions without the small fairing of the later variants.

V1000 I Convert 1975 – 84

One month after the 850 T3 entered service – in April 1975 – there was another premiere in Mandello. The first 1000-cc version of the big V-twin arrived as the V1000 I Convert. The new machine was based on the 850 version and had many equipment details of the 850 T3 California, differing from that machine only in having different paint, a flatter seat, a taillight incorporated into an oddly-shaped rear fairing, a tiny spoiler on the front roll bars, the instrument console, and the main brake cylinder on the outer right handlebar.

But, as the lengthy model name V1000 I Convert suggests, this first 1000 was a different animal. Let us first turn to the engine. The stroke was already rather long at 78 millimeters; a further lengthening was out of the question. An increase in bore was thus needed to achieve a full liter's displacement. Each cylinder now measured 88 millimeters in diameter. This resulted in a total displacement of exactly 948.8 cubic centimeters, just short of a full liter.

For the first time in a long while, Guzzi did not rely on hard, chrome-plated cylinders. The liners of the V1000 I Convert were made of cast iron with no coating. The cylinders were divided into two size classes: Class A measured between 88.000 and 88.009 mm, Class B between 88.009 and 88.018 mm. The diameter of the Class A pistons ranged from 87.920 to 87.929 mm, that of the Class B pistons from 87.929

The V1000 I Convert remained an experiment: the automatic transmission worked, nevertheless interest by motorcycle riders seemed to be minimal.

to 87.938 mm. Cast cylinders are known to wear if the running surfaces are damaged or worn out. For this reason, there are larger pistons, with 0.4 and 0.6 millimeters excess in diameter.

Apart from a new cylinder head seal and larger bores for the cylinders in the crankcase, the engine is unchanged. The camshaft port timings are the same as those of the 850 and the 30-mm carburetors are also from the smaller variants. Only the jetting has been changed to match the greater displacement. The increase in power output is thus minimal. As compression is slightly less than that of the 850 variants, at 9.2:1, the larger-displacement version delivers just two more horsepower to the crankshaft. The engine must turn 400 rpm slower to produce this power, however, and is redlined at 6,500 rpm.

V1000 I Convert

Production Period:	1976-1978
Number made:	1,929
Engine:	V-twin OHV/2 V
Displacement:	948.8 cc
Bore x Stroke:	88 x 78 mm
Compression:	9.2:1
Power output:	70 hp at 7,300 rpm
Mixture preparation:	Dell'Orto VHB, points
Transmission:	two-speed automatic, shaft
Frame:	steel tube, removable cradle braces
Wheelbase:	1470 mm
Front suspension:	telescopic fork
Rear suspension:	double swing arm, 2 shock absorbers
Front tire:	3.50H18
Rear tire:	4.00H18
Front brake:	dual disc, 300 mm
Rear brake:	disc, 242 mm
Empty weight:	225 kg
Tank capacity:	22.5 liters
Maximum speed:	206 kph

But all of this does not explain the long model name V1000 I Convert. The reason is not to be found in the engine but is hidden inside the crankcase: an automatic transmission. "One day the American police – one of the main customers for our police models – suggested that we equip these machines with automatic transmissions," recalled Umberto Todero. "During escort duties at slow speeds the rider very often had to use the clutch and it required more than the little finger to use ours." Company head Alejandro de Tomaso gladly accepted the cops' suggestion and pushed for the design of an automatic transmission – without giving much thought to the commercial possibilities of such a motorcycle. De Tomaso – an old car man, designer of the Panterra sports car – simply thought: "What's good for an automobile can't be bad for a motorcycle." And so a great deal of money was spent on a development that was almost universally rejected by "civilian" motorcyclists.

Let us nevertheless take a brief look at this development – even though it had no significance in subsequent development of the V series of motorcycles. I Convert, for *Idro Convert*, means something like "fluid converter". This component is located inside the clutch housing in the space normally reserved for the flywheel and the two-plate dry clutch. Delivered by Fichtel & Sachs, the device did not actually turn one fluid into another. Instead, on the Convert, it functioned as a sort of fluid coupling. That meant that there was no fixed connection between crankshaft and gearbox. The converter worked roughly like a slipping normal clutch. The only difference is that the latter is guaranteed to burn after a few tries, while the fluid converter manages it without any wear.

The whole thing functions something like this: the converter housing – it looks like two halves of plates laid on top of each other – is filled with hydraulic fluid and rigidly connected to the rear end of the crankshaft. The inside of these two bowls is fitted with turbine blades in a spiral arrangement. Inside there is also a turbine blade, which in turn is attached to the gearbox input shaft, thus more or less directly coupled with the rear wheel. When the crankshaft turns – with, of course, the entire converter assembly – the many turbine blades try to fling the hydraulic fluid around with them. And this, in turn, would most like to turn the turbine blade attached to the transmission with it. Thus a more or less "direct" connection is created between the crankshaft and transmission. As the crankshaft rotates faster, the transmission tries to keep pace, but because of the very "loose" connection created by oil, the transfer medium, the transmission never quite reaches the rotation speed of the crankshaft. At best it achieves 90% of the crankshaft rotation speed. The remaining energy is lost in the form of heat. The designers have therefore, provided the converter with a small oil circulation system with a small pump – powered by the camshaft, by the way – and an oil cooler.

In the transmission housing there is a normal dry clutch with seven friction and five steel plates, as seen on many Japanese motorcycles. Right behind it is a mini-gearbox with just two gears. This is constructed the same way as the four- and five-speed units we know from the other models. The first gear has an 18/24 gear set, the second a 22/22 gear set. These two gears are selected quite normally by means of a shift lever.

In practice, the whole story looks like this: when the engine starts, the rider pulls the clutch lever, engages the higher gear with the foot shifter, and then releases the clutch. If he now twists the throttle and releases the brakes, the machine slowly but surely begins to move – in a way that is familiar to almost every rider of an automatic moped or small Honda Dax. The first gear is hardly needed in normal operation; only now and then, when it is very steep or when a sidecar is attached, does one need to shift down.

Cutaway of the Convert's automatic transmission: at best the converter was capable of transferring ninety percent of the crankshaft's revolutions to the rear wheel.

Here is an excerpt from a Convert advertising brochure: "This wonderful motorcycle sets entirely new standards in motorcycle design. The machine offers a unique riding experience without a clutch – get on, give it the gas and hold on." Now that is probably exactly what doesn't interest the motorcycle rider – climbing on and just giving it the gas. With some astonishment, de Tomaso was forced to realize that the motorcycle buyer differs quite considerably from the automobile consumer. A motorcycle is simply not the most comfortable means of transportation. All of us have learned that lesson. And adding an automatic transmission doesn't make it any more comfortable. To make a long story short – the Convert was a flop! While the type was built until 1984 – for all of nine years – in Germany, at least, it remained a shelf-sitter.

V1000 G5 1978 – 85

A year and a half after the V1000 I Convert entered service, the Guzzi management was forced to concede that its 1000-cc flagship was unsaleable. The result was as simple as it was logical – the automatic transmission was replaced by a normal five-speed gearbox. The rest was unchanged, and the V1000 G5 was finished! The engine was absolutely identical to that of the Convert, while the gearbox was taken, unchanged, from the 850 T3.

V1000 G5	
Production Period:	1981-1984
Engine:	V-twin OHV/2 V
Displacement:	948.8 cc
Bore x Stroke:	88 x 78 mm
Compression:	9.8:1
Power output:	76 hp at 7,700 rpm
Mixture preparation:	Dell'Orto VHB, points
Clutch:	double plate
Gearbox:	5 speeds
Frame:	steel tube, removable cradle braces
Wheelbase:	1505 mm
Front suspension:	telescopic fork
Rear suspension:	double swing arm, 2 shock absorbers
Front tire:	100/90-18
Rear tire:	4.00H18
Front brake:	dual disc, 300 mm
Rear brake:	disc, 242 mm
Empty weight:	240 kg
Tank capacity:	25 liters
Maximum speed:	205 kph

Brochure for the V1000 G5: the 1000 with conventional gearbox sold much better than the nearly identical Convert.

There were also few modifications to the chassis: the 110 or 4.10 front tire was replaced by a 100 or 3.50 – in 18-inch format, of course.

The equipment was similar to that of the Convert in detail. But wait – the G5 also had a tiny tachometer, an instrument that the Convert rider had to and could do without. The G5 passed its type testing by the Italian ministry of transport in December. The model code VG in front of the chassis number was identical to that of the V1000 I Convert.

Despite having the same power – 61 hp at 6,500 rpm – the performance of the G5 actually had to be better than that of the Convert. For the latter's torque converter "consumed" about ten percent of engine output, which was converted into heat. Amazingly, the official maximum speed in the G5's approval documents was slightly less than that of the automatic version. In fact, the manual transmission version had a top speed of about 190 kph, while the Convert had to strike its sails at about 175 kph.

In 1990, 434 V1000 G5s and V1000 I Converts were registered in Germany. Because of the shared model code, it is impossible to separate the numbers into automatic and manual models. If one compares this number with the T3 versions still registered (1,261 machines), one could justifiably claim that the V1000 G5 was not exactly a big seller. Nevertheless, it was only built for a relatively short time. The 1000 stayed in production up to and including 1983. This figure includes many police motorcycles, however.

Despite less than overwhelming sales figures, the V1000 G5 remained in production for a long time, remaining in the company's range until 1983.

1000 SP 1978 – 84

It is 1976, BMW unveils the R100 RS. It is the first production motorcycle with a full fairing. The machine causes a stir and quickly becomes a sales success. "I can recall that the RS caused us some excitement and a lot of plain talking," recalled Umberto Todero. "After all, it had been we who, soon after the war, had recognized the importance of aerodynamics to motorcycles and built a suitable wind tunnel. For this reason we had always been ahead in this area. We simply failed to transfer this knowledge from racing to production."

1000 SP	
Production Period:	1979-1980
Number produced:	11,045
Engine:	V-twin OHV/2 V
Displacement:	948 cc
Bore x Stroke:	88 x 78 mm
Compression:	9.2:1
Power output:	61 hp at 6,500 rpm
Mixture preparation:	Dell'Orto PHF 36, points
Clutch:	double plate
Gearbox:	5 speeds
Frame:	steel tube, removable cradle braces
Wheelbase:	1470 mm
Front suspension:	telescopic fork
Rear suspension:	double swing arm, 2 shock absorbers
Front tire:	100/90-18
Rear tire:	110/90-18
Front brake:	dual disc, 300 mm
Rear brake:	disc, 242 mm
Empty weight:	238 kg
Tank capacity:	22.5 liters
Maximum speed:	208 kph

After being so rudely shaken up, the workers at Guzzi set about dusting off the old wind tunnel. The impossibly loud Piaggio aircraft engine – "We couldn't expect anyone to put up with the noise!" – was replaced, first by the engine from a torpedo boat and finally by a power-consuming 300-hp electric motor, which still blows fuses in the factory.

"We tinkered around with a fairing for half a year – always at night, for the factory's power supply couldn't run the electric motor during the day. We finally decided on a two-part solution. The upper part would move with the handlebars, while the lower part would be attached to the frame. This arrangement simply provided much better protection for the rider's upper body, for a fixed upper part would have to be mounted significantly further forward so that the handlebars could turn freely." The lower part was also mounted close to the frame. Seen from the front, the cylinders were in the open. After all, an unimpeded flow of cooling air was important. Two small spoilers were mounted in front above the cylinders. "We had discovered that the small things reduced the lift of the front wheel at high speed quite considerably. And that resulted in better directional stability." The fairing was made of fiberglass and the headlight and both front turn signals were incorporated into the swiveling upper section. The rearview mirrors were located above left and right next to the windscreen.

The design of the basic machine was simple, which was why it came with a very nice and complete tool kit. From the beginning, it had been obvious that the new top model would have a 1000-cc engine. After all, the new machine was aimed directly at its BMW competitor from Munich, which also had a 1000-cc engine. And they had the powerful Convert and G5 engine on the shelf. The five-speed gearbox of the V1000 G 5 also remained untouched. The latter's chassis was also adopted almost unchanged.

Only the equipment of the new V1000 SP – the letters SP stood for *Spada,* or sword – differs considerably from that of the other two 1000s. The exhaust pipes are upswept behind the rider's foot pegs. This arrangement had no impact on engine performance; like the G5 and Convert, the new bike had 61 hp at 6,500 rpm. The rear fender with rectangular taillight is taken from the final T3 models. The seat and the chrome bar at the end are also strongly reminiscent of the parts installed on the 850. One feature that was new was the comprehensively-equipped instrument panel. In addition to a speedometer and tachometer, there is a voltmeter on the outer right and a clock on the outer left. Beneath the instruments there are a total of eight warning lights. The ignition sits in the center of the plastic instrument panel and the filler cap is hidden by a locking cover. The candy-color switch units are new.

Of course, the V1000 SP also has the patented integral brake system. Exactly like the 850 T 4, the front brake calipers are behind the fork legs, not in front. New is an additional pressure relief valve, which is supposed to reduce wear on the rear disc brake. It had simply been too large for earlier machines equipped with this system.

The fairing of the NT looked very similar to that of the Le Mans II, and, in fact, the lower part was also identical. The fairing received good marks during motorcycle tests.

Although the new machine was really not all that similar to the Convert, it had the same model code VG. On 23 December, 1977, the V1000 SP was given type approval by the Italian authorities. It was imported into Germany by the Deutschen Motobecane in Bielefeld. In 1978 it cost 9,850 DM and was thus a full 1,600 DM more expensive than the 850 T3.

The new fairing received good marks in early tests. Peter Limmert in *Motorrad*: "When crouched behind the big fairing, one encounters a similar phenomenon as on the BMW R100 RS. The rider glides along with no wind resistance and finds himself underestimating his speed." And further on: "With the SP fairing, there is no turbulence behind the cockpit, causing the visor to open and the rider's jacket to flutter." Limmert did find one point to criticize, however. "Taller riders with long legs have difficulties positioning their knees, which rub against the fairing." In *PS*, Knut Briel expressed the fear that with the fairing the machine would be extremely vulnerable to wind. "Practical experience refuted this fear, and indeed the advantage of being able to install the upper part of the fairing close to the steering head carried weight.

This means a favorable position of the fairing for weight distribution and good weather protection and almost total absence of wind noise at high speed, all good conditions for touring."

In the spring of 1980, the SP was given an extensive makeover. The V1000 SP-NT, as the reworked machine was officially called, received a new, quieter exhaust system, nikasil cylinders – like the contemporary T4 – and a new paint scheme. The seat was replaced by the one from the V1000 G5.

Production of the faired 1000 continued until 1984. Not until the spring of that year was it replaced by the V1000 SP II. In July 1990, 320 examples of the first SP – including the NT models – were still registered in Germany.

1000 SP II — 1984 – 87

If only one has enough building blocks, one can make many different things with them. In Mandello at the beginning of the 1980s, the Guzzi makers were more and more adopting this "Lego block philosophy." By then, the series of motorcycles with the big V-twin engine had already seen more than fifteen springs. Of course, this building block system reduced the design costs for a new machine quite considerably. The 1000 SP II described here can serve as a good example.

The engine came unchanged from the California II. It was only slightly modified compared to the final production version of the SP-NT – even if it didn't look that way. The cylinders of the second edition of the SP were angular, while those of its predecessor had still been round. Apart from the angular cylinders, there was just the significantly reinforced crankcase and a new rocker arm bearing block of aluminum. However the performance parts – pistons, valves, camshaft, carburetors – remained unchanged from those of the original SP. What was responsible for the power increase of six horsepower? Well, the angular cylinders had a much larger cooling surface. And a cool engine produces more power than a hot one. It's as simple as that. The 1000 twin delivered a whopping 67 hp to the massive crankshaft at 6,700 rpm.

The transmission was also identical to that of the earlier model. The 7/33 final gear ratio had, by then, proved itself as a sort of standard ratio.

There was also nothing new to admire about the chassis. All of its components had proved themselves in other machines made by the company. Until then, the chassis had served the 850 T5. Only the 16-inch rear wheel of the smaller tourer had to give way to an 18-inch rim. The tubes of the patented Guzzi fork, with the encapsulated damping cartridges, had grown in diameter to 37 millimeters when the T5 was introduced, suspension traveled to 140 millimeters. The swing arms also did good service in the Le

Mans III. The two Koni shock absorbers, with three-position adjustable spring preload and rebound damping also adjustable in three stages, give the rear wheel 70 millimeters of travel. The wheelbase of 1505 millimeters is identical to that of the 850 T5. Because of the 16-inch front wheel, the diameter of the two front discs shrunk to 270 millimeters. And for simplicity's sake, a similar 270-mm disc was installed in the rear.

1000 SP II

Production Period:	1981-1984
Engine:	V-twin OHV/2 V
Displacement:	948 cc
Bore x Stroke:	83 x 78 mm
Compression:	9.2:1
Power output:	67 hp at 6,700 rpm
Mixture preparation:	Dell'Orto PHF 36, points
Clutch:	double plate
Gearbox:	5 speeds
Frame:	steel tube, removable cradle braces
Wheelbase:	1505 mm
Front suspension:	telescopic fork
Rear suspension:	double swing arm, 2 shock absorbers
Front tire:	110/90-16
Rear tire:	120/90-18
Front brake:	dual disc, 300 mm
Rear brake:	disc, 242 mm
Empty weight:	240 kg
Tank capacity:	23 liters
Maximum speed:	205 kph

The Guzzi makers also took the tank-seat combination from the T5 replacement parts shelf. The fairing we already know from the first variant on the SP theme. Only in the area of the cylinders did they acquiesce to minor modifications. The angular cylinders simply needed more room. The extensive instrumentation of the first SP was also adopted unchanged. On 9 April 1984, the machine – model code VH – received approval from the Italian authorities and entered production.

Surprisingly, the revised SP did not get the same outstanding marks from the specialist press that the first SP had received. Criticism of the chassis was understandable, because of experience with the 850 T5. Why the exact same fairing, which was praised when the first SP appeared, should now come in for harsh criticism, remains a mystery. Horst Vieselmann wrote in *Motorrad*: "The wide upper part is again attached to the handlebars, which is surely not an ideal solution because of the large mass around the steering axis. The somewhat unfavorable shape of the windscreen, whose sides are swept far back and through which the view is blurry, has the uncomfortable quality of generating considerable turbulence behind the rider's back. As well, because of the suction effect, as speed increases the rider must brace himself against the handlebars." Still, a few issues later, Helmut Rebholz and Fred Siemer recognized that: "The pillion rider is unaware of this concern (that of the poor view through the windscreen) or the grief of other similar motorcycles, on which the fairing protects the rider but leaves the passenger sitting in the storm."

The touring machine remained in production until 1988, when it was replaced by the considerably facelifted third SP variants.

Mille GT 1987 – 93

Mille Grazie – a thousand thanks – cried the collective Guzzi community in the late summer of 1987. The cause for so much celebration was the new Mille GT, which began leaving the assembly line in Mandello del Lario in September of that year. The Mille GT, a dream in black, aluminum and chrome, was it the return to long-forgotten fancied traditions, the return to the simple, powerful and reliable touring motorcycle – everything that the old V7 and V7 Special kept alive in the memory of the Guzzi fans?

The Mille was, in fact, supposed to build on precisely these traditions. And it seemed indicative of the disorientation the Italian maker sometimes displayed that the inspiration for this machine came from Germany. Though not the largest, the Federal Republic was an export market for Moto Guzzi, and the word of the German importer carried weight in Mandello. The staff of the Deutschen Motobecane believed they knew their Guzzi customers. And they didn't want a 16-inch experiment, no plastic frills. They wanted a simple, all-round motorcycle with the flair of the old road burners of the Sixties.

Mille GT: this was the dream of the Guzzisti at the end of the Eighties. Based on the 1000 SP II, Guzzi built a classic tourer with no fairing.

Mille GT

Production Period:	1985-1987
Engine:	V-twin OHV/2 V
Displacement:	948.8 cc
Bore x Stroke:	88 x 78 mm
Compression:	10:1
Power output:	81 hp at 7,500 rpm
Mixture preparation:	Dell'Orto PHM 40, points
Clutch:	double plate
Gearbox:	5 speeds
Frame:	steel tube, removable cradle braces
Wheelbase:	1514 mm
Front suspension:	telescopic fork
Rear suspension:	double swing arm, 2 shock absorbers
Front tire:	120/80V16
Rear tire:	130/80V18
Front brake:	dual disc, 270 mm
Rear brake:	disc, 270 mm
Empty weight:	244 kg
Tank capacity:	24 liters
Maximum speed:	207 kph

OK, they thought in Mandello, let's give the Germans, especially Eberhard Just, manager of Motobecane, the motorcycle of their dreams. After all, they had in place a well-organized building block system. And they would find a suitable base machine from which they could make a traditional one-thousand without spending too much money. In fact, the only motorcycle that met their requirements was the 1000 SP II, for a stripped-down California was not exactly what the Germans wanted.

And so they took an SP II, removed the fairing, installed a classic 18-inch wheel up front, screwed the instruments and the headlight of the small V75 Florida on the upper fork bridge, dipped the tank and side covers in a pail of black paint, embellished the whole thing with a few fine gold stripes – and the Mille GT was complete. The machine didn't even have to undergo new type testing. On 23 September 1987, it was certified as "*una nuova versione*," or a new version, of the 1000 SP II and, of course, was assigned the model code VH. In Italy it was as simple as that.

In fact, the differences between the new motorcycle and the SP II were minimal. The engine remained the same, and the Mille GT produced 67 hp at 6,700 rpm. Only the exhaust system underwent a number of minor modifications. The gearbox and final drive were also identical to those of the SP.

The same applied to the chassis, wheelbase, steering angle, castor – all of these values were identical to those of the faired version. We already mentioned the larger front wheel. At the same time, the two front brake discs were restored to their original size of 300 mm. The switches on the handlebars – often the subjects of fierce criticism – were provided by the German supplier Magura.

Originally, just 250 examples of the Mille were supposed to be built. The first machines were therefore given serial numbers between 1 and 250 on the seat rump. It was truly a special series. Sales were good, however, which guaranteed that more would be built. The GT sold like hotcakes in Germany – proof that the people at Motobecane knew what their customers wanted – and surprisingly also in Italy.

The specialist press showered the Mille with praise, especially its powerful V-twin engine, even though it was the same unit found in the SP II. But perhaps the absence of the fairing simply made the big V-twin more visible. The 1000 engine received excellent marks, especially for placid touring. "The Moto Guzzi even handles slow riding in column with bravura. There is no need for tiresome clutch work, the Mille GT still pulls sedately even at revs as low as about 500. There is even a pleasant sound experience: the rider can experience every single firing stroke acoustically. With this engine even a traffic jam becomes a pleasure." These lines about the classic Guzzi were written by Roland Schenk in *Motorrad.*

By the way, the German importer had also thought of the "Guzzisti," to whom the GT was nowhere near classic enough. Perhaps a set of spoked wheels instead of Borrani rims? There was, although the set cost about 1,100 Deutschmarks. Lafranconi pipes, baggage carrier, electronic ignition, three-inch rim in the rear – all of these things could be had in Bielefeld. And, for 108 DM, one could even buy two governors that reduced the Mille's 67 horsepower by 17. In Germany a 50-hp engine resulted in insurance savings.

Soon the Mille GT was leaving the factory in a fire-red paint finish with decorative gold stripes. On this version, even the steel-tube frame was painted red. There hadn't been anything like it since the legendary V7 Sport. Of course, this version left the factory on spoked wheels with valanced aluminum rims. With time, a pair of sensible rearview mirrors also found their way onto the motorcycle, for the original black and rather chunky items of the first version really didn't go with the Italian's classic outfit. The new, slim, chrome mirrors were much more impressive.

The Mille GT looks good even fully loaded. The well-balanced suspension and powerful engine made it a fine travelling companion.

Exactly like the SP III, the S1000 S, and the California III, after the IFMA 90 in Cologne, there was a Mille GT with an unregulated catalytic converter. As development costs for four different versions of the catalytic converter would have been too expensive, the Guzzi engineers developed just one model of this exhaust-cleaned engine. The 71-hp unit from the SP III formed the basis of the engine, which was then installed in all four of the motorcycles named above. The Mille GT's performance profited from the emission control measure. The classic 1000 was now propelled by 71 horsepower instead of the previous 67. A decision in favor of the catalytic converter model was thus not difficult. Anyway, Guzzis had been capable of using lead-free gasoline since early 1990.

The following are the thoughts that went through the mind of "Larry Rider," Reiner H. Nitschke, during a ride on the Mille GT: "Click – that was first gear. Cylinders shaking, the machine lifts gently from its still stiff springs. The coarse sand crunches beneath the cold tires. You carefully steer left onto the asphalt, which cuts through the yellow wheat fields like a long black beam. Your thighs press against the wide tank, the chrome circles of the instruments reflect the rays of the morning sun. You gently open the throttle, listen to the sonorous sound of the twin cylinders as they hurtle along over the shining asphalt. Euphoria rises in you. As if in a trance, you enjoy the solitude of the country road and the beauty of the mountains, whose staggered silhouettes draw ever closer. Scenes you dreamed about eighteen years ago, when you lingered in prayer near the green V7. Now, on the seat of the Mille GT, they come true."

1000 SP III 1988 – 92

"Being on a Guzzi has always had something of the riding of a bull about it, which has undoubtedly accounted for a bit of fascination. Here anyone who is bored with serenely gliding along will find contact with the roots of motorized transport. Something shakes and lives beneath the rider, every beat of the crankshaft shows that the rider can mobilize a piece of technology with a turn of the wrist, tempered metal parts combine to form a work of art, an energy converter created by human hands which, within a century, has conquered the world." These lovely words were written by Reiner H. Nitschke after his touring test ride on the SP 1000 III. Still enthused by the baroque shapes of a V7 Special, a V7 Sport or an 850 GT, a true "Guzzisti" surely found exaggeration in such lyrical sentences inspired by the smooth, fully-wired touring Guzzi.

But the year is 1990, and alongside the purring Japanese four-cylinders the antique technology of the "big" Guzzis – even if the SP III did have modern styling – seems a relic from the long ago days of motorcycling. And then one must resort to rather fancy words after testing such a machine – or?

In 1988 the 1000 SP – model code VN – entered its third round. This time, however, its relation to its predecessor is not so easy to recognize. There are some new features to be found on the SP III. For one, there is the familiar, but more powerful, 1000 twin-cylinder. While its main components are unchanged, it is now fed gas by two 36-mm Dell'Orto carburetors. Together with a higher compression ration of 9.5:1 and the larger Le Mans III valves, they are responsible for the latest SP variant having improved power – 71 hp at 6,800 rpm. Also, a solid-state electronic unit provides the ignition spark.

For the transmission, Moto Guzzi again turned to the proven, although in recent years the individual components of the gear train have been slightly reworked, all for better shiftability.

The twin-tube frame looks suspiciously similar to that of the Le Mans IV, with the frame tail upswept at the rear end of the seat. On the "old" chassis the upper frame tubes were dead straight from front to rear. The tube diameter of the patented Guzzi fork has meanwhile grown to 40 mm. Fork travel remains unchanged, however, at 140 millimeters. Two Koni shocks again help keep the back end under control.

The external appearance of the third SP generation is completely new: the only element bearing a certain relation to the SP II is the fuel tank. The seat, side covers, and in particular the fairing have all been redesigned. This time the large fairing is a one-piece affair, with both the upper and lower portions attached to the frame. The lower portion encloses the cylinders, but the cooling openings in front ensure sufficient fresh air reaches them. The rearview mirrors are again mounted high, next to the windscreen.

Within the fairing is the also redesigned instrument panel. The instrumentation itself, however, is the same as that of both of the older SPs – speedometer, tachometer, voltmeter, clock. At last the switches are of comparable quality to those standard on Japanese bikes. The seat is clearly stepped, with the passenger sitting one step higher than the rider. The whole thing is painted in noble gray or metallic-white. Standard equipment includes two plastic bags, which are provided by Givi. At 265 kg, the SP III is certainly not a lightweight.

And yet – the third SP III possesses extraordinary handling. Michael Pfeiffer noticed this during a comparison of the SP I and SP III in *PS* Magazine: "The SP III is also very stable; but what is amazing is how fleet-footed it is in the corners. We hadn't expected that, for our old SP wasn't exactly a paragon of maneuverability." Pfeiffer attributed this ease of handling in part to the rigid fairing: "... the moment of inertia about the steering axle is vanishingly low."

1000 SP III

Production Period:	1988-1992
Engine:	V-twin OHV/2 V
Displacement:	948.8 cc
Bore x Stroke:	88 x 78 mm
Compression:	9.8:1
Power output:	81 hp at 7,400 rpm
Mixture preparation:	Dell'Orto PHM 40, points
Clutch:	double plate
Gearbox:	5 speeds
Frame:	steel tube, removable cradle braces
Wheelbase:	1514 mm
Front suspension:	telescopic fork
Rear suspension:	double swing arm, 2 shock absorbers
Front tire:	100/90V18
Rear tire:	120/90V18
Front brake:	dual disc, 270 mm
Rear brake:	disc, 270 mm
Empty weight:	248 kg
Tank capacity:	24 liters
Maximum speed:	209 kph

The restyled seat with its pronounced step received some harsh criticism, however. The passenger kept sliding into the rider's back, pushing his knees against the rear edge of the fairing. Also, the rear end of the seat was found to be very hard. Reiner H. Nitschke found another point to criticize: "And very few potential Guzzi fans have forearms like an Italian prize fighter, consequently the stiff throttle must be rated as enjoyment-diminishing." The extremely tight return springs in the two 36-mm carburetors, which ensure that the rotary slides close properly when throttle is reduced, are responsible for this evil.

Since IFMA 90, there have also been big Guzzi touring bikes with catalytic converters. The two mini-catalytic converters sit at the beginning of the two exhaust pipes. The redesigned presilencer ensures that the hearty shock waves produced by the one-liter V-twin do not damage the sensitive catalytic converters.

The last SP variant against the backdrop of the Sierra Nevada: the stepped seat was not exactly comfortable, however.

850 Le Mans 1976 – 78

Who doesn't remember the melodious tones of the Italian racing machines of the Fifties and Sixties and the last remnant of them, the fabulous MV? Who has forgotten how the single-cylinder Guzzis with the trashcan fairing rumbled over the racetracks under Ken Kavanagh and Lorenzetti? In 1976, when he began his first Le Mans test, *Motorrad* test rider Franz-Josef Schermer reached far back into Guzzi history. A few pages of history could do no less.

On 11-12 September 1971, for example, Guzzi entered three factory racing machines in the legendary Bol d'Or, a 24-hour race which was then still held on the Circuit Bugatti in Le Mans, near Orléans. Brambilla and Mandracci rode the 750s to an outstanding third place. And this despite a crash during the night – at times during the race it rained buckets – and engine misfires at high rpm caused by a bent pushrod. Technically, the machine was based on the V7 Sport, had an oil pan spacer ring, which was supposed to avoid performance loss caused by the crankshaft splashing about in the lubricant, and

The 850 Le Mans is a much sought after motorcycle today and good examples sell for very high prices. At the time it had the most powerful engine of any Moto Guzzi production bike, producing an impressive 70 horsepower.

a slim half-shell fairing. The two courageous riders in their Belstaff gear still had to struggle with an antiquated drum brake on the front wheel.

Another example: two years later, Raimondo Riva of Lecco and Luciano Gazzola pushed a 750 S with double-disc front brakes and an 844-cc engine to the starting line of the 24-hour race in Barcelona. After 683 laps around the twisting and dangerous course in Montjuich Park, the pair was waved home in fifth place. One could confidently call this machine the prototype of what would later become the Le Mans.

850 Le Mans

Production Period:	1976-1978
Engine:	V-twin OHV/2 V
Displacement:	844 cc
Bore x Stroke:	83 x 78 mm
Compression:	10.2:1
Power output:	70 hp at 7,300 rpm
Mixture preparation:	Dell'Orto PHF 36, points
Clutch:	double plate
Gearbox:	5 speeds
Frame:	steel tube, removable cradle braces
Wheelbase:	1470 mm
Front suspension:	telescopic fork
Rear suspension:	double swing arm, 2 shock absorbers
Front tire:	3.50H18
Rear tire:	4.00H18
Front brake:	dual disc, 300 mm
Rear brake:	disc, 242 mm
Empty weight:	225 kg
Tank capacity:	22.5 liters
Maximum speed:	206 kph

The driving force behind the company's participation in long-distance racing was undoubtedly Lino Tonti. The increase in displacement of the company's racing machines was also his initiative. Ultimately, the rules permitted machines with displacements up to one liter, and the Sport, with its 750-cc engine, looked a little poor. As well, the necessary cylinders were already on the shelf, for the 850 GT – with a bore of 83 millimeters and a displacement of 844 cubic centimeters – had been in production for some time.

Even in normal street use, the 750 sport models hadn't exactly earned kudos for their torque. Almost every test report made mention of a slight torque weakness in the lower to mid-rpm range.

When Tonti presented his proposal for a new sport machine to the company management in the spring of 1975, he was already convinced that he should use an 850-cc engine. In fact, management welcomed Tonti's ideas with open arms. An 850 sport bike – that might be exactly the machine the company needed to give the brand an entirely new image and, of course, reach a new class of buyer. Stepping on the toes of its direct competitors in their own country – Ducati and Laverda – who had owned the sport bike market for years, was a possibility that intrigued company director de Tomaso. And so, Tonti was quickly given the green light to design a new sport bike.

Basically the matter was quite simple: a suitable chassis was available in the form of the 750 S3 and the 850 engine could be taken from the 850 T. Only a few modifications were needed for use in the new sport bike. Tonti used new pistons to increase compression to 10.2:1 and increased the size of the valves to 44 mm on the inlet side and 37 mm on the outlet side. Fat 36-mm Dell'Ortos with accelerator pumps – which enriched the mixture when the gas piston lifted by injecting a thin stream of gasoline – provided fresh gas to the engine. They drew fresh air through open plastic funnels. Timing was the same as that of the T3.

Although these modifications were minor, there was a noticeable increase in power. The sporty 850-cc engine produced 70 hp at 7,300 rpm. Maximum torque was again produced at relatively high rpm: the sport twin produced about 70 Nm (51.6 ft lb) at 6,500 rpm. The torque curve was, however, somewhat fuller in the lower rpm range than it had been on the 750 power plants. And after all, that was exactly what the increase in displacement was supposed to achieve. Also partly responsible was perhaps the newly designed exhaust system, with an intermediate pipe in front of and behind the oil pan. The entire exhaust was painted a sporty black.

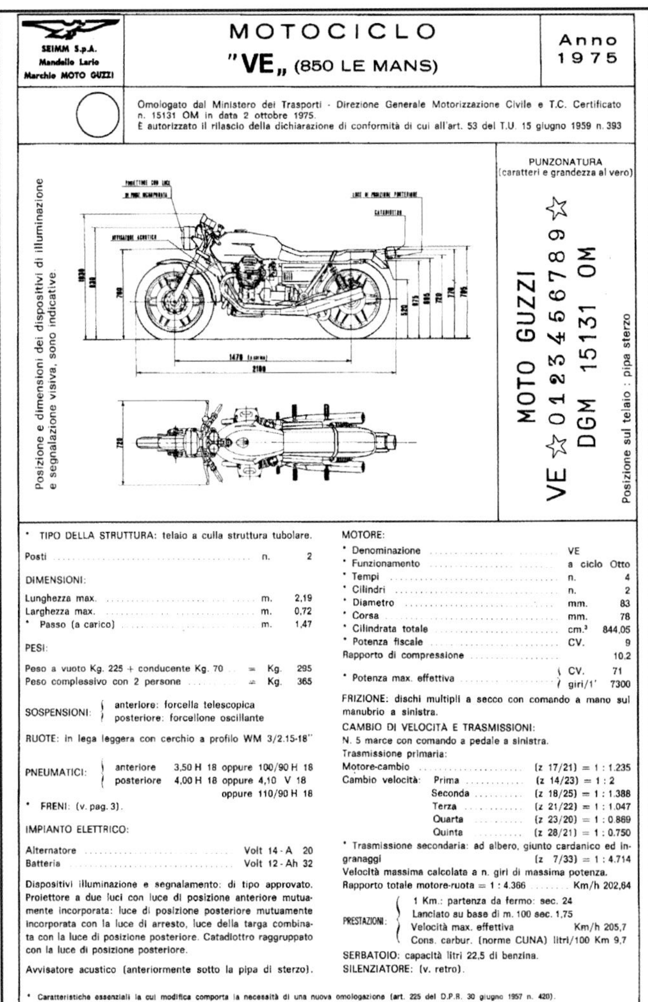

SEIMM S.p.A.
Mandello Lario
Marchio MOTO GUZZI

MOTOCICLO
"VE" (850 LE MANS)

Anno 1975

Omologato dal Ministero dei Trasporti - Direzione Generale Motorizzazione Civile e T.C. Certificato n. 15131 OM in data 2 ottobre 1975.
È autorizzato il rilascio della dichiarazione di conformità di cui all'art. 53 del T.U. 15 giugno 1959 n. 393

Posizione e dimensioni dei dispositivi di illuminazione e segnalazione visiva, sono indicative.

PUNZONATURA (caratteri e grandezza al vero)

MOTO GUZZI
VE ☆ 0123456789 ☆
DGM 15131 OM

Posizione sul telaio: pipa sterzo

* TIPO DELLA STRUTTURA: telaio a culla struttura tubolare.

Posti ..... n. 2

DIMENSIONI:

Lunghezza max. ..... m. 2,19
Larghezza max. ..... m. 0,72
* Passo (a carico) ..... m. 1,47

PESI:

Peso a vuoto Kg. 225 + conducente Kg. 70 ..... = Kg. 295
Peso complessivo con 2 persone ..... = Kg. 365

SOSPENSIONI: anteriore: forcella telescopica; posteriore: forcellone oscillante

RUOTE: in lega leggera con cerchio a profilo WM 3/2.15-18"

PNEUMATICI: anteriore 3,50 H 18 oppure 100/90 H 18; posteriore 4,00 H 18 oppure 4,10 V 18 oppure 110/90 H 18

* FRENI: (v. pag. 3).

IMPIANTO ELETTRICO:

Alternatore ..... Volt 14 - A 20
Batteria ..... Volt 12 - Ah 32

Dispositivi illuminazione e segnalamento: di tipo approvato. Proiettore a due luci con luce di posizione anteriore mutuamente incorporata: luce di posizione posteriore mutuamente incorporata con la luce di arresto, luce della targa combinata con la luce di posizione posteriore. Catadiottro raggruppato con la luce di posizione posteriore.

Avvisatore acustico (anteriormente sotto la pipa di sterzo).

MOTORE:

* Denominazione ..... VE
* Funzionamento ..... a ciclo Otto
* Tempi ..... n. 4
* Cilindri ..... n. 2
* Diametro ..... mm. 83
* Corsa ..... mm. 78
* Cilindrata totale ..... cm.³ 844,05
* Potenza fiscale ..... CV. 9
Rapporto di compressione 10.2
* Potenza max. effettiva ..... CV. 71; giri/1' 7300

FRIZIONE: dischi multipli a secco con comando a mano sul manubrio a sinistra.

CAMBIO DI VELOCITÀ E TRASMISSIONI:
N. 5 marce con comando a pedale a sinistra.
Trasmissione primaria:
Motore-cambio ..... (z 17/21) = 1 : 1.235
Cambio velocità: Prima ..... (z 14/23) = 1 : 2
Seconda ..... (z 18/25) = 1 : 1.388
Terza ..... (z 21/22) = 1 : 1.047
Quarta ..... (z 23/20) = 1 : 0.869
Quinta ..... (z 28/21) = 1 : 0.750
* Trasmissione secondaria: ad albero, giunto cardanico ed ingranaggi (z 7/33) = 1 : 4.714
Velocità massima calcolata a n. giri di massima potenza.
Rapporto totale motore-ruota = 1 : 4.366 ..... Km/h 202,64

PRESTAZIONI:
1 Km.: partenza da fermo: sec. 24
Lanciato su base di m. 100 sec. 1,75
Velocità max. effettiva Km/h 205,7
Cons. carbur. (norme CUNA) litri/100 Km 9,7

SERBATOIO: capacità litri 22,5 di benzina.
SILENZIATORE: (v. retro).

* Caratteristiche essenziali la cui modifica comporta la necessità di una nuova omologazione (art. 225 del D.P.R. 30 giugno 1957 n. 420).

Approval sheet for the 850 Le Mans: the slim machine was capable of 205 kph and weighed 225 kilograms.

The electrical system was largely the same, although the Bosch alternator now produced 280 Watts. Battery capacity was still 32 ampere hours. Switches and instruments were taken from the T3 touring model.

Compared to the 750 S3 and the 850 T3, there was nothing new in the gearbox. The gearing was also unchanged and all of the gear ratios were the same as those of the mentioned machines. The quite short 7/33 final ratio remained unchanged because of the significantly higher rpm level of the 850.

The chassis of the Guzzi should have become well known by then. It differed from that of the S3 only in detail. The main points of the chassis were: steel tube frame with removable cradle braces, the patented Guzzi fork with sealed damping cartridges, tapered-roller-bearing supported swing arms with the Guzzi-developed integral brake system with 300-mm discs in front and a 240-mm disc in back, and new light metal cast wheels. The rim sizes remained the same, however: front and rear the wheels were 2.15 inches wide and measured 18 inches in diameter. A 3.50 or 100/90 tire could be installed in front, with a 4.00, 4.10 or 110/90 tire in the back.

Brochure for the Le Mans: the machine shown here is one of the very rare silver-painted versions.

The 850's new dress was not all that sporty or exciting, however. The familiar S3 tank was painted red, the topside black. The side covers, the front of the plastic fairing, and the rear fender with circular tail light mount were also red. As initially envisioned, the seat was suitable for just one person, so pronounced and long was the hump at the rear. Nevertheless, the motorcycle was equipped with a set of foot pegs for a pillion rider. The machine was also fitted with a fairing – if that is what one wants to call the mini-fairing around the headlight. The center of this fairing was painted bright orange, underlining the motorcycle's sporty claim. The German TÜV had reservations about the garish paint scheme, however, which is why in this country the Le Mans only appeared without these added color accents.

The Italian ministry of transport issued the type approval for the 850 Le Mans on 2 October, 1975. The machine was issued the model identifier VE. Reiner H. Nitschke was the first German motorcycling journalist allowed to test-ride the new sport bike in Mandello. His test ride took him from Mandello towards Milan and from there over the unbelievably winding *Autostrada* A7 in the direction of Genoa. Nitschke, a passionate motorcyclist – and today editor in chief of *Tourenfahrer* (Touring Rider) magazine – liked the enormous torque of the 850 sport engine, though he had a difficult time making friends with the board-hard seat and the bent-over seating position.

The words of Franz-Josef Schermer sounded quite different: "Even during the obligatory ride through the city, I was impressed by the ease with which the motorcycle allowed itself to be steered. This impression was further strengthened on the country road, not to say on all. Changing direction was as effortless as I have ever experienced. There was no heaving from one lean to the other, no fear of approaching flat curves. The projecting parts of the machine hardly ever touched the ground, and when it did happen the machine stayed firmly on course."

Of course, this judgment was to be expected. After all, the 750 S3 and the Le Mans – which shared a common chassis – had very similar qualities. But a decisive advance was expected from the sporty 850 twin – and it did not disappoint. Franz-Josef Schermer: "Riding fast over country roads, with numerous quick passing maneuvers there was no need for tiresome downshifting; on the Le Mans, fourth and fifth gears have become all-round gears. Intake and exhaust noises are very pleasing, in no way bothersome, the mechanical noise of the engine is kept within limits." The motorcycle technicians measured a top speed of 202 kph during this test, exactly the same as the figure quoted by the manufacturer.

Where there is so much light there are usually also plenty of shadows, especially where Italian motorcycles are concerned. (They are found in the chapter on quality and workmanship.) There were a few very unpleasant things to discover on the Le Mans. Like several Guzzis before – and by the way after – it, the paint peeled in the area of the tank filler cap. Not only is this unsightly, but it is also the cause of so many "roadside repairs" – as Klacks Leverkus put it. For the tiny bits of peeled paint tend to clog the fine boreholes in the carburetors – always, of course, just as one is pulling into the passing lane.

There are other aggravations, including the alternator under the chrome cover between the two exhaust manifolds. The generator tends to overheat, especially at highway speeds, resulting in rotor damage and loss of the power supply. In 1978, the Le Mans received the ugly black alternator cover with cooling slots, which largely eliminated this problem.

One year after its debut, in January 1977, the one-man seat of the Le Mans was replaced by a rather longer example. The circular tail light integrated into the rear fender was forced to give way to a rectangular version. This was the Le Mans' only facelift during its three-year career.

With its aggressive, sporty design, contrasting fire-red and black paint scheme, narrow handlebars, mini fairing and racing seat, the Le Mans was exactly to the taste of the sport-oriented public. The Guzzi proved worthy of this trust by winning production motorcycle races and motorcycle rallies.

But the maintenance-free shaft drive and, in particular, the robust, simple engine also made the Le Mans a popular companion on the highways of Europe. Like all Guzzis with the big V-twin, the Le Mans also shone because of its great reliability and low fuel consumption.

The Le Mans cost 10,560 Deutschmarks when it appeared on the German market. With more than 1,100 sold, the sporty Le Mans, which so many experts had given little better than an outside chance of becoming a commercial success, was as big a hit as the 850 T3. In 1990, there were still more than 700 examples of the first Le Mans on the roads in Germany, and by then they had become real collector's items fetching correspondingly high prices on the used motorcycle market.

850 Le Mans II 1979 – 80

Moto Guzzi unveiled the Le Mans II, which was no more than a slightly modified version of the original Le Mans, at the IFMA in Cologne, in September 1978. This similarity was underlined by retention of the VE model identification. The most striking change was the fairing, whose upper part moved with the handlebars, while the lower part – like that of the 1000 SP – was attached to the frame and enclosed the entire engine block. Only the two cylinders were still exposed. For better alternator cooling, the chrome cover was replaced by a plastic version with cooling slots on the sides – as on late-production Le Mans I models. A modified exhaust resulted in increased power of 73 hp at 7,700 rpm. 208 kph appeared in the Le Mans II specification under the heading "maximum speed."

The Le Mans II was inferior in some respects to its predecessors, particularly with respect to the suspension: because of its wider fork bridge, the machine's directional stability was not as good.

The chassis also underwent minor changes. The front brake calipers moved behind the fork tubes and the fork bridges were made ten millimeters wider. In addition to the speedometer and tachometer, in the cockpit there was now also a clock and a voltmeter. Like the lower portion of the fairing, the entire instrument panel came from the SP. A red indicator light warned of low fluid level in the integral brake system.

The Le Mans II fell out of favor, however, on account of its chassis problems at high speeds. Light riders, in particular, had problems holding the machine on course at high speeds. For this reason, the bottom forkbridge was strengthened before the motorcycle was released to the public.

Then, at the end of 1980, Moto Guzzi improved the damping cartridges in the telescopic fork, which was also given pneumatic support, and the rear shocks. As well, on the final examples of the Le Mans II series, the hard chrome-plated cylinders were replaced by nikasil-coated versions.

850 Le Mans II

Production Period:	1979-1980
Engine:	V-twin OHV/2 V
Displacement:	844.05 cc
Bore x Stroke:	83 x 78 mm
Compression:	10.2:1
Power output:	73 hp at 7,700 rpm
Mixture preparation:	Dell'Orto PHF 36, points
Clutch:	double plate
Gearbox:	5 speeds
Frame:	steel tube, removable cradle braces
Wheelbase:	1470 mm
Front suspension:	telescopic fork
Rear suspension:	double swing arm, 2 shock absorbers
Front tire:	100/90V18
Rear tire:	110/90V18
Front brake:	dual disc, 300 mm
Rear brake:	disc, 242 mm
Empty weight:	238 kg
Tank capacity:	22.5 liters
Maximum speed:	208 kph

On the initiative of the German importer, Duilio Agostini, a local tuner situated next to the factory in Mandello, produced a special series of the Le Mans II. Grey cast iron cylinders with a bore of 88 mm increased displacement to almost 1000 cubic centimeters. Open Dell'Orto carburetors with a 40-mm inlet and accelerator pumps prepared the mixture. An aluminum spacer ring allowed the contents of the oil pan to be increased significantly.

The tuned twin-cylinder produced 85 hp at 7,600 rpm and propelled the machine to a top speed of 220 kph. Close to 150 examples of this special series were registered in Germany.

850 Le Mans III 1981 – 84

Moto Guzzi unveiled the third version of the Le Mans series in 1981. The amended model identification, VF instead of VE, showed that this was an entirely new motorcycle. The only components left unchanged from the preceding model were the frame, wheels, gearbox, and driveshaft.

The engine, in particular, underwent a thorough renovation. The engine housing was beefed up considerably, the cylinder stud bolts were spaced farther apart, which made possible the use of new nikasil-coated cylinders with considerably thicker walls. Inside were three-ring pistons, which once again were divided into three size classes. Class A ranged from 82.968 to 82.974 mm, Class B from 82.874 to 82.980 mm, and Class C from 82.980 to 92.986 mm in diameter. These dimensions are also valid for Le Mans II engines beginning with serial number 80390, which also had nikasil-coated cylinders.

The most striking thing, however, was the new, angular ribbing of the cylinders. These made the two cylinders look even more massive. Introduction of the hexagon shape was mainly for stylistic reasons, but in fact it increased the engine's cooling surface considerably. Another significant innovation is found beneath the valve covers, which were also angular:

the rocker arm bearing block is made of aluminum – like the head and cylinders – instead of steel. This measure was the result of the considerably stricter EU noise regulations. For mechanical noises played a not inconsiderable role in noise creation by such a Guzzi tractor. On the old round-cylinder machines, with a warm engine, this rocker arm bearing block and the cylinder head expanded to different degrees, with the result that during the warm-up phase valve play was subject to strong fluctuations, which in turn caused loud clattering. To avoid this, the Guzzi designers turned to the aluminum rocker arm bearing block for the third edition of the Le Mans.

The oil pan spacer ring of the Agostini Le Mans finally became standard on production motorcycles. With its help, crankshaft churning losses in the engine oil were reduced considerably. The engine simply blew less oil out through the casing ventilation.

The Le Mans III was the first European motorcycle to clear the hurdle of the new EU noise regulations. The Guzzi engineers developed a new exhaust system which was not only quieter than that of the II but also resulted in an increase in power to 76 hp at 7,700 rpm, in conjunction with a voluminous air filter system and much increased cylinder cooling area.

The best Le Mans of all time: the Le Mans III was a very mature and reliable motorcycle. It was the first Guzzi with the angular cylinder design.

There were several changes to the chassis. The front wheel was guided by the narrower fork of the Le Mans I, and in the rear the swing arms were lengthened by two centimeters. Both measures improved directional stability considerably.

The third edition of the sport bike also introduced some visual changes. The lower fairing shrank to two small spoilers above the cylinder heads. The short upper part was reminiscent of the fairing on the Le Mans I. The new, longer tank held 25 liters. The headlight was rectangular and a small spoiler was added at the end of the seat.

The redesigned cockpit was dominated by the large, white, Veglia tachometer. Together with a speedometer, voltmeter, and warning lamps, it took its place in a large plastic instrument panel. The colorful switches on the handlebars were the same as those of the Le Mans II, however.

The third Le Mans was the best Guzzi with the fat V-twin ever built. This is not just the author's opinion. Umberto Todero was quite sure of this: "The 850 with the angular cylinders – that was perhaps the best compromise between lots of torque and the ability to achieve high revs. As well, the moving parts in the small engine were not quite as large as those of the thousands. It simply ran smoother and revved higher. The relatively small valves provided good flow conditions in the induction tract. The big valves in the later 1000 engines were a mistake, which was in part forced upon us by marketing. That the fastest Guzzi racing machines still run with the small Le Mans III valves is probably proof enough."

From the very beginning, the Le Mans III showed itself to be absolutely mature and reliable. Thick layers of dust formed over the spare parts for this machine in the German importer's replacement parts warehouse in Bielefeld. The machine stayed in production for three years without a facelift.

The Le Mans III's performance was sparkling. A clocked top speed of 214 kph – the Veglia speedometer suggested 235 kph – was surely outstanding for an 850 twin-cylinder. The motorcycle's fuel consumption was also unbelievably low, often less than five liters per 100 kilometers. And to achieve this, one didn't even have to be too careful with the throttle.

The Le Mans III was to became the best-selling Guzzi ever in Germany. A staggering 2,504 were sold here, and by mid-1990 less than 300 had made their final trip to the crusher. This is further proof of the machine's outstanding reliability. If a motorcycle from Mandello ever truly earned the name "road burner," it was the third Le Mans. They were found in the

850 Le Mans III

Production Period:	1981-1984
Engine:	V-twin OHV/2 V
Displacement:	844.05 cc
Bore x Stroke:	83 x 78 mm
Compression:	9.8:1
Power output:	76 hp at 7,700 rpm
Mixture preparation:	Dell'Orto PHF 36, points
Clutch:	double plate
Gearbox:	5 speeds
Frame:	steel tube, removable cradle braces
Wheelbase:	1505 mm
Front suspension:	telescopic fork
Rear suspension:	double swing arm, 2 shock absorbers
Front tire:	100/90V18
Rear tire:	110/90V18
Front brake:	dual disc, 300 mm
Rear brake:	disc, 242 mm
Empty weight:	240 kg
Tank capacity:	25 liters
Maximum speed:	205 kph

Sahara, on all the highways of Europe, and countless examples ran on racetracks all around the globe.

In March 1983, Jan Leek, the author of this book, undertook a long-distance trip similar to the one made on the autobahn between Hamburg and Vienna on the V7 years earlier. It was supposed to go from Stockholm, Sweden to Venice and back. With him were a Laverda RGS 1000 and a BMW R 100 RS. Jan Leek recalled: "The racing began on the way there, just outside Göttingen in the Harz District. It was probably unavoidable on such a long ride on the autobahn. With very little throttle I was simply able to leave the BMW standing on a long hill. The Laverda stayed with me. We headed south with 220 kph on the clock. The Guzzi was already our favorite motorcycle. When the BMW began to wobble slightly, the Le Mans still ran straight and true. And when the rider on the Laverda was buffeted by the wind, one still sat completely relaxed on the Guzzi. South of Cortina one of my two colleagues – who owned a Guzzi privately – had a completely rusted right front disc after a long rainy period. He hadn't used the brake lever once. Three points impressed all of us about the Guzzi: the incredible effortlessness with which the machine ran at high speed, the small but unbelievably effective fairing, and most of all its low fuel consumption. The machine never consumed more than 6.5 liters per 100 kilometers during the entire 5,000 kilometer trip. For such a ride I would still choose a Le Mans III!" It would come as a surprise to few Le Mans III owners that the Guzzi completed the 5000-kilometer trip without mechanical problems.

The German Motobecane also provided a special model of the third Le Mans. Based on its successful experience gained in the German rally championship and the long-distance world championship, the German importer developed the DMB Le Mans III.

For its day the Le Mans III had a first-class chassis and suspension, something that Japanese motorcycles in particular were still unable to offer.

It had nikasil cylinders with a bore of 90 mm, Mahle forged pistons, a Schrick camshaft with sharper timing and longer valve stroke, 40-mm Dell'Orto carburetors, a straight-geared racing gearbox, and a taller final gear ratio. 95 horsepower helped the DMB reach a top speed of 227 kph. About eighty examples of the DMB Le Mans sowed fear and terror among the proud owners of big Japanese bikes.

Production of the Le Mans III continued until the end of 1984, and in the spring of 1985 it was replaced by the fourth variation on the Le Mans theme.

Accessory catalogue from Agostini, a Guzzi dealer in Mandello del Lario. Guzzis were and still are popular conversion projects. In the photo above is the German importer's DMB-Le Mans III.

The third Le Mans variant was also tricked out by the German importer: fairing with twin headlights, 1000-cc engine and adjustable seat.

1000 Le Mans IV	
Production Period:	1985-1987
Engine:	V-twin OHV/2 V
Displacement:	948.8 cc
Bore x Stroke:	88 x 78 mm
Compression:	10:1
Power output:	81 hp at 7,500 rpm
Mixture preparation:	Dell'Orto PHM 40, points
Clutch:	double plate
Gearbox:	5 speeds
Frame:	steel tube, removable cradle braces
Wheelbase:	1514 mm
Front suspension:	telescopic fork
Rear suspension:	double swing arm, 2 shock absorbers
Front tire:	120/80V16
Rear tire:	130/80V18
Front brake:	dual disc, 270 mm
Rear brake:	disc, 270 mm
Empty weight:	244 kg
Tank capacity:	24 liters
Maximum speed:	207 kph

1000 Le Mans IV 1985 – 87

In the spring of 1985, the Le Mans reached the absolute limit – the Le Mans IV, called the Le Mans 1000 internally, reached the dealers. The machine had received type approval in September 1984, but deliveries did not begin until early the next year. The differences from the pervious model were considerable. Indicative of this was the new model identifier VV. The Le Mans III had had a VF in front of its chassis number.

Let us first examine the engine. Obviously, its basic design remained the same. With a bore of 88 mm, however, the cylinders came from the California II or the 1000 SP II, if you will. The cylinders and pistons were divided into the familiar size classes of these models. The exact dimensions can be found in the chapter on that motorcycle. The valves in the cylinder heads – whose combustion chambers were 83 mm instead of 79 – were considerably larger: inlet 48 millimeters diameter, outlet 40 millimeters. They were activated by a new camshaft. Valve timing: inlet opens 29 degrees before top dead center, closes 60 degrees after bottom dead center, outlet opens 58 degrees before bottom dead center, closes 31 degrees after top dead center. Two big 40-mm Dell'Orto carburetors with accelerator pumps deliver fuel. Once again, a contact-controlled ignition provides the right sparks. The engine of the new Le Mans delivers an impressive 81 hp at 7,400 rpm. Maximum torque also reached new heights at over 80 Nm (59 ft lb).

The clutch and gearbox of the three earlier versions were adopted almost unchanged. The only difference: a softer spring in the switching unit which was supposed to improve shiftability of the gear train. The 7/33 final gear ratio was also retained.

The chassis: following the current trend, on their new creation, the Guzzi engineers installed a 16-inch front wheel for the first time. In the rear they continued to put their trust in the familiar 18-inch wheel. Instead of the WM hubs used before, which were unsuitable for the use of tubeless tires, Moto

Guzzi for the first time turned to MT hubs with tubeless Pirelli Phantom tires. The tube diameter of the new, air-supported telescopic fork grew to 40 millimeters.

While the patented integral brake system remained part of the Le Mans, the diameter of the front discs was reduced to 270 mm. The fairing and spoiler looked very similar to those of the Le Mans III, however, they came from the smaller Guzzi V65 Lario.

Like its predecessor, the big 1000 engine had the ability to impress. In a direct comparison though the 850 engine was somehow more fleet-footed and the Le Mans III was no less fast than the Four despite the latter's extra five horsepower. Apart from a minor torque weakness in the lower rpm range, one has to give the Guzzi engineers credit. Once again the machine is easily capable of exceeding 210 kph – though of course the speedometer still lies – and fuel consumption is still impressive. The Le Mans IV rarely exceeds six liters per hundred kilometers. And the shiftability of the gearbox is actually improved on account of the new spring in the switching unit.

But while the engine again basked in the sunlight, the chassis came in for fierce criticism. Horst Vieselmann of *Motorrad* wrote: "The 585-mm-wide stub handlebars continually try to turn into the turn, making a clean line almost impossible." Vieselmann correctly blamed this behavior, which took some getting used to, on the revised suspension geometry and the 16-inch front wheel: "It is therefore debatable whether the introduction of the small wheel can be characterized as advisable, especially as the theoretical advantages with respect to handling are more or less negated by the increases in wheelbase and castor."

The Le Mans IV came with the styling of the smaller V65 Lario. The rear frame tubes no longer ran straight back, instead they were upswept.

The tester also had something to say about the riding comfort of the Le Mans: "While the rear Koni shock does good work despite its small working stroke (68 mm), and absorbs small bumps even in its softest setting, even without air support the amply dimensioned telescopic fork, which is strengthened by an additional fork bridge, displays stiffness that is scarcely acceptable."

One year after the Le Mans IV was unveiled, an attempt was made to cure the ills of its running gear. It received new fork bridges, which shortened the wheel base to 1485 millimeters, but increased castor to 106 mm. New damping elements without air support were screwed into the telescopic fork and these responded better. Weights in the ends of the handlebars were supposed to reduce flutter on uneven roads. The fork stabilizer was float-mounted, which helped prevent the fork from tensing when the brakes were applied.

This conversion, which was offered to the owners of all older Le Mans IV models at no charge, improved the motorcycle's handling considerably. The machine still had a tendency to wobble, but only on worn tires. For 530 Deutschmarks the German importer

Ferrari on two wheels? In the photo studio the fire-red Le Mans IV looked good beside the much more expensive Ferrari.

also offered a conversion kit with the 18-inch tires of the latest model, which was supposed to eliminate the weaknesses of the Le Mans IV's suspension once and for all. The machine had to be in its original state for the conversion to be used, however.

At the end of his Le Mans IV test, Horst Vieselmann came to a melancholy conclusion that the many owners of the machine would surely agree with: "With respect to riding comfort and handling, the Le Mans IV rider must resign himself to conditions that are unfavorable or at least take getting used to. A fact which, given the largely good workmanship and fascinating engine of the big Guzzi, is a little sad."

1000 Le Mans V 1988 – 92

By the autumn of 1987, the Italians had had enough of the constant grousing about the Le Mans IV and with the new Le Mans – without a number after the name – that return to a proven suspension. The motorcycle had 18-inch wheels front and rear, like the original Le Mans. The rear tire was much wider than those of the first three Le Mans models: 120/90 V18. On the front wheel is a 100 tire. The latest Guzzi sport bike also received a half-shell fairing attached to the frame, an adjustable front wheel fork and, finally, sensible switch units.

The shortness of the preceding paragraph shows how minimal the modifications to the machine were. The approval sheet identified it as a modification of the *Motociclo Moto Guzzi Tipo VV* (Le Mans IV) rather than a new motorcycle. Approval for the then last model of the Le Mans was issued on 11 January 1988.

With the fifth variant, the Le Mans finally got back on a successful track. Even the motorcycle press acknowledged that the two-cylinder sport bike possessed the qualities of its earlier forebears. Wolf Töns wrote in *Motorrad*: "The Le Mans runs so consistently straight, even at top speed, that its seems as if a giant hand is guiding the 247 kilograms." He went on: "It follows the prescribed path as if pulled by invisible strings – as long as the surface is comparable to that of a good country road. Yes, even the current Le Mans has to carry on with the same insensible suspension elements as its predecessors. And it is no wonder, after all they are exactly the same."

The bike's workmanship also came in for criticism. Wolf Töns once again: "Perhaps a Guzzi simply demands of its owner that he wipes off the rain

1000 Le Mans V

Production Period:	1988-1992
Engine:	V-twin OHV/2 V
Displacement:	948.8 cc
Bore x Stroke:	88 x 78 mm
Compression:	9.8:1
Power output:	81 hp at 7,400 rpm
Mixture preparation:	Dell'Orto PHM 40, points
Clutch:	double plate
Gearbox:	5 speeds
Frame:	steel tube, removable cradle braces
Wheelbase:	1514 mm
Front suspension:	telescopic fork
Rear suspension:	double swing arm, 2 shock absorbers
Front tire:	100/90V18
Rear tire:	120/90V18
Front brake:	dual disc, 270 mm
Rear brake:	disc, 270 mm
Empty weight:	248 kg
Tank capacity:	24 liters
Maximum speed:	209 kph

drops (rust on the exhaust) with the rag he always carries with him. And he must also overlook the paint peeling off the front fender because of gasoline effect. And he also shouldn't curse out loud when he jams his fingers between the handlebars and fairing while maneuvering."

Even in its fifth incarnation, the Le Mans remained what it had always been: a sporty, somewhat classically-inspired twin-cylinder machine which feels equally at home on winding country roads or with two men and baggage on the autobahn between Hamburg and Vienna. A good dose of sportiness, combined with a solidity that sets it apart from most other sport bikes – that is what distinguishes the Le Mans. And even if the concept has become a little dated – the fascination remains.

Brochure for the Le Mans IV: was the Le Mans fairing ever tested in the wind tunnel? In any case, it functioned very well.

850 T3 California 1975 – 80

Brigette, lover of brimming Italian ice buckets, put the critics in their place: "It's the most beautiful motorcycle ever!" She's right, I thought, as I left the city upright – not lying flat with my nose on the tank and not sitting on the rear wheel, but sitting properly. With a little dignity even, like Don Camillo when he stalked Peppone. The two cylinders respond to rough handling of the throttle with knocking. I have to raise the foot to shift, to brake as well. There are no orgies of acceleration, neither can I show off with many cylinders. Somehow the builder of this machine prescribed to me how I should behave on it. And somehow it is fun, it is a different, a more beautiful kind of riding."

Wolfgang Fromm wrote these words after a brief spin on the California 850 T3. Offered alongside the standard T3, the 850 T3 California became one of the most beloved Moto Guzzis ever. It differed from the original version in having a windscreen, roll bars front and rear, footboards for the rider, two plastic bags and an elegantly upswept seat. The machine sold like hotcakes because of its exciting exterior. While many typically Italian details on this and all other T-series motorcycles – so-so bags, inaccurate speedometer,

The T3 California was very popular, largely because of its attractive styling. On account of its large windscreen, the machine was clearly slower than the naked 850 T3.

dim warning lamps, crummy switches – could drive a perfectionist to distraction, they scarcely bothered the true Guzzi fan.

But this wasn't the first California version made in Mandello. There was also an American version of the revered 850 GT, but the two motorcycles also differed only in their equipment package. The V7 California 850 – the bike's correct name – was given a sweeping black-and-white seat, curved handlebars, a windscreen, footboards for the rider, roll bars, luggage rack and two bags. The two versions were easily identified by their chassis numbers: the standard GT was given a combination of two numbers and two letters, while the California models were numbered consecutively from 11.111.

The same recipe was used once again with the T3 California. Technically the machine was identical to the standard T3. Only the two foot levers for the brakes and shifting gears had to be redesigned on account of the footboards. The brake pedal could bring a 30-ton diesel to a stop, so huge are its dimensions. The shift lever is once again designed as a rocker. Press back – shift up, press forward – shift back.

The two T3 variants differed quite considerably in performance, however. Instead of the 187 kph achieved by the naked version, the California reached just 158 kph. Mainly responsible were the terrible aerodynamics with the tall windscreen and the two drag-inducing bags. And as pleasant as the windscreen looked when the bike was standing still, on the road it could make the rider's life quite difficult. Norbert Bauer wrote in *Motorrad*: "Up to 80 or 90 kph there actually is a kind of calm behind

850 T3 California

Production Period:	1976-1978
Engine:	V-twin OHV/2 V
Displacement:	844 cc
Bore x Stroke:	83 x 78 mm
Compression:	10.2:1
Power output:	70 hp at 7,300 rpm
Mixture preparation:	Dell'Orto PHF 36, points
Clutch:	double plate
Gearbox:	5 speeds
Frame:	steel tube, removable cradle braces
Wheelbase:	1470 mm
Front suspension:	telescopic fork
Rear suspension:	double swing arm, 2 shock absorbers
Front tire:	3.50H18
Rear tire:	4.00H18
Front brake:	disc, 300 mm
Rear brake:	disc, 242 mm
Empty weight:	225 kg
Tank capacity:	22.5 liters
Maximum speed:	158 kph

With its large seat, the T3 California could comfortably accommodate two persons. Running boards provided plenty of room for the feet.

the screen. At higher speeds, however, a real storm breaks out, which threatens to lift the helmet from the rider's head, tugs at the glasses, or pulls up the visor of a full-face helmet if the pushbuttons are open. Behind the windscreen there is a powerful vacuum which increases with speed, pushing forward everything that is normally blown backward when riding a motorcycle."

Despite its rather modest performance – but the California was never designed for high-speed riding – the poor protection from the windscreen and its poor workmanship in places, the T3 California became a bestseller. And despite negative comments, even the motorcycle testers usually gave it a positive assessment. Franz-Josef Schermer: "One gets a comfortable, almost cozy feeling on the Guzzi California. The only other things one could ask for behind the windscreen would be a small minibar with stereo, television, cigars, and a nice barmaid."

Brochure for the T3 California: the plastic bags, seen clearly in this view, were not particularly stable and as well often leaked. The swept handlebars are extremely wide.

California II 1981 – 87

On 7 September 1987 the Italian ministry of transport approved a machine that would become one of the best-selling Moto Guzzis ever: the California II. Unlike its two predecessors, the V7 California 850 and 850 T3 California, the II was considerably more than a simple variant of an existing base model. The California II was a completely separate design. This is quite apparent if one looks at the other models then available. The last round-cylinder T4 tourer, the V1000 SP, was built at the same time, and the new Le Mans III with angular engine had been leaving the production Line for half a year. The California II was the second Guzzi with the modern rectangular engine, after the Le Mans III.

But the new California only had the usual things in common with the Le Mans engine – crankshaft, crankcase, electronics. The cylinders had a bore of 88 millimeters. Together with a stroke of 78 millimeters this resulted in a displacement of exactly 948.8 cubic centimeters. Once again, the cylinders and pistons were divided into three size classes – A, B and C. The cylinder liners were nigusil-coated. The two cylinder heads were completely new. While they shared the hexagonal design of the Le Mans, they had significantly smaller valves. They were exactly the same size as those of the familiar touring models, with 41 millimeters at the inlet and 36 millimeters on the outlet side. Complementing them were the familiar 30-mm Dell'Ortos with rectangular slides.

The Guzzi engineers hoped that this design would result in better performance than the 850 California had, plus improved torque at low revolutions. The bare performance figures confirm the potency of this first rectangular 1000: 67 horsepower at 6,700 rpm, maximum torque of 76 Nm (56 ft lb) was achieved at just 5,200 rpm. The 850 engines could not reach these two figures and also had to rev considerably higher.

Both the clutch and gearbox were proven components. They were taken unchanged – including the gear ratios – from the Le Mans.

The chassis and suspension had to submit to a thorough renovation, however. The T3 California occasionally showed a tendency to wobble at high speed. One of the reasons for this was its huge windscreen. Of course, the Guzzi designers didn't want to do away with it on the new Cali, as it was part of the bike. And so the otherwise unchanged twin-tube frame was considerably strengthened in the area of the steering head. The rear wheel swing arm was also lengthened significantly, and a welded cross-tube was added for improved stability. The wheelbase grew to a tremendous 1565 millimeters. If it didn't run straight after that.

The V1000 California II became a best seller: it was the first California with angular cylinders and nikasil-coated cylinders. Styling differed little from its predecessor.

Visually the California II differed little from its forerunners. The shape of the 25-liter tank was similar to that of the T models, while the seat was taken from the T3 California. The fenders, however, turned out to be much more voluminous. They were finished in the same color as the rest of the machine – black or white, and only the outer edges were chrome. Behind the seat there was a small chrome luggage rack. Roll bars front and rear were part of a California anyway. The same applied to the upswept handlebars. The two black plastic bags in the rear rounded out the picture. This Cali also had very large feet: 120 tires were mounted front and rear, of course with a diameter of 18 inches.

Weighing 280 kg, the motorcycle looked dazzling, which was surely part of the reason for its sales success. In the summer of 1990 – more than three years after production ceased – there were far in excess of 2,000 examples registered in this country (Germany). The California II thus ranked second on the domestic registry hit list – just behind the Le Mans III.

The California II, in fact, lived up to the expectations of its designers. At low rpm, the engine pulled like the proverbial tractor; fuel consumption was very low

at about six liters per 100 kilometers, and directional stability had become better. And, nevertheless, the big machine surprised with outstanding handling on winding country roads.

California II	
Production Period:	1979-1980
Engine:	V-twin OHV/2 V
Displacement:	948.8 cc
Bore x Stroke:	88 x 78 mm
Compression:	9.2:1
Power output:	67 hp at 6,700 rpm
Mixture preparation:	Dell'Orto VHB 30, points
Clutch:	double plate
Gearbox:	5 speeds
Frame:	steel tube, removable cradle braces
Wheelbase:	1470 mm
Front suspension:	telescopic fork
Rear suspension:	double swing arm, 2 shock absorbers
Front tire:	110/90V18
Rear tire:	120/90V18
Front brake:	twin disc, 300 mm
Rear brake:	disc, 275 mm
Empty weight:	250 kg
Tank capacity:	28 liters
Maximum speed:	157 kph

Not surprisingly, there were a few things about the bike that received criticism. Once again it was only the so-called little things that clouded the picture. The bags were not the sturdiest and when even slightly overloaded – capacity was ten kilos – they simply fell off. The warning lamps in the cockpit were still difficult to see in daylight, and finding neutral with the prominent rocker shifter was an art in itself. The California II was no faster than its 850-cc predecessors. The huge frontal area and the larger bags simply prevented better maximum speed values than the registered 157 kph. Perhaps they should have given the California a different, shorter, final gear ratio. In any case, the Le Mans III easily exceeded 210 kph with the same power plant.

The excessively tall final gear ration scarcely bothered the California rider, however. He certainly hadn't bought the fat Guzzi to race from point A to point B as quickly as possible. It conveyed a different, more casual style of motorcycle riding.

California III 1987 – 90

We now come to the next variant of this American-style touring machine: the California III. Once again the aim was to fit in precisely. The various versions of this third California could no longer be counted on one hand. We will first look at the carburetor version, as it was first on the market.

This next stage in the California styling can be dated to spring 1987. The engine was initially left as it was. The small amount of black paint added to the engine casing and crankcase surely do not count as modifications. There were, however, the two new 30-mm Dell'Ortos. They had round slides and an accelerator pump. This innovation had no effect on the engine's peak performance, however. As before, the 948-cc twin produced 67 hp at 6,700 rpm. Maximum torque rose, however, to 79 Nm (58.26 ft lb), which was achieved at just 3,200 rpm. This was due in large part to the newly designed, quieter exhaust system with upswept end pipes.

The gearbox also remained unchanged. There was a change in the final drive, where the 7/33 plate and bevel gear set was replaced by a shorter 6/32 pairing. This was a response to criticism of the California II for having an excessively tall final gear ratio. They obviously failed to take into account that the California III had considerably more oomph than its predecessor. Only fifty machines with the short final gearing made it to Germany – not surprisingly, these included the motorcycles made available to the specialist publications. And they promptly criticized the high rpm level, which also resulted in higher fuel consumption. Bad luck – for in fact only a very few motorcycles with the 6/32 gearing – all with approval for specific use – came to Germany. The German importer had complained about the too short gearing after the first test ride in Mandello, and all other California IIIs came with the standard 7/33 gearing.

The California III with and without fairing. The third generation of the California was not offered in Germany with the big fairing.

California III

Production Period:	1987-1990
Number built:	11,045
Engine:	V-twin OHV/2 V
Displacement:	948 cc
Bore x Stroke:	88 x 78 mm
Compression:	9.2:1
Power output:	67 hp at 6,700 rpm
Mixture preparation:	Dell'Orto PHF 36, points
Clutch:	double plate
Gearbox:	5 speeds
Frame:	steel tube, removable cradle braces
Wheelbase:	1470 mm
Front suspension:	telescopic fork
Rear suspension:	double swing arm, 2 shock absorbers
Front tire:	110/90V18
Rear tire:	120/90V18
Front brake:	twin disc, 300 mm
Rear brake:	disc, 275 mm
Empty weight:	250 kg
Tank capacity:	25 liters
Maximum speed:	163.6 kph

There weren't a lot of changes made to the chassis – model identification VW. Okay, the wheelbase is a little shorter, the steering head angle a little steeper, the castor, likewise, a little shorter, and up front there is a somewhat narrower 110 tire. The 40-mm forks are the same as those on the Le Mans IV and the brake discs are now mounted floating. More noticeable are the numerous styling retouches given to the big steamer. The tank holds twenty-six liters and is decidedly teardrop-shaped. The front of the seat is clearly lower, while the passenger sits one step higher than the rider. The straight-lined, somehow logical exterior of the earlier Calis has given way to a rather sporty, chopper-like design. Initially the plastic bags from the California II still hung from the rear of the machine, but one year later the California III was fitted with the gray Givi containers from the 1000 SP III. Also, the engine and gearbox lost their black crape. They did look a little sad, however.

The last two Cali variants exhibit few differences in handling. The rider sits a little lower and the suspension is clearly more comfortable. The California III is also much easier to maneuver than one would imagine on first seeing the big bike. The engine is

In terms of handling, there was little to choose between the California generations: one sat a little lower on the III and the suspension was clearly softer.

as powerful as ever, but pulls even better than the California II power plant at low revs. And with the taller, final gear ratio, fuel consumption is back in the familiar six liters per 100 kilometers rage.

In autumn 1989, Moto Guzzi unveiled a variant of the California with a large full fairing and top case. The German importer decided not to import this model, stating that the faired version was in direct competition with the 1000 SP III, and that German California owners wanted a machine on which the technology was visible. This assessment by the people in Bielefeld was not far off the mark.

In 1990 Guzzi brought out another version of the California III and it seemed custom made for German riders: the California III C. It was no more than a standard Cali with all the extra equipment removed. The C could stand for chopper or custom. And without a windscreen, roll bars, bags and luggage rack, the machine looked like a chopper. Apart from these absent details the machine was unchanged.

Beginning in 1991, the California III – and the III C – could be had with the 71-hp engine of the 1000 SP III. The reason for adoption of this engine was the introduction of the unregulated catalytic converter, which became available as an option at the beginning of 1991.

California III i.e. 1990 – 92

The revised model identifier – VY instead of VW – signified that the California i.e. was a new motorcycle. Let us discuss, in brief, everything that didn't change compared to the standard California: chassis, suspension elements, brakes, and styling. The only change that led to the new model identifier was the power plant, or more precisely the mixture preparation. The i.e. was the first Moto Guzzi without Dell'Orto carburetors, which were replaced by fuel injection.

Let us examine the Weber-Marelli system in detail. First the part that is responsible for preparing the mixture: a fuel line runs from the tank to a fuel pump, and from there through a filter, then through a pressure control valve that returns excess fuel to the tank, and from there to the electronically-controlled injectors, of which there is one in each intake duct. Now to the control system: injection quantity and timing are determined by various factors. Sensors take over measurement of air and oil temperature, air pressure, throttle valve setting, and engine revolutions. From this information a controller located under the seat calculates injection quantity and timing as well as the correct ignition timing.

California III i.e.

Production Period:	1987-1990
Number built:	11,045
Engine:	V-twin OHV/2 V
Displacement:	948.8 cc
Bore x Stroke:	88 x 78 mm
Compression:	9.2:1
Power output:	67 hp at 6,850 rpm
Mixture preparation:	Weber-Marelli fuel injection
Clutch:	double plate
Gearbox:	5 speeds
Frame:	steel tube, removable cradle braces
Wheelbase:	1470 mm
Front suspension:	telescopic fork
Rear suspension:	double swing arm, 2 shock absorbers
Front tire:	110/90V18
Rear tire:	130/90V18
Front brake:	twin disc, 300 mm
Rear brake:	disc, 275 mm
Empty weight:	250 kg
Tank capacity:	28 liters
Maximum speed:	160 kph

With the tank removed, the elderly V-twin looks like a heart patient in intensive care, yet there is no need to fear for the health of the power plant on account of the many hoses and cables. Quite the contrary – the electronic systems help give the antique machine new life. There wasn't much change in performance, just two horsepower more according to the specs, but engine behavior was much improved. The fuel-injected Guzzi accelerates from low to high revs much more smoothly than its normally aspirated cousins. More important for the future, however: with the help of fuel injection even such a dated engine was able to clear higher hurdles – in the form of stricter emission limits. The Weber-Marelli system brought one other benefit: the throttle twist grip forces were reduced to a poor remnant. Riding the California i.e. was clearly more carefree than on the carburetor version.

In 1991, fuel injection also became available on the other two California variants. There was the classic version with windscreen, roll bars, and bag as well as the completely naked Cali. Only the latter two were imported into Germany. Illogically, the fuel-injected California with catalytic converter did not appear here (Germany). The California was available with classic spoked wheels, however. And these wheels were so popular that the cast-wheel version was only available as a special order.

And what was it like? "Somehow the manufacturer prescribed how I should behave on this motorcycle. And somehow it was fun; it was a different, beautiful way of riding." Riding a California was certainly something quite special. "And actually there is no competing model for our California in the entire motorcycle market," declared Heinz Valentin of the former importer A & G. And perhaps this was true, only in the future Moto Guzzi would have to ensure that it did not water down the distinctive character of the Cali, for there are truly enough pretty soft choppers.

California 1100 — 1992

The Moto Guzzi construction set was now well established, and the engine of the 1100 Sport fit the California really well. The larger displacement and the increased torque that went with it suited the operating range of such a motorcycle quite well. And the concept was acknowledged, even though there was some delay. The model had been in production for three years when an American motorcycle magazine selected it cruiser of the year.

Meanwhile the manufacturer itself had recognized that the cruiser was more of a fashion trend and gave the Cali a number of improvements in its braking system and chassis. The factory celebrated its 75th birthday in 1996, with a special edition called the California 1100 i.e. Anniversario 75, with lavish equipment and a two-tone, red and silver paint job. The carburetor version was still available at that time. Nevertheless, the concept was successful, and one didn't have to be a manufacturer to see additional equipment variations in the future.

California 1100

Production Period:	1992
Engine:	V-twin OHV/2 V
Displacement:	1,064 cc
Bore x Stroke:	92 x 80 mm
Compression:	9.8:1
Power output:	75 hp at 6,400 rpm
Mixture preparation:	Weber IAW Alfa-N
Clutch:	double plate
Gearbox:	5 speeds
Frame:	steel tube
Wheelbase:	1575 mm
Front suspension:	telescopic fork
Rear suspension:	double swing arm, 2 shock absorbers
Front tire:	110/90-18
Rear tire:	140/80-17
Front brake:	twin disc, 300 mm
Rear brake:	disc, 270 mm
Weight:	268 kg (fueled)
Tank capacity:	19 liters
Maximum speed:	185 kph

Brochure for the California 1100: the 1100 could be had with fuel injection or the well-proven carburetors.

California EV 1997 – 99

When it was unveiled in 1997, this variant marked the highest development stage of the California and this remained unchanged for a long time. The 1,064-cc engine received strengthened pushrods and a new Magneti-Marelli multipoint ignition, along with 40-mm throttle valves

California EV	
Production Period:	1997-1999
Engine:	V-twin OHV/2 V
Displacement:	1,064 cc
Bore x Stroke:	92 x 80 mm
Compression:	9.8:1
Power output:	75 hp at 6,400 rpm
Mixture preparation:	Weber-Marelli, d=40 mm
Clutch:	double plate
Gearbox:	5 speeds
Frame:	steel tube cradle
Wheelbase:	1560 mm
Front suspension:	Marzocchi 45-mm telescopic fork
Rear suspension:	swing arm with two hydraulic shock absorbers
Front tire:	110/90-18
Rear tire:	140/80-17
Front brake:	twin disc, 320 mm
Rear brake:	disc, 282 mm
Empty weight:	270 kg (fueled)
Tank capacity:	19 liters
Maximum speed:	185 kph

Brochure for the California EV: when unveiled in 1997, this model marked the apex of development of the California series.

for the fuel injection system. The chassis also impressed, with two 320-mm brake discs up front with four-piston calipers. A Bosch-made pressure regulator was also part of the braking system, distributing braking forces as required and taking Guzzi's integral braking system into a new era. Also new were the 45-mm Marzocchi fork and the WP shock absorbers in the back.

The base EV was placed alongside the California Touring. It came with windscreen and watertight side bags as standard equipment, and had small arched leg shields on the standard roll bars. This version formed the basis of the EV 80, a special model with leather-covered bags and a burgundy-red seat released to mark the company's 80th anniversary, in 2001.

California Jackal 1999

The Jackal, introduced in 1999, was technically a very normal California but without some of its characteristic features. It was, so to speak, the naked bike among the cruisers from Mandello. Its uncluttered, simple, and harmonious lines were also reflected in its price, as the Jackal cost less than a standard California when it was introduced. With more than forty different available accessories, this could change quickly, upgrading the naked bike until it was unrecognizable. The paint, a shiny metallic titanium gray, underlined its archaic charisma.

The naked Jackal was very comfortable in the corners. It had an outstanding chassis and suspension, however it was less comfortable for a passenger.

California Jackal

Production Period:	1999
Engine:	V-twin OHV/2 V
Displacement:	1,064 cc
Bore x Stroke:	92 x 80 mm
Compression:	9.5:1
Power output:	75 hp at 6,400 rpm
Mixture preparation:	Magneti-Marelli injection
Clutch:	double plate
Gearbox:	5 speeds
Frame:	steel tube cradle
Wheelbase:	1575 mm
Front suspension:	telescopic fork
Rear suspension:	double swing arm, twin shocks
Front tire:	110/90-VB18
Rear tire:	150/80-VB17
Front brake:	dual disc, 320 mm
Rear brake:	disc, 282 mm
Empty weight:	246 kg (fueled)
Tank capacity:	19 liters
Maximum speed:	185 kph

The Jackal was free of all the ballast carried around by the other California models.

California Stone 2001 – 03

Derived from the California, the Stone (like its sisters) was based heavily on the first Jackal models. One significant difference from the Jackal was that the Stone had just one disc up front. This California derivative also had to do without the integral braking system. Equipment of the base model was spartan, and the instrumentation consisted of just a speedometer and a number of warning lights. Only the tank varied from the predominant color, gray.

California Stone	
Production Period:	from 2001
Engine:	V-twin OHV/2 V
Displacement:	1,064 cc
Bore x Stroke:	92 x 80 mm
Compression:	9.5:1
Power output:	75 hp at 7,000 rpm
Mixture preparation:	Weber-Marelli, d=40 mm
Clutch:	double plate dry clutch
Gearbox:	5 speeds
Frame:	steel tube cradle
Wheelbase:	1560 mm
Front suspension:	telescopic fork, non-adjustable
Rear suspension:	double swing arm, spring preload
Front tire:	110/90-VB18
Rear tire:	140/80-VB17
Front brake:	single disc, 320 mm
Rear brake:	disc, 282 mm
Empty weight:	260 kg (fueled)/Touring 280 kg
Tank capacity:	19 liters
Maximum speed:	185 kph

The Stone Metal version had a one-piece double seat, a chrome tank, and shocks with adjustable rebound damping. A wide range of accessories soon became available for the Stone, resulting in the appearance of the Stone Touring variants with bags and a low touring windscreen.

The Stone was simply equipped, like the Jackal.

A few accessories turned the Stone into the Stone Touring.

California Special/ California Sport/ California Sport Aluminum 1998-2003

Visually, the Special series resembled the Jackal models, but seen technically it was more like an EV, the successor of the California touring machine. While it looked a stripped-down EV, it did not have less equipment, only different. The low fender in the rear is noticeable, a replacement for the large chrome side racks of the EV. Instrumentation is also identical to that of the EV, as are the double discs in front and the integral brakes. One big difference is the footrests, like those of the earlier Jackal and later Stone series. The Special Sport shared the non-adjustable fork with the Stone. The Special Sport Aluminum had short, straight handlebars. The gold anodized valve covers provided a color accent, otherwise everything was aluminum or chrome.

California Special	
Production Period:	Special from 1998; Special Sport 2001-2003
Engine:	V-twin OHV/2 V
Displacement:	1,064 cc
Bore x Stroke:	92 x 80 mm
Compression:	9.5:1
Power output:	75 hp at 6,400 rpm
Mixture preparation:	Weber-Marelli, d=40 mm
Clutch:	double plate
Gearbox:	5 speeds
Frame:	steel tube cradle
Wheelbase:	1560 mm
Front suspension:	telescopic fork, non-adjustable
Rear suspension:	double swing arm, spring preload
Front tire:	110/90-18
Rear tire:	150/80-17
Front brake:	twin disc, 320 mm
Rear brake:	disc, 282 mm
Empty weight:	270 kg (fueled)
Tank capacity:	19 liters
Maximum speed:	185 kph

California Titanium/ Aluminum from 2003

Seen technically, these two models, unveiled in 2003, were the successors of the Special Sport Aluminum. The only difference, apart from the exclusive color of the titanium, was a small front wind deflector. In 2006 the two models were replaced by the Vintage and the Classic, whose opulent shapes were reminiscent of the first Californias.

California Titanium/Aluminum

Production Period:	from 2003
Engine:	V-twin OHV/2 V
Displacement:	1,064 cc
Bore x Stroke:	92 x 80 mm
Compression:	9.8:1
Power output:	75 hp at 7,000 rpm
Mixture preparation:	Weber-Marelli, d=40 mm
Clutch:	double plate dry
Gearbox:	5 speeds
Frame:	steel tube cradle
Wheelbase:	1560 mm
Front suspension:	telescopic fork, adjustable
Rear suspension:	double swing arm, spring preload
Front tire:	110/90-VB 18
Rear tire:	140/80-VB 17
Front brake:	twin disc, 320 mm
Rear brake:	disc, 282 mm
Empty weight:	255 kg (fueled)
Tank capacity:	19 liters
Maximum speed:	185 kph

California Classic/Vintage

Production Period:	from 2006
Engine:	V-twin OHV/2 V
Displacement:	1,064 cc
Bore x Stroke:	92 x 80 mm
Compression:	9.8:1
Power output:	54 kW at 6,400 rpm
Mixture preparation:	Magneti-Marelli IAW, 2 x 40 mm
Clutch:	double plate dry
Gearbox:	5 speeds, shaft drive
Frame:	steel tube cradle
Wheelbase:	1560 mm
Front suspension:	45-mm telescopic fork
Rear suspension:	double swing arm, twin shocks
Front tire:	110/90-VB 18
Rear tire:	150/70-VB 17
Front brake:	2 x 320 mm
Rear brake:	disc, 282 mm floating discs, 4 piston calipers
Empty weight:	251/263 kg dry
Tank capacity:	19 liters
Maximum speed:	180 kph

The Titanium and the Aluminum differed from the earlier Sport Special Aluminum mainly because of their exclusive paint schemes.

California Classic/Vintage from 2006

Here it is again: the classic California with the technology of 2006. It has all the styling elements of the 1970s, and all that powered by the 1064-cc engine, but with the latest technical aids and important modifications to the interior of the engine. So, apart from the usual modifications of every motorcycle generation – lighter and more powerful – the ratio between the stroke and the length of the connecting rods has been changed. This is fine work of the kind that would have pleased company co-founder Carlo Guzzi. The addition of a regulated catalytic converter enabled it to meet Euro 3 standards, even though the engine is still air-cooled. The lubrication system was optimized with the technology of the Breva engine, and despite its archaic look this is a very modern motorcycle. The Vintage model emphasizes the classic character of these two models very clearly and its design is almost identical to that of the first motorcycles delivered to the Los Angeles Police Department. From a distance, the illusion is perfect. The bags, the tall windscreen, and the high handlebars almost let the rider smell the palm trees in the California background.

It's back: the classic California. Both its components and color were strongly reminiscent of the beloved 850 T3 California.

A whopper of a motorcycle: although the machine looks massive resting on its stand, the big Guzzi handles itself well in the corners.

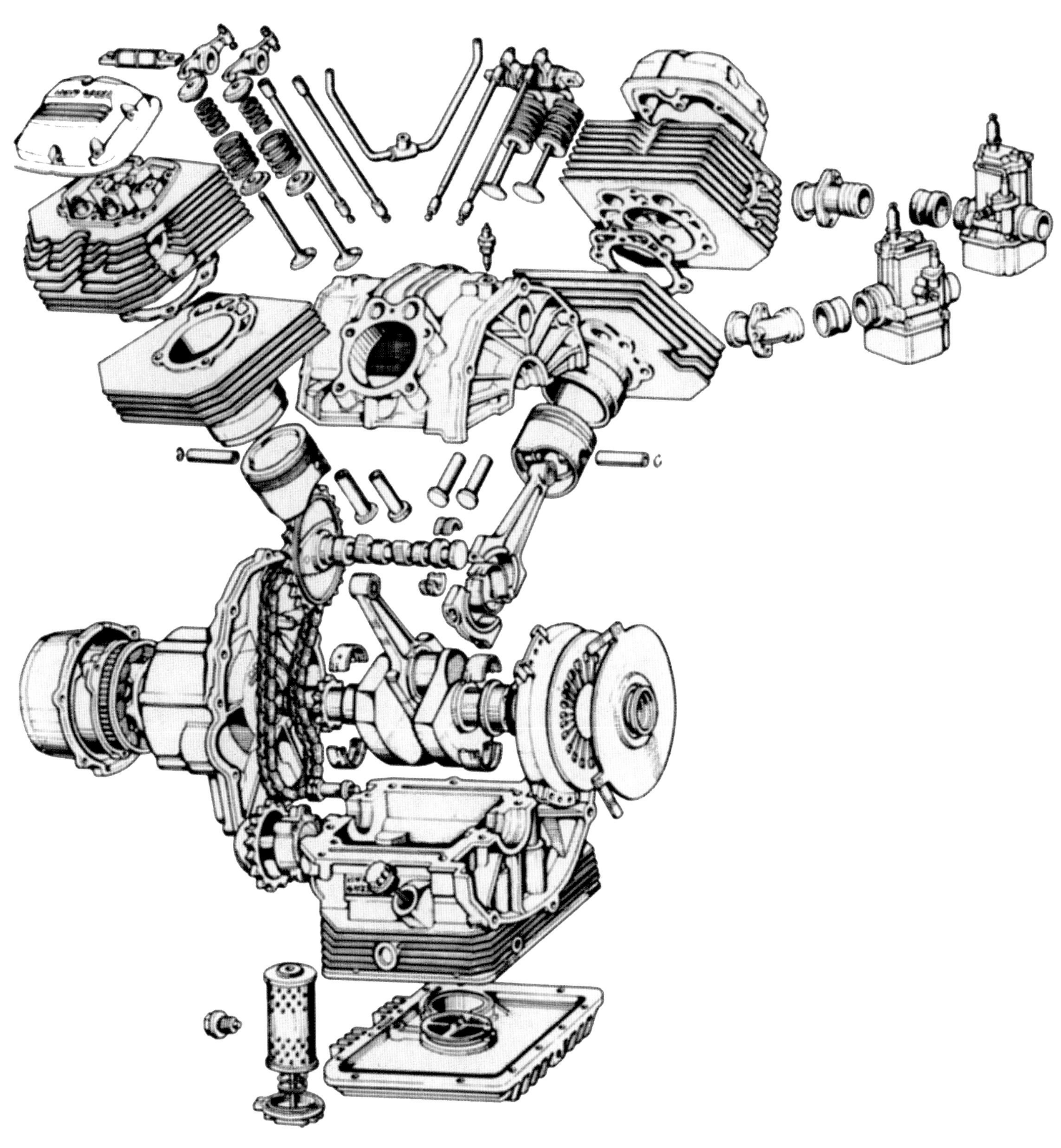

The Smaller Variants

V 35, II, III 1978 – 87

The V 35 was unveiled along with the V 50 in the autumn of 1976. Both were completely new designs. New Italian regulations introduced soon after its introduction placed 500s out of reach of young riders, which helped the V 35 achieve greater popularity. Although its general layout was similar to that of the larger machine, there were significant differences: the crankcase was split horizontally, the swing arm was mounted on the transmission case and was also cast aluminum. The versions II (1979) and III (1985) had several modifications, including nikasil-coated cylinders. The III differed from its predecessors mainly in appearance. The V 35 GT, Custom, Florida and Nevada, none of which were offered in Germany, were technically identical to the V 35 but with different tires. There were also the TT and NTZ off-road versions, plus the sporty Imola and Imola II.

V 35, II, III	
Production Period:	1978-1987
Engine:	2-cyl., OHV/twin valves
Displacement:	346 cc
Bore x Stroke:	66 x 50.6 mm
Compression:	10.8:1
Power output:	27 hp at 7,600 rpm
Mixture preparation:	electronic (later points), 2 x Dell'Orto VHB 24
Clutch:	dry clutch
Gearbox:	5 speeds
Frame:	steel tube
Wheelbase:	1410 mm
Front suspension:	telescopic fork
Rear suspension:	aluminum swing arm, 2 shock absorbers
Front tire:	3.00 18, 90/90-18, 100/90-16
Rear tire:	3.25 18, 100/90-18, 110/80-18
Front brake:	double disc
Rear brake:	disc
Empty weight:	175 kg (fueled)
Tank capacity:	16 liters
Maximum speed:	150 kph

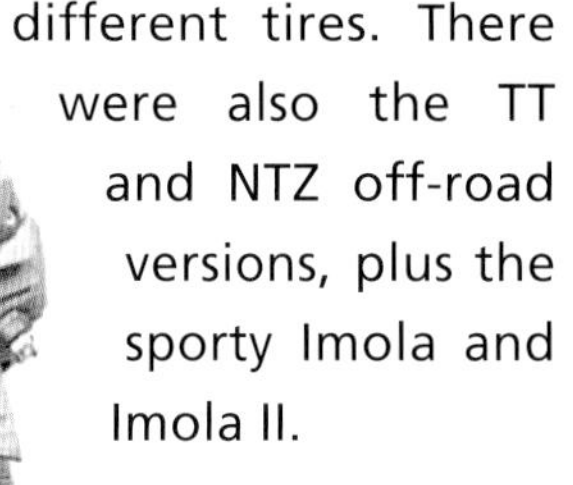

The outstanding technical feature of the small V models is the cast aluminum swing arm mounted on the transmission case. This greatly simplified removal of the engine.

V 50, II, III 1978 – 83

The larger version of the V 35 was called the V 50 and, apart from the stroke, it shared the same engine. The second (1979) and third (1981) versions had many technical improvements, such as nikasil-coated cylinders, a larger oil pan, a duplex chain for the valve train, and larger valves. The fork was given air support. The half-liter V models were only offered in Germany until 1983, as competition from the company's 650 was too strong.

V 50, II, III

Production Period:	1978-1979, 1980-1981, 1981-1983
Engine:	2-cyl., OHV/twin valves
Displacement:	490 cc
Bore x Stroke:	74 x 57 mm
Compression:	10.8:1, 10.4:1
Power output:	45 hp at 7,500 rpm, 49 hp at 7.600 rpm
Mixture preparation:	2 x Dell'Orto VHB 24, electric ignition, later points
Clutch:	dry clutch
Gearbox:	5 speeds
Frame:	steel tube
Wheelbase:	1410 mm
Front suspension:	telescopic fork
Rear suspension:	aluminum swing arm, 2 shock absorbers
Front tire:	3.00S18, 90/90S18
Rear tire:	3.50S18, 100/90S18
Front brake:	double disc
Rear brake:	disc
Empty weight:	183 kg (fueled)
Tank capacity:	16 liters
Maximum speed:	165 kph

V 50 Monza 1981 – 84

The V 50 underwent its first model upgrade and became the V 50 II when the Monza sport model appeared. The Monza shared the parts needed for sport use, such as the tank, fairing and seat, with the smaller V 35 Imola. Like the other V 50 models, the Monza was offered in Germany only until 1983.

V 50 Monza

Production Period:	1981-1984
Engine:	2-cyl., OHV/twin valves
Displacement:	490 cc
Bore x Stroke:	74 x 57 mm
Compression:	10.4:1
Power output:	45 hp at 7,500 rpm, 49 hp at 7.600 rpm
Mixture preparation:	2 x Dell'Orto carbs, points
Clutch:	dry clutch
Gearbox:	5 speeds
Frame:	steel tube
Wheelbase:	1420 mm
Front suspension:	telescopic fork
Rear suspension:	aluminum swing arm, 2 shock absorbers
Front tire:	3.25S18, 90/90S18
Rear tire:	3.50S18, 100/90S18
Front brake:	double disc
Rear brake:	disc
Empty weight:	174 kg (fueled)
Tank capacity:	16 liters
Maximum speed:	175 kph

V 50 Custom 1982 – 86

With its high handlebars and stepped seat, the Custom followed Moto Guzzi's policy of offering entire families of motorcycles instead of single machines: Normale, Custom and Sportiva models of each motorcycle would be offered. Over the years, however, it was found that the normal version usually lacked popularity and was therefore dropped. The machines themselves were largely identical technically; in the case of the Custom the only difference was the lengthened swing arm compared to those on the other V 50s. It had become necessary to accommodate the fat rear tire – a necessity on a chopper.

V 50 Custom	
Production Period:	1982-1986
Engine:	2-cyl., OHV/twin valves
Displacement:	490 cc
Bore x Stroke:	74 x 57 mm
Compression:	10.4:1
Power output:	49 hp at 7.600 rpm
Mixture preparation:	2 x Dell'Orto VHB 24, points
Clutch:	dry clutch
Gearbox:	5 speeds
Frame:	steel tube
Wheelbase:	1460 mm
Front suspension:	telescopic fork
Rear suspension:	aluminum swing arm, 2 shock absorbers
Front tire:	100/90-18
Rear tire:	130/90-16
Front brake:	double disc
Rear brake:	disc
Empty weight:	192 kg (fueled)
Tank capacity:	16 liters
Maximum speed:	151 kph

The look of the V50 C fit in well with the cruiser style of the 1980s. Though not to everyone's taste, it sold better than the standard version.

V 65, SP, GT 1981 – 87

When the V 65 appeared in 1981, all it had in common with the V 50 was its frame. The engine, for example, was larger in all aspects – including the carburetor – and the gear ratios in the transmission were appropriate for the larger displacement. The forks were supported by the bridges of the Le Mans, and the swing arm was lengthened. The damping elements of the fork legs were interconnected. The fully-faired SP appeared at the same time. Apart from the fairing and the modified seating position, it was identical to the V 65 Normale. The third version, the GT, arrived in 1988 along with the V 35 GT and the Mille GT. Improvements included electronic ignition and the somewhat longer fork.

V 65, SP, GT	
Production Period:	1981-1987 (GT: 1988)
Engine:	2-cyl., OHV/twin valves
Displacement:	644 cc
Bore x Stroke:	80 x 64 mm
Compression:	10:1
Power output:	52 hp at 7,050 rpm
Mixture preparation:	2 x Dell'Orto PHBH 30, points
Clutch:	dry clutch
Gearbox:	5 speeds
Frame:	steel tube
Wheelbase:	1440 mm
Front suspension:	telescopic fork
Rear suspension:	aluminum swing arm, 2 shock absorbers (Paioli)
Front tire:	100/90H18
Rear tire:	110/90H18
Front brake:	double disc, 260 mm
Rear brake:	disc, 235 mm
Empty weight:	173 kg (SP 178 kg, GT 165 kg) (fueled)
Tank capacity:	15.5 liters
Maximum speed:	175 kph

The V65 SP is a wonderful mid-class tourer with low weight, excellent engine performance and outstanding protection against wind and weather.

V 65 Custom, Florida 1983 – 92

The Florida was the first custom variant of this series to arrive in Germany, in 1986. The first Custom with the 650 engine, which was not offered in Germany, was built from 1983 to 1986, and apart from its engine it resembled the V 50 Custom. The new Florida, however, was outfitted with numerous optical gimmicks and went more in the direction of the later California models. It was available in Germany until 1992.

V 65 Custom	
Production Period:	1983, 1986, 1986-1992
Engine:	2-cyl., OHV/twin valves
Displacement:	644 cc
Bore x Stroke:	80 x 64 mm
Compression:	9.1:1
Power output:	48 hp at 7,500 rpm (also 27 hp at 5,200 rpm)
Mixture preparation:	2 x Dell'Orto PHBH 30, electronic ignition
Clutch:	dry clutch
Gearbox:	5 speeds
Frame:	steel tube
Wheelbase:	1470 mm
Front suspension:	telescopic fork
Rear suspension:	double swing arm, 2 shock absorbers
Front tire:	100/90V18
Rear tire:	130/90V16
Front brake:	double disc, 260 mm
Rear brake:	disc, 260 mm
Empty weight:	197 kg (fueled)
Tank capacity:	15 liters
Maximum speed:	152 kph (27 hp: 125 kph)

The V65 Florida comes with many eye-catching features and was sold in Germany until 1991.

V 65 Lario 1983 – 89

The Lario was unveiled in 1983, along with the four-valve Imola, and its technology also gave legs to the 650 V-twin engine. Visually, it closely resembled – rightly – the Le Mans III, apart from its 16-inch wheels. Despite its capabilities and performance, the Lario always remained in the shadow of the Le Mans and was also made at a time when the company was mired in a serious crisis. In 1980 it was replaced by the 750 Targa. The Lario was only sold in Germany until 1985.

V 65 Lario	
Production Period:	1983-1989
Engine:	2-cyl., OHV/twin valves
Displacement:	644 cc
Bore x Stroke:	80 x 64 mm
Compression:	10.3:1
Power output:	60 hp at 7,800 rpm
Mixture preparation:	2 x Dell'Orto PHBH 30, 2 points
Clutch:	dry clutch
Gearbox:	5 speeds
Frame:	steel tube
Wheelbase:	1455 mm
Front suspension:	telescopic fork
Rear suspension:	aluminum swing arm, 2 shock absorbers
Front tire:	100/90V16
Rear tire:	110/90V16
Front brake:	double disc, 270 mm
Rear brake:	disc, 235 mm
Empty weight:	199 kg (fueled)
Tank capacity:	18 liters
Maximum speed:	180 kph

The V65 Lario is a very pretty thing. Unfortunately, the valves sometimes stick in the guides.

V 65 TT, 650 NTX 1984 – 86

Moto Guzzi did not remain untouched by the off-road wave, which also affected the 650 series. The V 65 TT, or *Tutto Terrano*, had the same specifications as the V 35 TT. Compared to the Normale, this was reflected in the shorter final gear ratio, the strengthened frame, and the suspension with all-terrain spring travels. A typical feature of the TT was the absence of the integral braking system. The V 65 TT was built for two years and imported into Germany before it was replaced by the 650 NTX in 1987. Almost identical in design, it differed mainly in having a much larger tank with integrated fairing and black-painted power plant.

V 65 TT, 650 NTX	
Production Period:	1984-1986, 1986
Engine:	2-cyl., OHV/twin valves
Displacement:	644 cc
Bore x Stroke:	80 x 64 mm
Compression:	9.8:1
Power output:	45 hp at 7,500 rpm
Mixture preparation:	2 x Dell'Orto PHBH 30, electronic ignition
Clutch:	dry clutch
Gearbox:	5 speeds
Frame:	steel tube
Wheelbase:	1455 mm
Front suspension:	telescopic fork
Rear suspension:	double swing arm, 2 shock absorbers
Front tire:	3.00-21
Rear tire:	4.00-18
Front brake:	disc, 260 mm
Rear brake:	disc, 260 mm
Empty weight:	184 kg, 200 kg (fueled)
Tank capacity:	14 liters, 32 liters
Maximum speed:	160 kph, 170 kph

The V65 TT (left) was only made for two years and then replaced by the 650 NTX (above). The main difference was the fairing.

750 NTX 1987

The concept of the 650 NTX, combined with the 750-cc V-twin engine, led to the largest Enduro from Mandello to date. The big NTX was distinguished by its large fairing, which extended to beneath the engine. The 750 Enduro, with its twin-valve engine, had little success on the market, however. In Italy it was widely used as a police motorcycle.

V 75 1985 – 86

When the V 75 was unveiled in Germany in 1986, customers could chose between 27, 50 or 59-hp versions. The new four-valve bike shared the layout of the V 65 Lario but with a new suspension, including a 16-inch front wheel and an 18-inch rear wheel. The basic model didn't remain long in the program, however the SP, which was derived from it, continued in production until the mid-1990s.

750 NTX	
Production Period:	1985-1986
Engine:	2-cyl., OHV/twin valves
Displacement:	744 cc
Bore x Stroke:	80 x 74 mm
Compression:	10:1
Power output:	50, 59 hp at 6,400, 7.300 rpm
Mixture preparation:	2 x Dell'Orto PHBH 30, Bosch electronic ignition
Clutch:	dry clutch
Gearbox:	5 speeds
Frame:	steel tube
Wheelbase:	1470 mm
Front suspension:	telescopic fork
Rear suspension:	double swing arm, 2 shock absorbers
Front tire:	3.00-21
Rear tire:	4.00-18
Front brake:	disc, 260 mm
Rear brake:	disc, 260 mm
Empty weight:	200 kg (fueled)
Tank capacity:	32 liters
Maximum speed:	170 kph

V 75	
Production Period:	1985-1986
Engine:	2-cyl., OHV/four valves
Displacement:	744 cc
Bore x Stroke:	80 x 74 mm
Compression:	10:1
Power output:	27, 50, 59 hp at 4,600, 6,400, 7.300 rpm
Mixture preparation:	2 x Dell'Orto PHBH 30, Bosch electronic ignition
Clutch:	dry clutch
Gearbox:	5 speeds
Frame:	steel tube
Wheelbase:	1470 mm
Front suspension:	telescopic fork
Rear suspension:	double swing arm, 2 shock absorbers
Front tire:	100/90V16
Rear tire:	120/80H18
Front brake:	double disc
Rear brake:	disc
Empty weight:	200 kg (fueled)
Tank capacity:	17 liters
Maximum speed:	138, 175, 188 kph

Nevada 750 1989 – 03

Of the four models with the 750-cc engine, only the Nevada survived into the new century. The 750 Targa had the optics of the Le Mans IV; on the other hand the 750 Strada (1994-1996) had the technology of the first V 75, but with the twin-valve engine and larger wheels. The similarity with the bigger Strada was unmistakable. The 750 SP (1989-1996) was hidden behind a large fairing in the style of the big Spada. It reached 170 kph and had 110/90-18 and 120/80-18 tires. The small SP always suffered from in-house competition and was not a sales success. The Targa (1991-1992) was much loved in the press but it received a lukewarm reception from buyers. The true survival artist, however, proved to be the cruiser variant, the Nevada. For a long time it seemed to have been forgotten and in 1990 the German importer dropped it from the program. But it came back. The growing popularity of cruiser models helped give the economical model a second chance in Germany at the end of the 1990s. Meanwhile, the Nevada had undergone several facelifts and variants, including the Nevada Club 750 with a different seat and a large selection of colors. The motorcycle's technology had also been carefully modernized over time.

Nevada 750	
Production Period:	1989-2003
Engine:	2-cyl., OHV/four valves
Displacement:	744 cc
Bore x Stroke:	88 x 74 mm
Compression:	9.6:1
Power output:	49 hp at 6,200 rpm (27 hp at 5,800 rpm
Mixture preparation:	2 x Dell'Orto PHBH 30, Motoplat electronics
Clutch:	dry clutch
Gearbox:	5 speeds
Frame:	steel tube
Wheelbase:	1505 mm
Front suspension:	telescopic fork, 38 mm
Rear suspension:	double swing arm, 2 shock absorbers
Front tire:	100/90V18
Rear tire:	130/90H16
Front brake:	double disc, 270 mm
Rear brake:	disc, 260 mm
Empty weight:	197 kg (fueled)
Tank capacity:	16 liters
Maximum speed:	165 kph

The cruiser variant, the Nevada, turned out to be a real survival artist.

The Targa, the SP and the Strada were not particularly successful models.

In Italy there was also a 350 version of the Nevada, however it was not available in Germany.

750 I.E. Nevada Classic from 2004

That the Nevada name was not allowed to disappear from the model palette is clear – with more than 35,000 examples built, from the Custom V35/50 to the Nevada Club 2003, it was a very popular story. When the manufacturer revised the popular Nevada in 2004, it did not stop at a mere facelift. The basis of the new design was the Breva, which had earned praise from the press for its handling. The engine and entire drive train formed the basis of the new Nevada, along with the Breva's chassis. The rest of the 441 parts were designed in keeping with the cruiser concept, though with fewer cruiser features than usual. The rider's seating position was upright and visually it was more similar to a "normal" motorcycle. With 53 Newton-meters of torque (39 foot-pounds) at 3,600 rpm, the Nevada was no slowpoke. Fuel injection made possible the use of a three-way catalytic converter.

750 I.E. Nevada Classic	
Production Period:	from 2004
Engine:	2-cyl., OHV/four valves
Displacement:	744 cc
Bore x Stroke:	80 x 74 mm
Compression:	9.6:1
Power output:	48 hp (35 kW) at 6,800 rpm
Mixture preparation:	electronic fuel injection
Clutch:	single-plate dry clutch
Gearbox:	5 speeds
Frame:	steel tube cradle
Wheelbase:	1467 mm
Front suspension:	telescopic fork
Rear suspension:	double swing arm, 2 shock absorbers
Front tire:	100/90-18
Rear tire:	130/90-16
Front brake:	disc, 320 mm
Rear brake:	disc, 260 mm
Empty weight:	184 kg
Tank capacity:	14 liters
Maximum speed:	approx. 160 kph

Breva V 750 I.E. from 2003

Newly introduced for the 2003 season, the Breva represented a new approach for Moto Guzzi. With its modern chassis and its small, newly developed engine, it deviated clearly from the company's previous philosophy. And it rode that way too – light, maneuverable and with bite. Despite its small dimensions, there was even a comfortable place for a passenger. The engine doesn't quite produce 50 horsepower, but at least it is all there. Power is developed over a broad rpm range, usually a feature of the bigger engines. Technically, the twin-cylinder is very modern and, of course, is equipped with a three-way catalytic converter.

Breva V 750 IE	
Production Period:	from 2003
Engine:	2-cyl., OHV/four valves
Displacement:	744 cc
Bore x Stroke:	80 x 74 mm
Compression:	9.6:1
Power output:	48 hp at 6,800 rpm
Mixture preparation:	Weber-Marelli
Clutch:	single-plate dry clutch
Gearbox:	5 speeds
Frame:	steel tube cradle
Wheelbase:	1449 mm
Front suspension:	telescopic fork
Rear suspension:	aluminum double swing arm
Front tire:	110/70-17
Rear tire:	130/80-17
Front brake:	double disc, 260 mm
Rear brake:	disc, 260 mm
Empty weight:	182 kg (fueled)
Tank capacity:	approx. 18 liters
Maximum speed:	175 kph

The Breva's small windscreen provided amazingly good protection against the airflow.

The styling of the Breva is not really exciting.

Available Guzzi accessories include the bags with top case shown here.

V7 Ippogrifo

The *Ippogrifo*, which owes its name to the mythical beast the Hippogryph (half horse, half eagle), is a motorcycle that never made it to the market but was often displayed. Designed in accordance with the popular street fighter concept, its 750-cc power plant was originally designed as a lightweight engine for aircraft. Despite its rather modest 58 hp, the engine propels the machine to almost 200 kph. Among the technical innovations of this design study are its torque-supported swing arm with the shock absorber on the right and a 6-speed gearbox. This was apparently not enough, however, to excite the enthusiasm of the motorcycle community.

A real eye-catcher, shown many times to the press and public, but never in production: the V7 Ippogrifo.

MOTO GUZZI S.p.A.
Via E. V. Parodi, 57
Mandello del Lario
LECCO (Italy)
Tel. +39 341 709111
Fax +39 341 709220

MOTO GUZZI

MOTO GUZZI FLASH

DIE NEUE
V7 IPPOGRIFO

NOUVELLE
V7 IPPOGRIFO

Ein aus dem Flugzeugbau abgeleiteter Motor für die neue Guzzi, deren Name an das Fabeltier Hippogryph - halb Adler, halb Pferd - erinnert.

Un moteur provenant de l'aéronautique pour la nouvelle Guzzi, qui prend le nom italien de cet animal légendaire, l'hippogriffe, mi-aigle, mi-cheval.

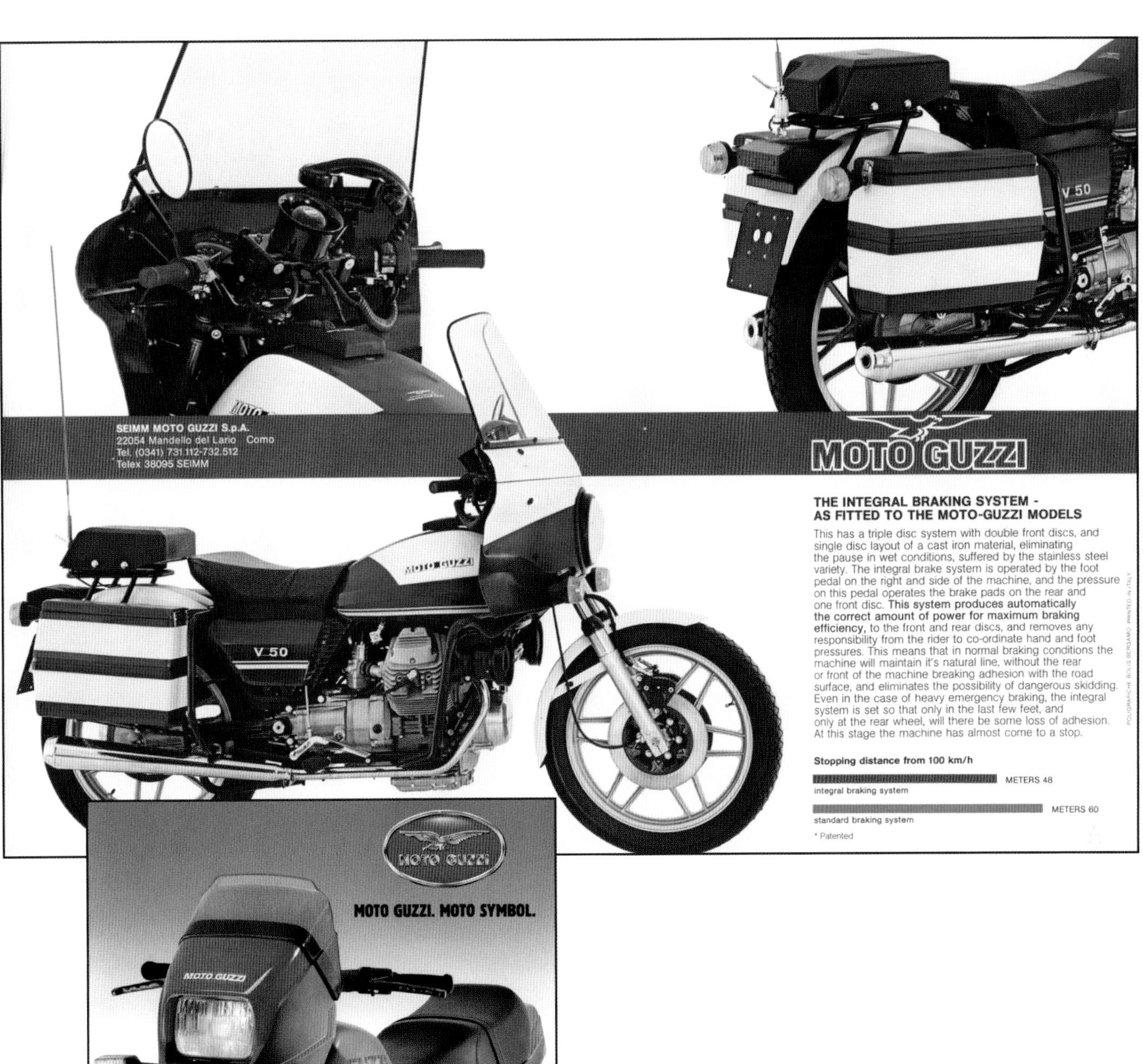

SEIMM MOTO GUZZI S.p.A.
22054 Mandello del Lario Como
Tel. (0341) 731.112-732.512
Telex 38095 SEIMM

MOTO GUZZI

THE INTEGRAL BRAKING SYSTEM - AS FITTED TO THE MOTO-GUZZI MODELS

This has a triple disc system with double front discs, and single disc layout of a cast iron material, eliminating the pause in wet conditions, suffered by the stainless steel variety. The integral brake system is operated by the foot pedal on the right and side of the machine, and the pressure on this pedal operates the brake pads on the rear and one front disc. **This system produces automatically the correct amount of power for maximum braking efficiency,** to the front and rear discs, and removes any responsibility from the rider to co-ordinate hand and foot pressures. This means that in normal braking conditions the machine will maintain it's natural line, without the rear or front of the machine breaking adhesion with the road surface, and eliminates the possibility of dangerous skidding. Even in the case of heavy emergency braking, the integral system is set so that only in the last few feet, and only at the rear wheel, will there be some loss of adhesion. At this stage the machine has almost come to a stop.

Stopping distance from 100 km/h

METERS 48
integral braking system

METERS 60
standard braking system

* Patented

POLIGRAFICHE BOLIS BERGAMO PRINTED IN ITALY

Moto Guzzi produced motorcycles based on the smaller V engines with typical police equipment.

V7 Special from 2008

A sensation in autumn 2007; a petite motorcycle was unveiled at the Milan show that had all the lines of a V7 Sport. It was called the V7 Special and was supposed to rekindle memories of its Guzzi ancestors from the 1960s. Flat seat, classic S tank, spoked wheels, triangular side covers – it could hardly be more classic. The new V7 Special is powered by the small V-twin that is found in the current 750 Breva. The flat seat promises comfort, even for two grown men.

V7 Special	
Production Period:	from 2008
Engine:	2-cyl., OHV/four valves
Displacement:	744 cc
Bore x Stroke:	80 x 74 mm
Compression:	9.6:1
Power output:	48 hp at 6,800 rpm
Mixture preparation:	Weber-Marelli injection
Clutch:	single-plate dry clutch
Gearbox:	5 speeds
Frame:	double cradle
Wheelbase:	1449 mm
Front suspension:	telescopic fork
Rear suspension:	aluminum double swing arm
Front tire:	110/70-17
Rear tire:	130/80-17
Front brake:	disc, 320 mm
Rear brake:	disc, 260 mm
Empty weight:	182 kg
Tank capacity:	approx. 22 liters
Maximum speed:	175 kph

From almost every angle, the new Special reminds the viewer of the V7 Sport of the early 1970s.

Step into the Future

Daytona 1000 1991 – 95

When the Daytona entered production in autumn 1991, it marked the beginning of a new era in the construction of large twin-cylinder motorcycles by Moto Guzzi. Its engine and chassis were based on those of the racing prototype by the already almost legendary Doctor John, a dentist and racing enthusiast who had established himself as a product developer for Moto Guzzi. Let us briefly look at this four-valve machine in detail. It was the first production Guzzi to have a bore greater than 90 millimeters. This gave a displacement of exactly 992 cubic centimeters, about 50 cc more than the company's pervious Thousands.

The camshaft moved from the depths of the crankcase up to the cylinder head. The twin camshafts are not directly over the combustion chambers, consequently it cannot be called an overhead camshaft engine. Mechanical engineers call the arrangement selected by Todero a CIH, or cam in head, arrangement. Todero also developed an OHC version, which got as far as the test bench. Its cylinder heads were clearly too wide, however, and in any case this option was too expensive.

Dr. John Wittner's racing machine (top left) is clearly recognizable as the inspiration for the first Daytona prototypes (above). The production version (left and top), however, displays clearly more modern styling.

Daytona 1000

Production Period:	1991-1995
Engine:	2-cyl., CIH/four valves
Displacement:	992 cc
Bore x Stroke:	90 x 78 mm
Compression:	10:1
Power output:	93 hp (68 kW) at 8,000 rpm
Mixture preparation:	Weber-Marelli ignition-injection system
Clutch:	double-plate dry clutch
Gearbox:	5 speeds
Frame:	central tube frame of chrome-molybdenum
Wheelbase:	1480 mm
Front suspension:	Marzocchi telescopic fork, 41 mm
Rear suspension:	cantilever swing arm, torque support, Koni shocks
Front tire:	120/70 ZR 17
Rear tire:	160/60 ZR 18
Front brake:	double disc, 300 mm, floating
Rear brake:	disc, 260 mm, fixed
Empty weight:	240 kg (fueled)
Tank capacity:	23 liters
Maximum speed:	224 kph

The two camshafts are driven by two toothed belts. These rotate below on a pulley that sits on the end of an intermediate shaft, which is located where the camshaft used to be. The two camshafts of the Daytona engine each operate four valves per cylinder by way of short mushroom tappets and rocker arms with adjusting screws.

A Weber-Marelli system takes care of ignition and fuel injection. The lower engine casing is largely unchanged. The same applies to the gearbox, although the flywheel is lighter.

The chassis: central tube with attached aluminum side plates which also serve as swing arm mounts, cantilever swing arms with a horizontal central shock absorber and torque support on the shaft drive. In principle this chassis later became the model for the chassis of all of the V10 and V11 models covered later in this chapter and also for the two Sport variants.

No Japanese superbike, but a motorcycle that is very comfortable to ride on country roads: the Daytona is no bike for racetrack competition.

Daytona RS 1996

After four years in production, the Daytona changed in the direction of the recently introduced 1100 Sport, with the pointed seat being the most obvious feature. Other changes included the enclosed swing arm mount behind the gearbox and the oil cooler in front of the engine. In short: Guzzi had jazzed up the entire machine, but in doing so moved its flagship very close to the 1100 Sport. The technical changes included an upside-down fork from White Power, a larger and more effective front brake (from the 1100 Sport) and increased engine power (102 hp).

Daytona RS	
Production Period:	1996
Engine:	2-cyl., CIH/four valves
Displacement:	992 cc
Bore x Stroke:	90 x 78 mm
Compression:	10.5:1
Power output:	102 hp (75 kW) at 8,400 rpm
Mixture preparation:	Weber-Marelli Alfa-N
Clutch:	double-plate dry clutch
Gearbox:	5 speeds
Frame:	central tube frame of chrome-molybdenum
Wheelbase:	1475 mm
Front suspension:	White Power telescopic fork
Rear suspension:	cantilever swing arm, torque support
Front tire:	120/70 ZR 17
Rear tire:	160/60 ZR 18
Front brake:	double disc, 320 mm, floating
Rear brake:	disc, 282 mm
Empty weight:	223 kg (fueled)
Tank capacity:	19 liters
Maximum speed:	240 kph

Thanks to its slim rear end, the Daytona RS is more attractive than its predecessor. Engine performance is only slightly enhanced at 102 hp, but the WS fork improves handling.

Sport 1100 1994 – 96

Introduced in 1994, the 1100 Sport had increased in displacement thanks to the venerable twin-valve engine of the California. Its chassis was identical to that of the first version of the Daytona 1000, however it had larger brake discs in front (320 mm) and a narrower frame tail. The Sport was designed for the less demanding Guzzi customers, for whom the Daytona was too expensive. Nevertheless, the Sport – despite twin-valve technology and mixture preparation by carburetor – was hardly cheaper than the Daytona. Most customers however liked the look of the Sport much better than the Daytona. The new seat and the tank, which was four liters smaller, gave the Sport a much more modern look. For purists, the two Dell'Orto carburetors were also an important factor in deciding on a Sport.

V1100 Sport	
Production Period:	1994 - 1996
Engine:	2-cyl., OHV, twin valves
Displacement:	1064 cc
Bore x Stroke:	92 x 80 mm
Compression:	10.5:1
Power output:	90 hp (66 kW) at 7,800 rpm
Mixture preparation:	2 Dell'Orto PMH 40, electronic ignition
Clutch:	double-plate dry clutch
Gearbox:	5 speeds
Frame:	central tube frame of chrome-molybdenum
Wheelbase:	1495 mm
Front suspension:	Marzocchi 41-mm telescopic fork
Rear suspension:	cantilever swing arm with torque support
Front tire:	120/70 ZR 17
Rear tire:	160/60 ZR 17
Front brake:	double disc, 320 mm, floating
Rear brake:	disc, 260 mm
Empty weight:	232 kg (fueled)
Tank capacity:	19 liters
Maximum speed:	225 kph

Curiously the slim 1100 Sport appeals to Guzzi buyers better than the more powerful Daytona.

Sport 1100i 1996

In 1996 the 1100 Sport (like the Daytona 1000) appeared in new clothes. The Guzzi engineers fitted it with the familiar Weber-Marelli fuel injection and hollow-spoke wheels with three spokes, and completed the new chassis with high-quality suspension elements from White Power. Essentially, all that remained of the old Sport 1100 was the twin-valve engine, and even it had been reengineered. For example, the lubrication system now had a separate oil cooler. Changes were also made to the clutch.

Sport 1100i	
Production Period:	1996
Engine:	2-cyl., OHV, twin valves
Displacement:	1064 cc
Bore x Stroke:	92 x 80 mm
Compression:	9.5:1
Power output:	90 hp (66 kW) at 7,800 rpm
Mixture preparation:	Weber-Marelli Alfa-n
Clutch:	double-plate dry clutch
Gearbox:	5 speeds
Frame:	central tube frame of chrome-molybdenum
Wheelbase:	1475 mm
Front suspension:	White Power telescopic fork
Rear suspension:	cantilever swing arm with torque support
Front tire:	120/70 ZR 17
Rear tire:	160/70 ZR 17
Front brake:	double disc, 320 mm, floating
Rear brake:	disc, 282 mm
Empty weight:	221 kg (fueled)
Tank capacity:	19 liters
Maximum speed:	230 kph

The days of the stiff throttle are gone. Beginning in 2006, the 1100 Sport was only available with fuel injection, which not only improved exhaust emissions but also brought with it much reduced actuating forces.

V10 Centauro GT and Sport 1996

In Greek mythology, the centaur was a creature that was half man, half horse, and when the Centauro was introduced in autumn 1996 it was greeted with mixed feelings. Technically it was a Daytona with a four-valve engine; it was designed, however, for greater torque and therefore produced seven horsepower less than the sport machine. In return, it developed 70 Nm (51 ft lb) of torque at 3,000 rpm, while the peak value of 88 Nm (64.9 ft lb) was reached at 5,800 revs. The chassis was similar to that of the Daytona, with White Power suspension parts and the same massive brake system. A second variant, with a cockpit fairing and carbon fiber exhaust mufflers, appeared in 1997 and was sold in several countries as the Centauro Sport.

V10 Centauro	
Production Period:	1996
Engine:	2-cyl., OHV, four valves
Displacement:	992 cc
Bore x Stroke:	90 x 78 mm
Compression:	10.5:1
Power output:	95 hp (70 kW) at 8,200 rpm
Mixture preparation:	Weber-Marelli
Clutch:	double-plate dry clutch
Gearbox:	5 speeds
Frame:	central tube frame of chrome-molybdenum
Wheelbase:	1475 mm
Front suspension:	White Power telescopic fork
Rear suspension:	cantilever swing arm with torque support
Front tire:	120/70 ZR 17
Rear tire:	160/60 ZR 17
Front brake:	double disc, 320 mm, floating
Rear brake:	disc, 282 mm
Empty weight:	224 kg (fueled)
Tank capacity:	18 liters
Maximum speed:	218 kph

This Centauro with small windscreen was not available in Germany and was sold elsewhere as the Centauro Sport. The machine had the engine of the Daytona.

Wide fork legs, potent engine: the Centauro was a true muscle bike. It is not a real two-up machine, but otherwise it offers plenty of riding enjoyment.

V11 Sport from 1999

This jewel entered production in the summer of 1999, and with its green-painted chassis parts and red frame, it clearly had the traits of the legendary 750 Sport of 1972. Hidden beneath the fuel tank is a slightly modified Centauro frame, but all other components were developed specifically for this machine. Engine layout is the same as all the other big displacement Guzzis of that time, but in terms of engine output – the V11 Sport produces an impressive 90 hp – it clearly outdoes all of them. Development of the concept progressed through several special models. The naked basic Sport disappeared from the lineup in the 2004 season, as the newly introduced model variants of the Café Sport better suited the wishes of customers.

V11 Sport	
Production Period:	from 1999
Engine:	2-cyl., OHV, four valves
Displacement:	1064 cc
Bore x Stroke:	92 x 80 mm
Compression:	9.5:1
Power output:	90 hp (70 kW) at 7,800 rpm
Mixture preparation:	Weber-Marelli IAW, 1.5 Multipoint
Clutch:	double-plate dry clutch
Gearbox:	6 speeds
Frame:	central tube frame of chrome-molybdenum
Wheelbase:	1475 mm
Front suspension:	Upside-Down telescopic fork
Rear suspension:	central suspension, double swing arm with torque support
Front tire:	120/70 ZR 17
Rear tire:	160/60 ZR 17
Front brake:	double disc, 320 mm
Rear brake:	disc, 282 mm
Empty weight:	230 kg (fueled)
Tank capacity:	20 liters
Maximum speed:	210 kph

The color of the first V11 Sport, in particular, was reminiscent of the 750 Sport of 1972. Several modifications to the suspension improved its initially wonky riding behavior.

V11 Rosso Mandello 2001

This special model was unveiled at the Intermot in Munich in September 2000. Technically it was a V11 Sport, but offered something more for the eye. Compared to the Sport, it was upgraded with a number of carbon and red anodized aluminum parts. Limited to 300 machines, the series was built to celebrate the company's anniversary in 2001. The name not only referred to the model's red parts, but also to the birthplace of the company.

V11 Rosso Mandello	
Production Period:	2001 only
Engine:	2-cyl., OHV, twin valves
Displacement:	1064 cc
Bore x Stroke:	92 x 80 mm
Compression:	9.5:1
Power output:	91 hp (67 kW) at 7,800 rpm
Mixture preparation:	electronic fuel injection, CDI
Clutch:	single-plate dry clutch, hydraulic
Gearbox:	6 speeds, shaft drive
Frame:	central tube frame, engine-bearing
Wheelbase:	1471 mm
Front suspension:	Marzocchi Upside-Down telescopic fork, 40 mm
Rear suspension:	Sachs fully-adjustable cantilever swing arm
Front tire:	120/70-17
Rear tire:	170/60-17
Front brake:	double disc, 320 mm, 4-piston Brembo
Rear brake:	282 mm disc, 2 caliper pistons
Empty weight:	219 kg (fueled)
Tank capacity:	approx. 22 liters
Maximum speed:	over 200 kph

V11 Sport Scura 2002

Limited to 300 examples, the Rosso Mandello quickly sold out. After the takeover by Aprilia, the factory stoked the fire and unveiled the Sport Scura. It was a high-grade version of the Rosso Mandello. The Scura had Öhlins suspension parts and less carbon fiber than the Mandello, but a clearly higher price than the standard V11: in 2002 the basic V11 cost 11,190 Euros in Germany, the Sport Scura 12,750 Euros. This was quite a lot for a machine that offered no more than the only slightly less fancy base model.

V11 Sport Scura	
Production Period:	2002
Engine:	2-cyl., OHV, twin valves
Displacement:	1064 cc
Bore x Stroke:	92 x 80 mm
Compression:	9.5:1
Power output:	91 hp at 7,800 rpm
Mixture preparation:	Weber-Marelli
Clutch:	twin-plate dry clutch
Gearbox:	6 speeds
Frame:	central tube frame, engine-bearing
Wheelbase:	1471 mm
Front suspension:	Öhlins fully-adjustable telescopic fork
Rear suspension:	Öhlins central shock absorber
Front tire:	120/70-17
Rear tire:	170/60-17
Front brake:	double disc, 320 mm
Rear brake:	282 mm disc
Empty weight:	220 kg (fueled)
Tank capacity:	approx. 22 liters
Maximum speed:	over 200 kph

Rosso Mandello (left) and Sport Scura (above) are optically upgraded versions of the V11 Sport. The Scura even comes with a high-grade Öhlins fork.

V11 Café Sport/Ballabio/Coppa Italia

The V11 Sport was replaced by the Cafe Sport for the 2004 season. Ostensibly it was only a machine with a slightly different seating position, but that still meant a great deal. In the press, where the Sport had so far aroused little interest, the Café Sport became a favorite of testers on account of its upright seating position. The straight handlebars turned the Sport into a fun machine, even though the rest of its technology was practically unchanged – with small but important differences: the rear hub had become larger, and there a 180 tire transferred the torque to the asphalt. The wheelbase is also greater: these modifications were previously first seen on the Le Mans. Two versions, the Café and the Ballabio, differed only in having expensive Öhlins suspension parts and carbon fiber details from the Café Sport. The third variant is the Coppa Italia – not an ice bucket but a Café Sport finished in an eye-catching scheme of the Italian national colors.

The higher handlebars make the V11 Café Sport into an entirely different motorcycle than the base model. The upright seating position provides no end of riding enjoyment.

V11 Café Sport/Ballabio/Coppa Italia

Production Period:	from 2003
Engine:	2-cyl., OHV, twin valves
Displacement:	1064 cc
Bore x Stroke:	92 x 80 mm
Compression:	9.8:1
Power output:	91 hp at 8,200 rpm
Mixture preparation:	Weber-Marelli, d=45 mm
Clutch:	twin-plate dry clutch
Gearbox:	6 speeds
Frame:	central tube
Wheelbase:	1490 mm
Front suspension:	Öhlins fully-adjustable telescopic fork
Rear suspension:	Öhlins central shock absorber
Front tire:	120/70-17
Rear tire:	180/55-17
Front brake:	double disc, 320 mm
Rear brake:	282 mm disc
Empty weight:	226 kg (fueled)
Tank capacity:	approx. 21 liters
Maximum speed:	over 200 kph

Except for its wonderful paint scheme, the Coppa Italia is the same motorcycle as the Café Sport, even down to the Öhlins suspension parts.

V11 Le Mans from 2001

When the Le Mans arrived in 2001, it represented more than a bow to the old Le Mans models, whose career began at the end of the 1970s. It was the first new model under Aprilia management and the improved quality control led to noticeably better riding stability, which longtime Guzzi owners noted with gratitude. A somewhat more elongated frame, new struts between the engine and frame, plus a wider rear tire helped the Le Mans to a clear advantage over the V11 Sport. Thanks to its improved chassis, the new Le Mans is much more than a V11 with a noticeably large fairing, even if the look is the same. The V11 Le Mans Tenni is a special model released in the first model year and named for motorcycle racer Omobono Tenni. The machine has a matte gray fairing, white number plate, and a suede-covered seat. It also has the light racing clutch and a redesigned gearbox.

V11 Le Mans	
Production Period:	from 2001
Engine:	2-cyl., OHV, twin valves
Displacement:	1064 cc
Bore x Stroke:	92 x 80 mm
Compression:	9.8:1
Power output:	91 hp at 8,200 rpm
Mixture preparation:	Weber-Marelli, d=45 mm
Clutch:	twin-plate dry clutch
Gearbox:	6 speeds
Frame:	central tube
Wheelbase:	1490 mm
Front suspension:	fully-adjustable telescopic fork
Rear suspension:	central shock absorber
Front tire:	120/70-17
Rear tire:	180/55-17
Front brake:	double disc, 320 mm
Rear brake:	282 mm disc
Empty weight:	226 kg (fueled)
Tank capacity:	approx. 21 liters
Maximum speed:	220 kph

Visually the Le Mans differs from the base V11 in its voluminous fairing. Less noticeable is the wider rear tire. The Tenni is a special model named after the racer of the same name who won great success for Moto Guzzi in the 1930s.

The V11 Le Mans is a sport bike on which a passenger can feel comfortable. The large fairing provides good protection from the airflow.

V11 Le Mans Rosso Corsa/ Nero Corsa/Le Mans from 2003

Since 2003 all Moto Guzzis have been equipped with regulated three-way catalytic converters, including the second generation of the Le Mans series. The base model is largely similar to the first model, but the two Corsa variants Rosso and Nero – differ only in color; both have more exclusive Öhlins suspension parts and a Bitubo steering damper. The Rosso Corsa is the more elite model of the two as it has a suggested chessboard pattern in two shades of red under a clear coat.

V11 Le Corsa	
Production Period:	from 2003
Engine:	2-cyl., OHV, twin valves
Displacement:	1064 cc
Bore x Stroke:	92 x 80 mm
Compression:	9.8:1
Power output:	91 hp at 8,200 rpm
Mixture preparation:	Weber-Marelli, d=45 mm
Clutch:	twin-plate dry clutch
Gearbox:	6 speeds
Frame:	central tube
Wheelbase:	1490 mm
Front suspension:	fully-adjustable telescopic fork (Corsa = Öhlins)
Rear suspension:	central shock absorber (Corsa = Öhlins)
Front tire:	120/70-17
Rear tire:	180/55-17
Front brake:	double disc, 320 mm
Rear brake:	282 mm disc
Empty weight:	226 kg (fueled)
Tank capacity:	approx. 21 liters
Maximum speed:	220 kph

MOTO GUZZI

V11 LE MANS
V11 LE MANS ROSSO CORSA

In addition to the base model (above), since 2003 there have been two variants of the Le Mans: the Nero Corsa (far left) and the Rossa Corsa (left), both with Öhlins suspension parts.

Quota 1000 1992 – 1997

Moto Guzzi tried to swim with the wave of big Enduros with the huge Quota Mille. Huge not just because of its general dimensions, but mainly because of its seating height (which was criticized in every test report). The specially developed box frame with linkage for the rear shock absorber has removable cradle braces and is painted entirely in silver. The 1000-cc fuel-injected engine is designed more for torque than top end performance and in this respect is similar to the off-road tourers of the competition, which are also available with rigid fairings and space without end. Unfortunately, the Quota was given a cool reception by the buyers, and by the beginning of the 1990s it was not available in several markets, including Germany.

Quota 1000	
Production Period:	1992-1997
Engine:	2-cyl., OHV, twin valves
Displacement:	948.8 cc
Bore x Stroke:	88 x 78 mm
Compression:	9.1:1
Power output:	71 hp at 6,600 rpm
Mixture preparation:	Weber-Marelli combined ignition and fuel injection system
Clutch:	twin-plate dry clutch
Gearbox:	5 speeds
Frame:	steel tube
Wheelbase:	1610 mm
Front suspension:	Marzocchi fully-adjustable telescopic fork
Rear suspension:	central shock absorber, double swing arm
Front tire:	90/90-21, tube
Rear tire:	130/70-18, tube
Front brake:	double disc, 280 mm, 2 caliper pistons
Rear brake:	260 mm floating disc, 2 caliper pistons
Empty weight:	256 kg
Tank capacity:	20 liters
Maximum speed:	190 kph

Quota 1100 ES 1997

By 1997 it was time for a new Quota. It followed the concept of its predecessor but incorporated some sensible modifications. Noticeable were the larger 1064-cc engine, which developed 92 Nm (67.85 ft lb) of torque at 3,800 rpm, the Boge shock absorber with infinitely variable adjustable damp base, and, in particular, the lower seat height. The Quota got good marks for its braking system; as on its predecessor, steel flex lines were used, but both front discs were larger, at 296 mm in diameter.

Quota 1100 ES

Production Period:	1997
Engine:	2-cyl., OHV, twin valves
Displacement:	1064 cc
Bore x Stroke:	92 x 80 mm
Compression:	9.5:1
Power output:	74 hp at 6,800 rpm
Mixture preparation:	Weber-Marelli combined ignition and fuel injection system
Clutch:	twin-plate dry clutch
Gearbox:	5 speeds
Frame:	steel tube
Wheelbase:	1600 mm
Front suspension:	Marzocchi fully-adjustable telescopic fork
Rear suspension:	central shock absorber, double swing arm
Front tire:	90/90-21
Rear tire:	130/80-R17
Front brake:	double disc, 296 mm, 2-piston caliper
Rear brake:	260 mm floating disc, 2-piston caliper
Empty weight:	264 kg (fueled)
Tank capacity:	20 liters
Maximum speed:	190 kph

The Quota was Moto Guzzi's attempt to get in on the attractive enduro market. The heavy Guzzi was unable to match the qualities of a BMW GS, however.

Stelvio from 2008

Surprise at the Milan motorcycle show in autumn 2007: after almost ten years, Moto Guzzi makes a new beginning in the direction of big Enduro. Visually the Stelvio is much more attractive than the Quota ever was. With a 19-inch front wheel and tubeless tires front and rear, it is clearly trimmed more for street use. Up front, suspension and damping are provided by a big 50-mm, upside-down fork; in the rear there is a single swing arm with progressive articulation and central shock absorber.

The Stelvio is powered by the newly developed four-valve engine with a displacement of exactly 1151 cubic centimeters and an output of 110 hp, which helps it achieve a top speed of more than 200 kph. The windscreen is adjustable, as is the two-part seat. Of course, there is also a baggage system for the new flagship for long trips with two up.

Stelvio	
Production Period:	from 2008
Engine:	2-cyl., OHV, four valves
Displacement:	1151 cc
Bore x Stroke:	95 x 81.2 mm
Compression:	11:1
Power output:	110 hp at 7,500 rpm
Mixture preparation:	Weber-Marelli combined ignition and fuel injection system
Clutch:	twin-plate dry clutch
Gearbox:	6 speeds
Frame:	steel tube
Wheelbase:	1550 mm
Front suspension:	upside-down fully-adjustable fork
Rear suspension:	central shock absorber, single swing arm
Front tire:	110/90 ZR 19
Rear tire:	180/55 ZR 17
Front brake:	double disc, 320 mm, 4-piston caliper
Rear brake:	260 mm floating disc, 2-piston caliper
Empty weight:	214 kg
Tank capacity:	18 liters
Maximum speed:	over 200 kph

Current Models

Breva 850 from 2006

After the half-hearted introduction of the Breva 1100, a model that almost disappeared in the shadow of the exciting Griso, the engineers knew how to use the entirely successful engine design for a smaller model. The result was two models, one of them the Breva 850, which was not a bigger Breva 750 but a faired 1100. In the spring of 2006 the newcomer shared the technology of the Breva 1100. The engine even had the same bore of 92 millimeters, which resulted in outstanding torque and a very smooth-running engine.

Handling was actually not supposed to change, but the different engine characteristics made themselves felt on the road. The rider feels no shortage of power, as torque remains adequate at 66 Newton meters (48.67 foot-pounds) at 7,000 revolutions. The engine is also lively, which results in sporty handling.

Breva 850	
Production Period:	from 2006
Engine:	2-cyl., OHV, twin valves
Displacement:	877 cc
Bore x Stroke:	92 x 66 mm
Compression:	9.8:1
Power output:	72 hp at 7,700 rpm
Mixture preparation:	Weber-Marelli IAW, 2 x 40-mm,
	Weber IW 031 fuel injectors, Lambda
	sensor, double ignition
Clutch:	dry clutch
Gearbox:	6 speeds, shaft
Frame:	steel tube with cast sections
Wheelbase:	1495 mm
Front suspension:	45-mm telescopic fork, adjustable spring preload
Rear suspension:	single swing arm, central shock
	absorber, fully adjustable
Front tire:	120/70 ZR 17
Rear tire:	180/55 ZR 17
Front brake:	2 x 320-mm floating discs, 4 pistons, ABS
Rear brake:	282-mm disc, 2 caliper pistons, ABS
Empty weight:	231 kg dry
Tank capacity:	23 liters
Maximum speed:	200 kph

Breva 1100 from 2006

There had not been a normal touring motorcycle, a mainstream motorcycle for all uses, in the Moto Guzzi program for a long time. The aggressive propulsion system with the new Evo engine at its heart sits in a frame of tubes and cast pieces. With its less than spectacular optics, it is not exactly a typical Guzzi but it is a modern one. It is equipped with the most modern mixture preparation system and emission control in accordance with Euro 3 rules. The suspension is designed to be less sporty than normal, and the only adjustable feature of the fork is spring preload, which is sufficient for the operational purpose it is aimed at. In addition, a Matrix display makes it possible to communicate with the motorcycle: infotainment without the rider having to take his hands from the handlebars. Exclusive touring accessories complete the package.

Breva 1100	
Production Period:	from 2006
Engine:	2-cyl., OHV, twin valves
Displacement:	1064 cc
Bore x Stroke:	92 x 80 mm
Compression:	9.8:1
Power output:	112 hp (84 kW) at 7,800 rpm
Mixture preparation:	Weber-Marelli, electronic
Clutch:	dry clutch
Gearbox:	6 speeds
Frame:	take-apart double cradle with cast sections
Wheelbase:	1500 mm
Front suspension:	telescopic fork, adjustable spring preload
Rear suspension:	single arm, progressive linkage, rebound and preload adjustable
Front tire:	120/70-17
Rear tire:	180/55-17
Front brake:	discs, 320-mm
Rear brake:	disc, 282 mm
Empty weight:	233 kg (with touring windscreen and center stand)
Tank capacity:	24 liters
Maximum speed:	over 200 kph

Visually the 1200 Breva is almost identical to its smaller cousins. The new engine produces about eight more horsepower.

Breva 1200 from 2008

Unveiled at the EICMA in autumn 2007, the Breva 1200 replaced its 1100-cc predecessor for the 2008 model year. Increased bore and stroke raised displacement to exactly 1151 cubic centimeters. Claimed engine output is 95 hp at 7,500 rpm. Maximum torque of 100 Nm (73.75 ft-lb) is reached at 5,800 rpm, with the new power plant providing 85% of its maximum torque over a band between 2,300 and 4,800 rpm. The chassis and braking system do not differ from those of the Breva 1100, and visually the two models are almost indistinguishable.

Breva 1200	
Production Period:	from 2008
Engine:	2-cyl., OHV, twin valves
Displacement:	1151 cc
Bore x Stroke:	95 x 81.2 mm
Compression:	11:1
Power output:	95 hp at 7,500 rpm
Mixture preparation:	Weber-Marelli, electronic
Clutch:	dry clutch
Gearbox:	6 speeds
Frame:	take-apart double cradle with cast sections
Wheelbase:	1500 mm
Front suspension:	telescopic fork, adjustable preload
Rear suspension:	single arm, central shock absorber, fully adjustable
Front tire:	120/70-17
Rear tire:	180/55-17
Front brake:	discs, 320 mm
Rear brake:	disc, 282 mm
Empty weight:	233 kg (with touring windscreen and center stand)
Tank capacity:	24 liters
Maximum speed:	over 200 kph

Griso 850 from 2006

When the Griso 1100 was introduced in autumn 2005, almost unchanged from the concept study first shown in Munich in 2002, the motorcycle community was split. Is it a street fighter, a work of art, or an ugly motorcycle? No one knew exactly, but interest was sufficient for a second variant to be introduced in 2006. The Griso 850 had the same power plant as the small Breva, with the same bore as the 1064-cc engine, but a markedly shorter stroke. Engine power and torque were both better than those of the Breva 850, but at somewhat higher rpm. This made it lively, with sensitive behavior even in difficult passages. The motorcycle is very balanced, and one moves between cars in heavy city traffic effortlessly and fully controlled. When production began, it differed visually in having a black frame, which on the 1100 was a metallic color. The bigger engine also had a larger oil cooler on the right side of the crankcase, where the 850 had just the ribbed case.

Griso 850	
Production Period:	from 2006
Engine:	2-cyl., OHV, twin valves
Displacement:	877 cc
Bore x Stroke:	92 x 66 mm
Compression:	9.8:1
Power output:	76 hp at 7,600 rpm
Mixture preparation:	Weber-Marelli IAW, 2 x 40-mm, Weber IW 031 fuel injectors, Lambda sensor, double ignition
Clutch:	dry clutch
Gearbox:	6 speeds, shaft
Frame:	steel tube
Wheelbase:	1554 mm
Front suspension:	43-mm telescopic fork, fully adjustable
Rear suspension:	single arm, central shock absorber, fully adjustable
Front tire:	120/70 ZR 17
Rear tire:	180/55 ZR 17
Front brake:	2 x 320-mm floating discs, 4 pistons, ABS
Rear brake:	282-mm disc, 2 caliper pistons, ABS
Empty weight:	227 kg dry
Tank capacity:	17.2 liters
Maximum speed:	200 kph

The small Griso has the same engine as the 850 Breva. The motorcycle looks very balanced and the chassis and suspension are very well harmonized with the smaller engine.

Griso 1100 from 2006

The Griso was unveiled as a concept bike at Intermot 2002, initially with the old four-valve engine of the Daytona. Two years later, there was finally clarity: the street fighter with fighter soul arrived in 2005. Around the newcomer: 1064 cc V-twin with small chassis fairing dominated by two imposing steel tubes embracing the tank. Moto Guzzi got the idea from looking at the competition's power cruisers: big engine, little equipment. The engine is the center of attention and, with its two-in-one exhaust, it is supposed to exude aggressiveness. The chassis also signals performance, with a fully-adjustable fork and fully-adjustable center shock. The seat offers meager space for a passenger, but that does not matter – what matters is naked technology. Symbols of the Griso are the 1100 engine, which is almost completely new inside, and the 650 Watt alternator between the cylinders.

Griso 1100	
Production Period:	from 2005
Engine:	2-cyl., OHV, twin valves
Displacement:	1064 cc
Bore x Stroke:	92 x 80 mm
Compression:	9.8:1
Power output:	88 hp at 8,000 rpm
Mixture preparation:	Weber-Marelli, electronic
Clutch:	dry clutch
Gearbox:	6 speeds
Frame:	double cradle, tubular steel
Wheelbase:	1543 mm
Front suspension:	telescopic fork, fully adjustable
Rear suspension:	single arm, fully adjustable shock absorber
Front tire:	120/70-17
Rear tire:	180/55-17
Front brake:	discs, 320 mm
Rear brake:	disc, 282 mm
Empty weight:	229 kg
Tank capacity:	17 liters
Maximum speed:	over 200 kph

Griso V8 from 2006

Here is another innovation from the winter of 2006-07: the big Griso updated with the technology of the eight-valve engines from the sport models of the 1990s, but with the layout of the first Griso from 2005. This engine had the camshaft mounted high and valve movement controlled by very short pushrods. It is a potent package, fully matching the Griso's intended operating range: fast riding. The 1996 predecessor engine with the same layout produces just under 100 hp, and with the light costume of the Griso promises more agile handling and enjoyable experiences.

Griso V8	
Production Period:	from 2006
Engine:	2-cyl., OHV, four valves
Displacement:	1151 cc
Bore x Stroke:	95 x 81.2 mm
Compression:	11:1
Power output:	110 hp at 7,500 rpm
Mixture preparation:	Weber-Marelli IAW, 2 x 45-mm,
	Weber IW 031 fuel injectors,
	Lambda sensor, double ignition
Clutch:	dry clutch
Gearbox:	6 speeds, shaft
Frame:	steel tube cradle
Wheelbase:	1554 mm
Front suspension:	43-mm USD, adjustable preload,
	rebound, compression
Rear suspension:	single arm, central shock absorber,
	fully adjustable
Front tire:	120/70 ZR 17
Rear tire:	180/55 ZR 17
Front brake:	2 x 320-mm floating discs, 2 pistons
Rear brake:	282-mm disc, 2 caliper pistons
Empty weight:	227 kg dry
Tank capacity:	17.2 liters
Maximum speed:	over 200 kph

The Griso models are all exceptional back-road bikes. The four-valve engine provides plenty of power.

1200 Sport from 2007

No, the 1200 Sport is not a sport bike by the standards of the new century. But anyone interested in tradition and sport riding is at home here. The engine is identical to that of the 1200 Norge but with a higher redline. The suspension is identical to the 1200 Norge's, and only the fork's preload is adjustable. Fuel injection is the latest version. The motorcycle has a classic design layout: cockpit fairing, stub handlebars, humped tank and everything in a compact package. The paint schemes are attractive, either red or black, with white fields necessary for starting numbers. It is no super sport bike, but it is more than adequate for sporty jaunts and may be seen as a fun toy.

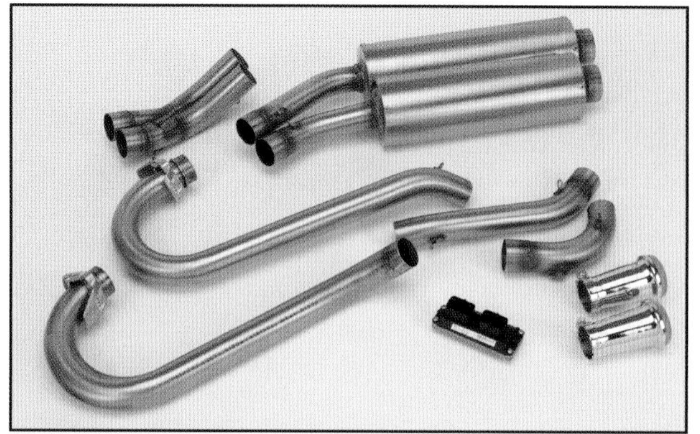

1200 Sport	
Production Period:	from 2007
Engine:	2-cyl., OHV, twin valves
Displacement:	1151 cc
Bore x Stroke:	95 x 81.2 mm
Compression:	9.8:1
Power output:	95 hp at 7,800 rpm
Mixture preparation:	Weber-Marelli IAW5A, 2 x 45-mm,
	Weber IWP 162 fuel injectors,
	Lambda sensor, double ignition
Clutch:	dry clutch
Gearbox:	6 speeds, shaft
Frame:	steel tube cradle
Wheelbase:	1485 mm
Front suspension:	45-mm telescopic fork, adjustable preload
Rear suspension:	single arm, central shock absorber, fully adjustable
Front tire:	120/70 ZR 17
Rear tire:	180/55 ZR 17
Front brake:	2 x 320-mm floating discs, 4 pistons, ABS
Rear brake:	282-mm disc, 2 caliper pistons, ABS
Empty weight:	229 kg dry
Tank capacity:	23 liters
Maximum speed:	over 200 kph

Moto Guzzi offers comprehensive tuning packages for buyers inclined towards sport or touring use. In the photo on the far left is an exhaust kit.

The 1200 Sport is the sportiest motorcycle in Moto Guzzi's current lineup. The big machine's handling is much lighter than its impressive dimensions would suggest.

1200 Norge from 2006

In 1928 the Guzzi brothers designed an ingenious rear wheel suspension, four tension springs in a metal box, for their GT touring model. As a general test of the new system, Giuseppe Guzzi rode the motorcycle to the North Cape. The model was subsequently dubbed the Norge (Norway). When, in autumn 2005, Mandello unveiled a new GT machine based on the big Breva but with greater displacement, it revived the name. It had everything the touring rider could want: bags, full fairing, and accessories including GPS in combination with Blue Tooth for mobile communications. The standard ABS can be switched off.

The base technology is identical to that of the Breva 1100, although the suspension is stiffer because of the greater weight. The mentioned increase in displacement brought increased torque and simpler passing, not just on the highway. The GTL version has a complete luggage system, while the T version does not.

1200 Norge	
Production Period:	from 2006
Engine:	2-cyl., OHV, twin valves
Displacement:	1151 cc
Bore x Stroke:	95 x 81.2 mm
Compression:	9.8:1
Power output:	95 hp at 7,500 rpm
Mixture preparation:	Magneti-Marelli IAW5A, 2 x 45 mm, Weber IWP 162 injectors, Lambda sensor, double ignition
Clutch:	dry clutch
Gearbox:	6 speeds, shaft
Frame:	steel tube double cradle with cast sections
Wheelbase:	1495 mm
Front suspension:	45-mm telescopic fork, adjustable preload
Rear suspension:	single arm, central shock absorber, fully adjustable
Front tire:	120/70-ZR 17
Rear tire:	180/55- ZR 17
Front brake:	2 x 320 mm floating discs, 4 pistons, ABS
Rear brake:	282 mm disc, 2 caliper pistons, ABS
Empty weight:	246 kg (dry)
Tank capacity:	23 liters
Maximum speed:	over 200 kph

In keeping with the name Norge, in 2006 Moto Guzzi organized a tour to the North Cape, in which many models with this name took part. The motorcycle's basic technology is identical to that of the Breva.

Bellagio 940 from 2007

When this new model was unveiled in the spring of 2007, Moto Guzzi openly admitted that it was intended to be a direct competitor for the Harley-Davidson 1200 Sportster. With adjustable suspension, double discs in front and six horsepower more than the Sportster, it had the horses to do it. Also unique was the newcomer's displacement, which at that time was shared by no other Guzzi – 940 cc. The Bellagio is very modern, with double ignition and electronic mixture preparation, making it Euro 3 compatible. The six-speed gearbox transmits the power to the patented single swing arm with no load change reactions. The tire selection represents a mixture of trend and rideability: an 18-inch front tire and a decently-wide 180/55 rear tire not only ensure classical lines, but are also a design concept that is becoming more and more noticeable. The machine also handles very elegantly at a sporty pace.

Bellagio 940	
Production Period:	from 2007
Engine:	2-cyl., OHV, twin valves
Displacement:	935.6 cc
Bore x Stroke:	96 x 66 mm
Compression:	10:1
Power output:	74.7 hp at 7,200 rpm
Mixture preparation:	Magneti Marelli, digital
Clutch:	dry clutch
Gearbox:	6 speeds, shaft
Frame:	tubular twin cradle
Wheelbase:	1570 mm
Front suspension:	Marzocchi 45-mm telescopic fork, adjustable
Rear suspension:	central shock absorber, 110-mm suspension travel
Front tire:	120/70-18
Rear tire:	180/55-17
Front brake:	2 x 320 mm, two pistons
Rear brake:	282-mm disc, two pistons
Empty weight:	224 kg
Tank capacity:	19 liters
Maximum speed:	200 kph

MGS-01 Corsa from 2005

After the success of the special models by the company Ghezzi et Brian, located south of Mandello, which had the old technology of the five-speed models, Giuseppe Ghezzi was given the task of coming up with a development of the Guzzi concept for the racetrack. Designed for national twin-cylinder races, the MGS was unveiled in autumn 2003 as a 122-hp racing machine, much to the joy of Guzzi enthusiasts. This figure was later raised to 128 hp. During the winter of 2003-2004 the display example was fitted with various lights, but by then it was clear: this was a pure racing machine and there was no approval for street use. In addition to the slim frame, the Öhlins suspension parts front and rear, it was the engine that got the most attention. Details like Cosworth pistons, Carillo connecting rods and proper bearings instead of previous shells were the hallmarks of a true racing engine. Thanks to its short wheelbase and exclusive chassis, the machine, ready to ride at 200 kg, was well-suited for club racing or various four-stroke racing series.

MGS-01 Corsa	
Production Period:	from 2005
Engine:	2-cyl., OHV, four valves
Displacement:	1225 cc
Bore x Stroke:	100 x 80 mm
Compression:	11.6:1
Power output:	128 hp at 8,000 rpm
Mixture preparation:	Marelli IAW 15M, electronic digital
Clutch:	sintering double disc
Gearbox:	6 speeds
Frame:	rectangular section single-beam ALS 450
Wheelbase:	1450 mm
Front suspension:	Öhlins telescopic fork 43 mm, fully adjustable
Rear suspension:	aluminum plate swinging fork
	Öhlins monoshock absorber, four adjustment positions
Front tire:	120/60-17, Michelin slicks S1246A
Rear tire:	180/55-17, Michelin slicks S1835A
Front brake:	discs, 320 mm, radial caliper
Rear brake:	disc, 220 mm
Empty weight:	192 kg
Tank capacity:	18.5 liters
Maximum speed:	not known

Although it doesn't exactly fit the Moto Guzzi brand image, it is wonderful that the company has a pure racing machine in its lineup. The MGS-01 Corsa is suited for nothing else but fast laps on the racetrack.

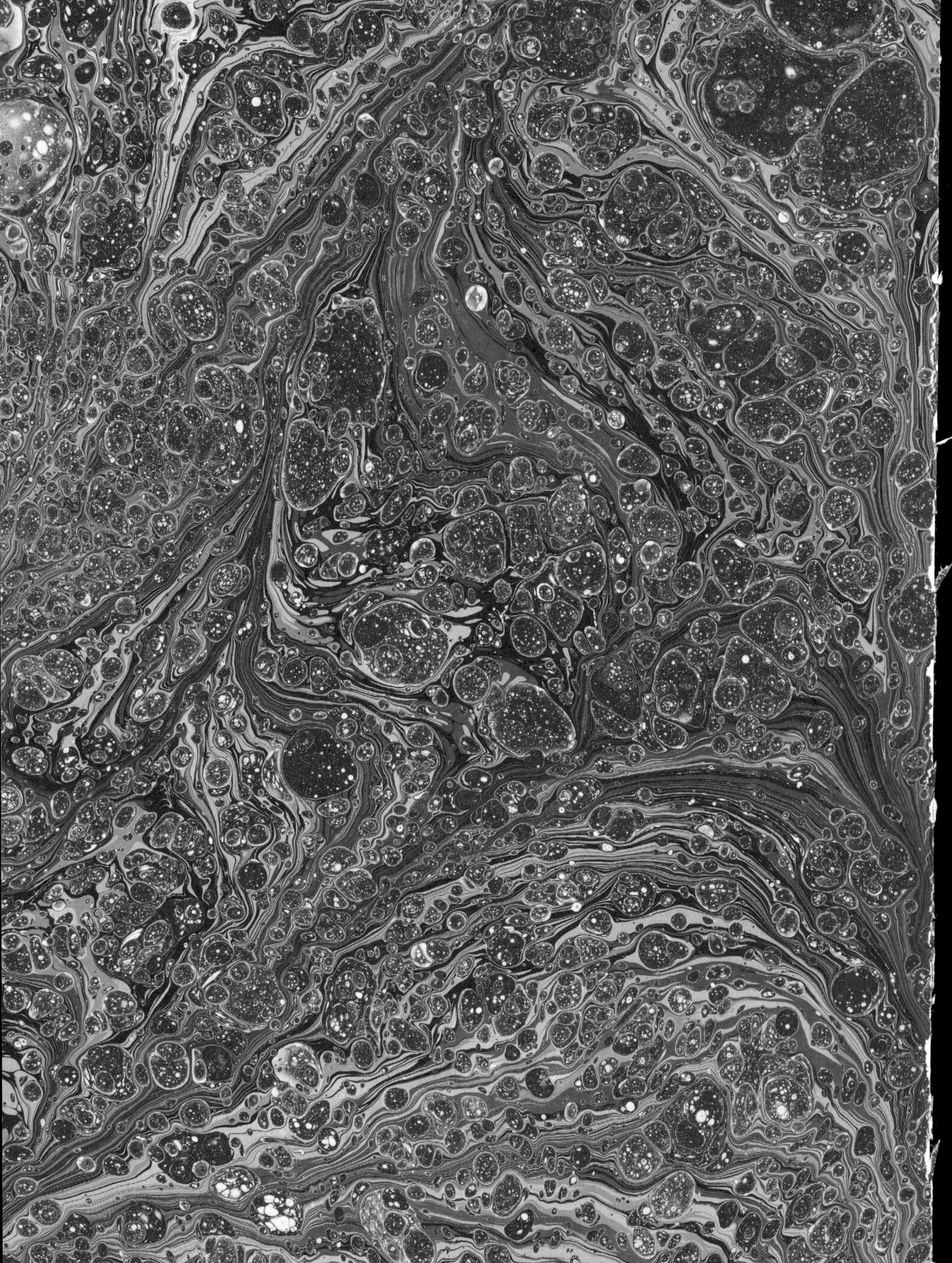